Acts that Prove

Causes of Human Suffering From the Perspective of Reincarnation

A Series of Spirit Communications
with commentary by
Amalia Domingo Soler

Translated by Yvonne Crespo Limoges

ACTS THAT PROVE CAUSES OF HUMAN SUFFERING FROM THE PERSPECTIVE OF REINCARNATION A SERIES OF SPIRIT COMMUNICATIONS WITH COMMENTARY BY AMALIA DOMINGO SOLER

iUniverse books may be ordered through booksellers or by contacting:

iUniverse
1663 Liberty Drive
Bloomington, IN 47403
www.iuniverse.com
844-349-9409

ISBN: 978-1-6632-4215-0 (sc)
ISBN: 978-1-6632-4216-7 (e)

Library of Congress Control Number: 2022912668

Print information available on the last page.

iUniverse rev. date: 07/14/2022

ACKNOWLEDGEMENTS

When my mother Yolanda taught me to pray, it provided me great comfort; and thus began my spiritual life. Thanks Mom!

I am indebted to my father, Edgar Crespo, for introducing me to knowledge of spiritual realities which provided logical answers for me to some of life's many existential questions; these have especially helped me to have more resignation and faith in supporting life's challenges.

To my daughter Alysia Mikesell Pape, thank you, I am forever grateful for your technical computer expertise, and most importantly, your financial backing to publish this book.

I want to thank my son Michael Limoges for his enthusiastic support of my efforts, especially since this information will now be available to young people. Moreover, for the wonderful discussions we had regarding the moral lessons herein.

After reading the book, much appreciation goes to Michael E. Tymn for his thought-provoking perspectives and our discussions on various philosophical fine points brought up in some of the chapters.

I want to extend my love and heartfelt appreciation to Norberto Prieto and Maria Del Carmen Prieto for their longtime friendship, the sharing of their collective spiritual wisdom with me and their sincere encouragement to translate this book.

DEDICATION

To all who suffer, and wonder why. May you find within this book some answers, but most of all some consolation and hope.

TABLE OF CONTENTS

INTRODUCTION

A Series of Spirit Communications revealing Past Lives

We all suffer; and we see so much suffering, unfairness and inequalities in our world. Some people are born rich, others poor; some live long healthy lives, others suffer with agonizing diseases; some people live uneventful lives, while trouble seems to follow others wherever they go; some live to a very old age, while some are born into this world only to live a few hours or days; freak accidents or unexpected sickness cause premature deaths; innocent bystanders are randomly killed; children live with horrific diseases; natural disasters terribly affect some and not others and other worse situations, and, we ask, why?

If we believe in an All-Loving, All-Just and All-Powerful Creator, why do we suffer, seemingly so randomly? All three major religions say we only live one life, and the cause of suffering we are told is a mystery only God knows. Yet, as science has continued to increase its knowledge about the material world and its laws, the scientific establishment is reluctant to seriously study the spiritual aspects of life, which is left to the religions where we find the causes of suffering still unknown and we are solely to have blind faith. However, just as science strives to find the cause for every material effect, our own minds naturally seek the same thing in moral and spiritual matters. Therefore, I offer this translation from the Spanish-speaking world that may provide some answers to spiritual and moral questions and the cause of human sufferings from the perspective of reincarnation.

In 19th century apostolic Roman Catholic Spain - a poet, writer and editor named **Amalia Domingo Soler** wrote of the human dramas (sufferings, heartaches, terrible tragedies and more) around her, and she discovered many of the root causes of these terrible circumstances and events were found in the past-life existences of the people involved.

However, this only was after she underwent great emotional pain, blindness, poverty and suffering in her own personal life, herself desperately looking for life's answers and for consolation. She found what made sense to her when she was introduced to the information compiled by French educator and paranormal researcher **Allan Kardec** (1804-1869). This provided knowledge of a spiritual science and moral philosophy Kardec called **SPIRITISM**. It is the study of the interaction between our material world with spirits in the spiritual world (plane or dimension) via the faculty of mediumship, and the moral teachings revealed by superior spirits (that are in accordance with the purest teachings of Jesus). The main principles are:

— the existence of an Eternal, Unique, All-Powerful, All-Knowing, All-Loving Creator (First Cause of All Things)
— the existence of material and spiritual laws from the same source, the Creator
— that our spirits (souls) are reborn into material bodies to learn, advance, evolve and progress (which can be painful) through the natural process of the law of reincarnation
— there is a material world and a spiritual world (an afterlife where spirits go after the death of the physical body)
— the mediumship faculty that some people obviously have provides communication between the two planes of existence (material and spiritual)
— the existence of a plurality of life on other worlds
— the purpose of material life is for us to learn, develop, mature in all ways, and evolve to the point where we do not have to suffer anymore or have to reincarnate again

Ms. Soler found these ideas to be very logical. There was a reason why she suffered. This knowledge explains where we come from, our purpose on Earth, why we suffer, and where we go after physical death; that we are spirits that choose to incarnate in a human body in the material world with the purpose to intellectually, spiritually and morally progress. When our physical bodies die, our spirit continues to exist in an afterlife or spirit world (so we never die) and the love for our loved ones and their love for us, never dies. And, there is the natural law of cause and effect which is in essence is what the Bible and other religions teach, "we reap what we sow" based on the quality of our thoughts, words and/or deeds. If we suffer and cannot find a reason for it due to something we may have done in this life, it may be due to something we did in a past existence or some lesson we ourselves chose to undergo. [1]

Ms. Soler attended numerous seances in Spain where spirits communicated and where mediums provided informative answers to her sincere and serious questions, and this is what comprises the majority of the chapters in this book (all the material is from her writings and magazines published approximately between 1879 to 1899) and translated from the Spanish into English. These spirit communications explain the moral law of cause and effect. Many of the responses were given to her by her own spirit guide, who called himself - **Father Germain.** That spirit and others, offer insight into many tragic circumstances and events that had their original cause in each victim's past life and/or lives, and in addition, we discover from the spirits what happened to some of them when they returned to the spirit world. And, although Spanish is a beautiful romance language which can be very poetic and lovely, at times, during this mid-to-late 1800s book, some of the dialogue is very direct, vivid and extremely straightforward.

In the present day, many polls conducted reveal there are many people who believe in the existence of a spirit or soul (a consciousness separate from our brain/body), the existence of spirits, the faculty of mediumship, out-of-body experiences (OBEs), near-death experiences (NDEs), spirit influences and spirit obsession, different types of psychic phenomena, as well as many more who now believe in reincarnation.

Long ago, many peoples, including Jews and some early Christians, believed in reincarnation; it may very well be that Jesus was speaking of reincarnation when he said:

---

[1] A book published in 1999 entitled *Reaching to Heaven: A Spiritual Journey Through Life and Death* by spiritual medium James Van Praagh teaches and explains in modern times, the same moral and spiritual laws and lessons through spirit communications. The spirits continue teaching us in every age!

"Very truly I tell you, no one can see the kingdom of God unless they are born again." – John 3:3, Bible

****

At spirit seances, spirits teach that the Creator is All Love and All Just and never punishes; it is WE who do it to ourselves. We were given free will. Also, we have our spirit protectors and other loving spirits who encourage, guide and protect us as much as they are permitted on our material and spiritual journey that is LIFE. In our countless lifetimes, we have been many things: rich, poor, athletic, disabled, powerful, beautiful, plain, etc., etc., and have done and experienced many things. We have, and will continue to explore in many lives, different aspects of life, such as: the arts, science, business, spirituality, philosophy, the trades, engineering, athletics and the list goes on and on. We are here to learn in all aspects, but foremost to learn how to be good.

The spirits explain that the natural law of reincarnation provides that the challenges that we suffer have a *just cause*; and we each are our own judge, jury and executioner and we are the architect of our own destiny. Through the centuries in a myriad of lives, we have done much wrong, made poor choices, but the door of redemption is never shut; it is up to us through our own willpower to learn, change, make amends, develop, progress, overcome and evolve ever towards goodness and wisdom for as long as it takes; each lifetime is a continuing opportunity for progress and to receive the merits of our own efforts to reach (through charity, peace and love) spiritual purity, true happiness and nearness to the Creator.

If we believe this to be true, the faster we should all better ourselves, be good and do good, so we suffer less the consequences of our poor choices and the sooner we can reach a happier state of being in this and future lives. Furthermore, we also receive all the many spiritual and material rewards, for all the good we think, say and do. How hopeful this is when we may be in suffering and see so much suffering!

The moral and spiritual philosophy that the spirits teach us has significant consequences for all of humanity and the destiny of our planet. Yet, human progress is very, very slow, thus the necessity for a myriad of lifetimes towards our final redemption, progress and evolution. The means of reaching true happiness, whether slow or fast, is in our own hands!

In conclusion, if you read this book and consider it a work of fiction, the ideas herein may nevertheless still prompt you to explore its concepts as a possible explanation of the unfair and tragic situations so many seemingly good people endure in our world.

Nevertheless, as the good spirits always tell us, never accept what your reason rejects!

Yvonne Crespo Limoges

BIOGRAPHY

AMALIA DOMINGO SOLER

(November 10, 1835 – April 29, 1909)

Spiritist Editor, Author, Poet, Social Reformer from Spain

The story of her life is widely known by Spiritists through her own writings and many articles written about her. Amalia and her mother were financially supported by her father, who had abandoned them both prior to her birth on November 10, 1835 in Sevilla, Spain. Unfortunately, she was discovered to be blind several days later. Doctors tried everything to no avail, but a homeopath was able to provide some sight for her. Yet, throughout Amalia's life, she always had imperfect sight (with many periods of blindness), especially if she worked too much due to sewing or writing. Amalia's mother loved her daughter dearly and was totally devoted to her; and, by age 5 she had taught her to read and she started writing at age 10. Her first poems were published at age 18.

Once her father died, they lived off a small inheritance, but as those funds dwindled, her mother came down with a terminal illness. Amalia prayed fervently to God so she would be able to care for her mother until her end, and so she would not have to die in a hospital. Her prayers were answered, and she was at her mother's side when she died. Amalia was 25 years old.

During those long days of great heartache and loneliness, and since she was poor and practically blind, one of her mother's friends advised that she enter a convent and become a nun to devote herself to God. Another, told her she should marry. They said otherwise she would have to work sewing, and that situation could not last long due to her poor eyesight. However, Amalia refused both suggestions, even though she was practically penniless and her eyesight was in poor shape.

Fortunately, her father's relatives agreed to let her live with them and pay her to sew, and she resigned herself to live that way. Later, they said they couldn't afford it and she had to leave. Then, a childhood friend told her to come live with her in a city far away. It was a great disappointment. Finally, she moved to Madrid and started publishing her poetry at age 28. She lived frugally, but when she ran out of money, she eventually had to start pawning her clothes. Meanwhile, her eyesight grew worse. She was forced to seek out those people who she previously had done some work for, to get food to eat. Her life was hard and she had never had to live like this before. Some of these people told her she should put herself in an asylum. The idea of suicide crossed her mind.

However, she continued to barely make a living sewing, selling her writings, and delivering letters and packages all at various times. She suffered hunger and periods of blindness. Eventually, she became unable to pay for a place to stay and she had to pawn all her clothes. She stated that, "then began for me an uninterrupted series of sufferings and inexplicable humiliations." [2] She again contemplated suicide. Eventually, she found a place to stay for free at the studio of two painters.

---

[2] Domingo Soler, Amalia. *Memories of a Woman. Memorias de una Mujer.* Editora Amelia Boudet. Jan.1,1990. Spain. p. 43

Then, she remembered about the religions – the Roman Catholic church and the reformed Lutheran. She visited different churches trying to find consolation, help and answers to the suffering she endured. She eventually found some comfort at an Evangelical Church which she frequently attended and made some friends there. One of the ladies took her to see another homeopath, and he told Amalia her eyes were so bad that she had to rest them for a whole year, and he would give her free medicine. The church ladies felt sorry for her and gave her alms, although she sometimes received complaints from some.

During this time an old friend of her mother's told her about a society of ladies that did philanthropic work. They gave out coupons one could use to exchange for food. She was able to receive these and when she went to El Palacio where the charity work was done, one day when she got there, she saw so many poor, and she thought:

"I arrived at the palace where the charity work was being carried out, I entered a large courtyard, and I saw hundreds of poor people from all walks of life, because something (which I could not explain at that time) in those moments (which were for me supreme moments), I recovered a part of my lost sight and I could see perfectly the scene before my eyes. There were poor people of all conditions, many women humbly dressed in their mantilla, who like me carried death in the soul, many old men with their ragged overcoats that looked like ghosts escaped from their graves… I believe that in those moments I paid a large part of the debts contracted in a hundred centuries, because I suffered such anguish. It has no name in the human language. I wanted to flee, but at the same time I said: no, it is necessary to go to the end to know the strength that my soul has, and I went over to pick up my portion, in the company of an old man who said sadly to me: Oh, lady! How horrible is the crucifixion of misery!" [3] It was then that she seriously contemplated why so many people were born so unfortunate and others so fortunate.

Discussing this topic with her eye doctor, he gave her a magazine about Spiritism (a moral philosophy and spiritual science that came out of France) that spoke about talking to the dead and the evolution of the soul. This changed her life forever. Her eyesight had improved after she had rested them for so long (now she could sew to support herself) and

---

[3] Ibid, pp. 55-56

she found the answers she needed to live. Her body and soul had received light! [4]

As time went on, her eyesight permitting, she read all the magazines she could and finally all the books by Allan Kardec (French educator and paranormal researcher) on Spiritism (*The Spirits' Book*, *The Mediums' Book*, *The Gospel according to Spiritism*, *Heaven and Hell - or Divine Justice according to Spiritism*, etc.). She attended Spiritists groups, mediumship sessions, and started writing on Spiritist topics about and for women, children, the poor, prisoners, on Spiritist principles, public rebuttals to officials of the Catholic Church which condemned Spiritism (her newsletter was suspended for weeks at times), and about human tragedy and its causes. She became the editor of a Spiritist journal by women and for women - the *Light of the Future* (*Luz del Porvenir*) founded in 1879, from where many of the stories in this book come from, and conducted worldwide correspondence with many people, throughout numerous Spanish-speaking countries (some were Spain's colonies at that time). She became a very important figure in the Spiritist movement in Spain, Spanish-speaking countries and still is with Spiritists worldwide.

At the first **International Spiritist Congress of 1888** (September 8 -11) in Barcelona, Spain, **Amalia Domingo Soler** was one of the Vice Presidents alongside the famous Spiritist medium and healer **Miguel Vives** (known as the "Apostle of Goodness") where over 2,000 people attended. [5] The original Spanish translator of Allan Kardec's Spiritist books from the French, **José María Fernández Colavida** (known as the "Spanish Kardec") was Honorary President, and the two Presidents were **Viscount of Torres Solanot** (writer, journalist, founder and organizer of many Spiritist groups in Spain) and **P. G. Leymarie** (from France, who stayed involved in the

---

[4] Ibid. p. 72

[5] https://grupoespiritaisladelapalma.files.wordpress.com/2010/12/primer-congreso-internacional_espiritista_1888.pdf (This pdf file is the written record in Spanish of the entire Congress and clearly lists it as a **Spiritist Congress**, who the leaders were, what discussions and principles were discussed, as well as the centers and delegates from various countries attending, even from the United States - from Tampa, Florida and New York.)

administering the continuing works of Kardec and the Society's magazine, the *Spiritist Review* (*Revue Spirite*) after Kardec's death).[6]

Amalia Domingo Soler's biography is in the 1915 edition of the *Universal Illustrated European-American Encyclopedia of Espasa Calpe* (*Enciclopedia Universal Ilustrada Europeo-Americana de Espasa Calpe)* a highly reputable encyclopedia of Spain as a writer of the 19th century. [7] Her writings were printed in Spiritist and regular magazines; her articles and books are still published to this very day. Many of her books in Spanish are given out for free by Spiritist societies. Many contain spirit communications relayed to her by mediums at the seances she attended, with explanations from the spirit world about the causes of why specific people suffered in particular ways in their life, due to their actions (or inactions) in past lives.

The spirit guide of her spiritual works went by the name of **Father Germain**, dictated his life story (when on earth as a priest) which she wrote down through the use of an unconscious medium named Eudaldo Pagés, who she worked with for many years. This famous Spiritist classic, in novel form - ***Memoirs of Father Germain*** (*memorias del padre germán*) – was

---

[6] The *International Spiritualist Federation* website mentions the 1888 Barcelona Congress as a Spiritualist one: https://www.theisf.com/about/history. In the early years of paranormal study, in books, the terms "spiritualist and Spiritist phenomena" were used sometimes interchangeably, but a clear distinction emerged when Spiritualism became a religion and Kardec clarified what Spiritism was. Also, there were (and still are) two schools of thought – those who believe in reincarnation and those who do not. Generally, those from England and the United States did not believe, however, those primarily from France (and its colonies like Viet Nam, which formed the religion of Caodaism - a syncretism of Spiritism with Taoism, Buddhism, Confucianism and Christianity), Spain and most Spanish-speaking countries (previously Spanish colonies, which also included the Philippines), Portugal and Brazil, Italy and France more easily accepted reincarnation and have Spiritists still. Nowadays, belief in reincarnation has increased all over the world, and here in the United States of America a 2018 report by the Pew Research Center found 33% of Americans believed in it.
See: https://www.pewresearch.org/fact-tank/2018/10/01/new-age-beliefs-common-among-both-religious-and-nonreligious-americans/

[7] https://studylib.es/doc/377316/librepensamiento-y-espiritismo-en-amalia-domingo-soler *Librepensamiento y espiritismo en Amalia Domingo Soler, escritora sevillana del siglo XIX*, Publicado en Archivo Hispalense (Sevilla, Diputación de Sevilla), Tomo LXXXIII, nº 254, septiembre - diciembre de 2000, pp. 75-102.

the first of her books translated into English, by my father **Edgar Crespo**. When Father Germain lived on Earth, he was a medium, believed in reincarnation and many good spirits assisted him in his dangerous confrontations with the Catholic Church authorities; the book is a beautiful true-life story where he teaches the Universal Religion of Love, but it also provides intrigue, adventure, hope, consolation and moral lessons. He also speaks of the love of his life during that time, "the pale girl with the black curls," of which he could not be with due to having already made his vows to God as a Catholic priest.

My father, **Edgar Crespo**, also translated for the first time into English from Spanish a book by the man who Ms. Soler respected very much and mentioned above (they knew each other well and visited each other's Spiritist centers) - **Miguel Vives**. His book of only 61 pages is a treasure for those of any faith who want to try and become a good person, and how to act: before the Creator, Jesus, one's Family, Humanity, how to deal with the temptations of life and more - entitled *A Practical Guide for the Spiritist* (*Guía Práctica*) [*Practical Guide*].

Eventually, President Luis Llach of the Spiritist center Ms. Soler attended - *La Buena Nueva* [*The Good News*] invited Ms. Soler to live with his family (wife and two children) so she could fully dedicate her life solely to her writings. She died over 110 years ago in Barcelona, in 1909.

Ms. Soler, known to Spiritists as the "Grand Dame of Spiritism" and the "Chronicler of the Poor" is still greatly respected and her work cherished, in addition her writings are still published and distributed worldwide to this day!

TRANSLATOR'S NOTE

I am not a scholar or a professional translator, but I have translated and/ or edited numerous Spanish and Portuguese articles, and several books into English since at least 1973. I am a 5th generation practicing Spiritist and medium (of over 40 years) and a 5th generation American of Spanish, Italian and French heritage.

This Spiritist classic, famous among Spiritists worldwide, made a tremendous moral impact on me (I promised my father I would translate it; he transitioned in 2008). Its 19th century text, in my mind, is a companion to her book he translated into English Ms. Soler's *Memoirs* of *Father Germain* (2006). And, it is Father Germain (her spirit guide) that is the spirit which mostly responds to Ms. Soler's questions in this book.

It is a collection of human incidents (usually tragic) that Ms. Soler wrote down, asked the spirits about them and wrote down their response. The 19th century Spanish dialogue can, at times, be very blunt due to the culture. The stories were originally printed in her magazine then placed in book form known in Spanish as **Hechos Que Prueban** which in English could be translated as either, *Facts that Prove* or as *Acts that Prove*. I chose the latter as more appropriate because the chapters report actions that occurred or that people took, and then the spirits tell of the effects (or consequences) of those acts in previous lives, whether for good or bad. The first chapter only, is where Ms. Soler presents a letter from a medium who submitted eleven short separate spirit communications of which are numbered.

As translator, I have tried to be as faithful to the text as possible, but I did make a few adjustments. Throughout this book Ms. Soler uses the word "space" (as many Spiritists did back then for the spiritual dimension), but for the purposes of a more contemporary reader's understanding I use "spirit world" or the "afterlife" instead. I left the names of cities and names in Spanish.

In addition, since Spanish has three types of quotation marks and the texts and conversations when translated into English made it difficult to know who was saying what; I felt it necessary, as needed, to add in **bold print** who was speaking: whether Ms. Soler, another person(s) or whether it was a spirit communication, which is not in the original text. In the Table of Contents, I added descriptions with the chapter titles for easy reference. The Preface, is part of a statement Ms. Soler made in Chapter 15.

Finally, all the footnotes are mine. She lived in predominately Roman Catholic Spain, so there are various Biblical references, Spanish sayings and other terminologies that needed clarification. I explain and clarify certain situations involving spirit and mediumship events discussed in some of the chapters - from the perspective of Spiritism. There are a few translator's notes. I did this especially for those not familiar with its spiritual and moral principles. I believe Ms. Soler (as a Spiritist) would not be opposed by my attempt for current day readers to have a clearer understanding of the spiritual/moral concepts in her writings. In addition, I added a commentary regarding why we should study spirit communications. I have also provided a list of suggested readings.

Before God, I feel I have translated this book to the best of my ability. I consider it a sacred work and am very grateful for the helpful spiritual inspiration I believe I received. I pray its moral and spiritual value is not diminished by any of my imperfections and that its Divine Light of the spiritual knowledge of the whys and wherefores of Life will still radiate brightly in this first English edition.

Yvonne Crespo Limoges

PREFACE

"We are continually receiving letters in which our brothers and sisters, the Spiritists, asking "the why" of many times truly dramatic events, and some of them more than dramatic, tragic, frightening and horrible [...]

The communications that we are given by the spirits serve as teachings, and more than teachings, as consolation. A comfort of which humanity is thirsty! Since there are many afflicted ones, many incarnated [those living on earth] as well as disincarnated ones [spirits in the spirit world], who have reported to us the good that our writings have produced. We continue to write not to receive applause from those who are happy, but to be useful to the unfortunates, whose number is incalculable."

Amalia Domingo Soler

CHAPTER ONE

CLAIRVOYANCE AND SPIRIT COMMUNICATIONS

Ms. Soler:

Continuing with our custom of publishing all the good that we know concerning Spiritism, we have extracted sections of an extensive letter we have received giving us an account of new communications and clairvoyance obtained by a medium, one that we have already occupied ourselves within our article "Spiritual Protection." [8]

Since earthly life is a series of hardships, it is of much benefit to read and meditate on these communications from the spirit world that impel us towards resignation and hope.

There is so much suffering...so it is very necessary to know to have hope, having confidence in God's mercy, and in the enormous force of our own unwavering willpower.

This brother writes in his letter about various visions wherein the medium not only sees beautiful luminous spirits whose contemplation transports the medium to other regions but, are received with sweet words

---

[8] A topic she must have addressed in a previous article of her Spiritist magazine *Luz del Porvenir* [*Light of the Future*]. The word *Clairvoyance* in the title means "clear vision" and is a *psychic ability*, one of gaining knowledge through what parapsychologists call extrasensory perception (ESP). *Mediumship* is the ability to hear, see, feel spirits and/or have the facility for trance mediumship. Most mediums are also psychic.

that make one realize that beyond the Earth there is another life of love and infinite progress.

The medium, in order to obtain visions and spirit communications, isolates completely from human misery, separates from bitter memories and sad thoughts, and solely thinks of God's greatness.

At various spirit sessions, he being outside of this material world, has listened to communications given by diverse spirits that we have copied in continuation below:

Several Spirit Communications

Number One:

"The humbler and simple one is, the less the world knows you, because humanity wants vanity, ostentation and material things. The distractions of the Earth are for those of this world; you have already found divine joy within the kingdom of God.

"The humble should feel satisfaction in carrying their crosses [life's sufferings] otherwise in what way could you resemble the Master [Jesus]? In what way, can you prove you are submissive and resigned, and what testimony can you give to the Father that you respect His Law? We should be like the navigator traveling on high seas, that in the middle of a tempest when the waves come so furiously that it appears, they will sink the boat (for behind one wave, comes another and another), but the navigator resists and struggles until he overcomes because he knows he may lose his life. How unfortunate are those who lose their composure!

"Same for you; the trials of life are as tempests, and at times it appears that they will annihilate you. How unfortunate for you if you are driven to despair! Ask for strength and struggle with valor! And, just like the navigator who passed through the storm, singing along to his rolling ship, who now can enjoy tranquil and happy days; you will live happy when you have triumphed over your trials and sufferings, and in the kingdom of God." [9]

---

[9] For Spiritists, the "kingdom of God or heaven" is where happy, good and moral spirits are. in the spirit world.

Number Two:

"Don't expect anything good in this world, because many want to surrender themselves to the cult of vanity and apart themselves from virtue. Have courage and resignation to carry the cross of your captivity.

"Lift up your thoughts and remember the multitude of martyrs, and remember the road of Bitterness, the Calvary Mount, the Cross, and the Death. [10] Have you arrived at that level of those extreme circumstances? Strengthen your willpower, love your pain, love the sorrows and anguish, and obey the law, for the father has made everything good, and one day, even if centuries from now, all will turn to light, happiness and peace."

Number Three:

"Come to me, for I will help elevate your prayers to the Father. You give thanks now when circumstances satisfy you; that is good. But also, give it when you are in tribulation and pain oppresses you; and give it with serenity and love, for that is precisely what elevates you.

"Reject all categories of thoughts that are not honorable before God."

Number Four:

"What do you ask for? Aren't you satisfied with today? Give thanks to God. If you had more than enough you would lose yourselves or make use of it contrary to your desires. Don't think of tomorrow, for tomorrow will be a new day. When you do this, your sufferings, trials and pain don't afflict you, nor cause you to fall. Think of it as if you had made a step towards your perfection; but if you worry about tomorrow and your sufferings it makes you lose your calmness of spirit, to know your soul's progress has remained stationary."

---

[10] The last days of sufferings of Jesus of Nazareth on Earth.

Number Five:

"Come to me those who feel overburdened and I will relieve your sadness, for I will alleviate and provide rescue by our Father. For that, there is no need of riches or titles, but only abnegation, love, and sacrifices. Ask for me, I will come; for I have come from the Father who loves us all and is with us, if we are with Him.

"Don't complain about your trials, because who are you to grumble? Give thanks to God and resign yourself to the Divine Law."

Number Six:

"The Earth that the Father has conceded you for your purification could make you happy, if all the poor and the rich, thought every day the following: 'Why have I come to the Earth?' However, you have been neglectful and deficient in the [divine] Law. The passions, pride and cruelty have taken a hold of humanity and in place of making the world in which you live an Eden, it has been converted into a hell. I say hell, because in Creation there are no other hells than those what rebellious souls have made; where they suffer and will suffer, because instead of peace you have war, instead of loving each other, you have made each other suffer. And, the greater part of humanity act like animals: growling and tearing each other to pieces. This conduct has resulted in tears, blood, horrors, crimes, sufferings, punishments and confusions for centuries and centuries."

Number Seven:

"If those who would obey the divine law want to avoid expiation and arrive at days of peace, be gentle and humble of heart and be resigned to your trials. Separate yourself from temptation and be strong in virtue and work. Spread peace and love to attract those who would oppose you in this struggle, as wild beasts are destroyed; for if you succeed in carrying the light where there is so much darkness, you will merit recompense from Up High."

Number Eight:

"Unite yourselves closely, and respect one another, and observe...those that you see that by their virtue, humility and their abnegation make themselves worthy of being chosen of the Father. Take them before you as a guide, and follow them, so finally none of you are lost and all are eligible to enter the kingdom of God."

Number Nine:

"Be careful on speaking when you are sad and disheartened for the pains that you suffer upon the Earth, if your words are not in praise of God, because the Father has done all well under the law of justice; and as the stars cannot change course, neither can your destiny be changed. Therefore, when you are sad and depressed, withdraw to a quiet place, and devote yourself to prayer, and I will come and console you, and others will also come to console you."

Number Ten:

"Why do you look so eagerly upon the earth for hours of calm and of peace? Don't you know that it is not a place of peace, but of struggle? Expect always those hours of trial and suffering but await them with a serene spirit and with courage, and in that way, you will not become so disappointed regarding the struggles and oppression of life.   " Y o u , who love the Master so much, don't you know that upon the Earth he did not find one hour of peace? Why do you so anxiously desire much of what is not upon this world? Remember, you are in a place of trials, expiation and of sorrows; adjust to this suffering, and resign yourselves so that you can find peace in the kingdom of the Father."

Number Eleven:

"All who want to follow me should carry their cross with love, and don't think going to one place or another you can escape it. Wherever you so, so goes your cross; and if you try to escape from it, you will then carry two of them, that of your expiations and the other of your rebellion."

Ms. Soler continues:

Up to this point were the spirit communications; [and] finishing the letter of our brother, he leaves us with this last comment:

"We do not insist in demonstrating the truth of the manifestations received of this fine medium; we only set them forth as they are for your consideration so that you can take what you feel is good and leave what you feel is not."

Ms. Soler's final comments:

For our part, we believe these spirit communications deserve to be read and studied, because within them they advise us regarding the most difficult, which are regarding resignation and serenity during the battles of life.

We all know how to give advice regarding resignation to others, and all are good seamen when on solid ground, but when our own boat takes in water, the majority of people may wish they were never born. So, when some who are dissatisfied argue that the spirits always tell us the same thing, "that we be good, humble, and resigned" ... we say, what other thing can they express, if the most that is lacking within us is kindness, humility, and resignation? He who is not good, does not love humanity; he who is not humble, is not tolerant; and he who is not resigned cannot wait regarding his own progress. Therefore, we believe that Spiritist books should be an inexhaustible stream of sweet and consolatory teachings.

The wise write about their scientific observations, and the spirits know how to read the alphabet of Infinity. So, save some pages to be filled by spirit communications that advise the troubled to keep calm, and have hope during their sufferings and in their distress. Humanity, what are we? Castaways, shipwrecked upon the sea of life; and may the Spirits of Light be our pilots!

CHAPTER TWO

ONE HUNDRED AND FIFTY YEARS

Article from a newspaper:

"A beggar of 150 years old died in Belgoroff (Russia). His interesting novel-like life had truly fantastic episodes. This man, named Andrés Basilica, started begging at fifteen years old. First, he made himself one-handed, later deaf, next lame, much later blind, and from seventy-years old onwards, he acted as a deaf-mute practically perfect.

"Well then, by virtue of such deceptions, the good of Andrés Basilica obtained altogether a fortune of several thousand rubles, with which he acquired three inns that he put in the name of one of his sons; all while continuing to beg without harm, like any fool. Going from one city to another, he acquired a house and a car, and handed it over to his children. Then, he would begin to walk to another province, where he continued his life of a "lucky beggar."

"He died, as we said, at one hundred and fifty years old; leaving eight children a fortune, between farms and money, of two million rubles."

Ms. Soler:

The newspaper item that preceded these lines caught my attention when I read it, and I exclaimed in horror, what a long expiation, one hundred and fifty years!

What history can this spirit have? It must be very troubled, and there must have been much sin to deserve so many years of torture, because we have to confess that life is burdensome when one reaches twelve lustrums[11]; and at sixty years, for how strong an organism can be, it begins to decline, multiple ailments announce old age. Juvenile illusions, like the flowers of a day, wither, leaves fall off and all that is left of them is a melancholy memory, and at times one feels the lamentations of Campoamor[12]: "Suffer so much, for so little…" that life without illusions does not have enchantment, it does not have charm, it has no attraction, it is a slow sickness, without great crises, but sickness in the end. Sensing that the Russian beggar would have a sad history, I asked the spirit guide of my literary works if I was right in believing that the large course of his life on Earth was atonement for previous faults, and the spirit told me:

Spirit communication:

"The present is always a corollary of the past, as the future is of the present. Life is a series of events intimately linked within you. Life is like a bundle of yarn without a loose end, and it never breaks no matter how tangled it gets. It is not necessary to do to it what was done by Alexander, cutting the Gordian knot with his sword; such is the nature of this knot, of this tangled bundle of life, that although violence wants to break it and it appears that it may break, there are some invisible threads so resistant, that these do not break, and not even death can break them. This spirit, by stages or by force, is paying off its debts in innumerable incarnations (not valuing being a scholar and considered a true notable in the scientific world) because sentiment had not been united with his science and the strict fulfillment of duty. Great among the greats, he returned to Earth and as compensation, each is given recompense depending on their works.

"He who had lived ultimately deceiving and pretending to have physical defects has shined in this world over many centuries. When Greece flourished, there among the groupings of illustrious men, the materialist Ataulfo stood out. He, who searched for the secret for the

---

[11] The word "lustrum" was used to denote a 5-year period in the Ancient Roman language.

[12] Ramon Campoamor was a 19th century poet and playwright from Spain.

prolongation of life, who detested death, and even more so than death old age. He, who would say that it was humiliating and shameful to let physical decay dominate; and that intelligence should search for heroic remedies to conquer the struggle of the debilitated organism; that man should not be resigned to die, like the irrational immolators die [sacrificing themselves] before their gods. Ataulfo, who was the master and teacher of many sciences, with his disciples were dedicated to finding tonics and medicines that would strengthen debilitated bodies due to the weight of the years. He (without understanding it at that time) dreamed of eternal life. He wanted to live many centuries, and since he did not comprehend that his spirit could live not bound to his body, all his earnest desire was to fortify his body and devise diverse specifics in order to be reborn like he said.

"His studies and experiments produced many victims, he sacrificed many innocent beings; tender children and beautiful young people, because the old man needed to drink the rare blood of a virgin, mixing said blood with a small quantity of the powder of humans, or rather they were the pulverized bones of children. He committed in that existence many crimes, but he committed them without as great a responsibility for himself [13] (because he did not kill because he liked to kill). He did not delight in the agony of his victims, he prevented them suffering and solely wanted to find the means to live for ages. According to his theory, if men managed to live for many centuries continually acquiring new knowledge, the Earth would be a paradise because it would be enhanced by every man due to his inventions and their incessant discoveries. He dreamed, I repeat, about the truth of life, but did not agree with seeing a sage die at the height of his maturity. He lamented the lost energy, initiatives that would be paralyzed and at all costs he wanted to fight death. He loved life with true idolatry; and upon reaching old age, not due to the concoctions he took, but by the hygienic methods he subjected himself, he reached middle age. He was a model of self-control; he admirably regulated his hours of work, of complete rest and meditation. He glimpsed the streams of eternal life; he suspected that there was a force superior to all, but that force was not to his liking. He wanted to be great on his own, he was the personification of pride and he wanted everything due to his own efforts. When he broke

---

[13] If compared to one who actually *enjoys* killing.

*ee from his physical body, completely useless by the enormity of his years, his amazement knew no bounds. He was so stunned to see what he had never dreamed of, the life of a detached spirit from the body. If one may use the phrase, Ataulfo went mad on finding eternity with its distinct laws, of some which he even knew.

"How small the prideful sage saw himself!... When he understood that centuries were much shorter than the seconds on the clock of Time. He, who had committed so many assassinations to prolong life for a few years, was full of life without that physical body whose preservation had made him commit so many abuses.

"He quickly returned to Earth, eager for new discoveries, and arrived in penetrating a temple of glory for his inventions and discoveries all aimed to prolong human life without pain, without loss of strength. Although no longer employing his previous methods of sacrificing children and virgins for the sake of science, he imposed on others; causing the ruin of many families, because he seized the wealth of many to undertake long journeys, promising large profits that never came to fruition. He forgot very easily his clients. His pride blinded him, and he believed that he did them a great favor (although stripping them of their property) in order to seek a scientific truth by some means of associating them with his glorious enterprises.

"He became very learned. He turned from that world when travel became an accumulation of impossibilities and difficulties to conquer. Yet, his heart was dry, the sweetness of love was totally unknown to him. The time arrived when he felt coldness in his soul, and he found himself all alone in the spirit world with his science. He heard the warnings from his spirit guide, and finally he was convinced that knowledge without love is like a fountain without water; like a tree whose top reaches to heaven but gives no shade or fruit.

"He recognized the greatness of God, and with the spirited eagerness matching his sympathy towards science, he commenced a series of existences of expiation, dying many times sacrificed at an early age. He who sacrificed so many innocents, ultimately wanted to endure all the time possible in humiliation upon the Earth (because he was previously blinded by his pride, and believed he was greater than all of humanity), and, at the same time pay back a minimal part of what had been seized by him.

When he begged, it was not for him to live comfortably, but so his children could live, those whose wealth he had plundered in other times to satisfy his whims and vanity. The learned man of yesterday who took so much care concerning the vitality of his physical body, in this last existence he used it to deceive, to mislead, so as to extract fruit from an apparent defect. There are many considerations provided of the different uses made of the physical body of this great sage of yesterday! You had reason to believe that the spirit of the beggar had a long history! Science without love, leads to so many cliffs! Goodbye."

Ms. Soler:

How much instruction there is within the above spirit communication!... Victor Hugo already has said that without love, the sun would extinguish; and I say, that one who does not love, does not live. [14]

---

[14] Victor Hugo (1802-1885) studied law, but became a French poet and novelist, of which his most famous novels were the *Hunchback of Notre Dame* and *Les Misérables*. Also, Victor Hugo attended spirit seances with some family and friends when he lived on the isle of Jersey.

CHAPTER THREE

EVERYTHING IS JUST

Ms. Soler:

A friend of mine currently living in Mérida, Yucatan [Mexico], sent us (with his letter) a small obituary that sadly affected us, to the extent that we asked the spirit that generally guides our work if something could be said concerning that profoundly unfortunate being, whose existence was so horrible. Our invisible friend, seeing that our question had no other motive than of learning, and a desire to serve us a useful lesson did give us some details.

In continuation, transcribed below is the aforementioned letter, which read:

Arcadia Góngora

Nature uses often appalling mockery for humanity.

Already deep within the household, or in the public front, evil sentiments usually make a bloody mockery of the king of Creation - man; and, who the Supreme Creator formed in its own shape and likeness according to the biblical phrase. Usually, it leads from the throne where Nature placed him, unto the last and dirty steps of degradation.

One has seen individuals of the human species (on all steps of the social scale) carrying on, as not even the dullest of animals would have conducted themselves.

Put a hand on a chick of whatever bird, or over the litter of whatever quadruped animal, or on the cub of the most ferocious beast, and you will see how the parents pounce on you; and, they despair if they find themselves unable to take revenge or defend their young. Also, if their young get sick or go astray, with what affection or distress, they care, cure or seek them out!

However, one has seen fathers, and what is most monstrous still, mothers that remain indifferent and cold before the agony or the dead body of a child. Or, they forget or abandon them to the extremes of life, as if they had never conceived them or nourished them from their breast… People have been seen dying in such conditions. Fortunately, it is not the norm with the existence of societies. Such gloomy reflections are suggested concerning the recent conclusion of a drama, that as a result of the central character not being humble or having developed comportment in the shadows of human poverty, every thoughtful person and humanitarian spirit will be left touched.

In a village, on the 13th day of the present month, has ceased forever the suffering of a man known by the name of Arcadio Góngora.

It appears that it has been thirty-two years since he completely lost his reason, victim of a certain inherited organic predisposition, by an undetermined misfortune.

He was an arrogant young man of twenty-eight to thirty years old, full of life and health. Unfortunately, his insanity inoffensive and calm at first, after a while made him hostile and dangerous, an such was the case that they had to chain him to a post like a wild beast for his own tranquility and that of his family. There, they would bring him his miserable food from where he never moved, and there…he lived as if an animal, and on occasions, in worse conditions than that.

It had been about ten years that I knew of him. Yet, the impression he then produced in my presence, still it has not been erased, nor do I think it will ever be erased from my mind.

He was with his right elbow resting on his knee, and his cheek in the palm of his hand, sitting in a small hammock which was all the furniture within the crumbling, unkempt and bleak thatched-hut dwelling; sad and isolated from the others, like a pariah or like one infested with the plague… his foot clamped tightly between a ring and the end of a chain attached to an iron pole. His hair, whiskers and beard grown unkempt, fell to his shoulders; his chest and back frame formed some features that should have been good, but then they were disfigured. His black terrifying eyes were almost jumping out of their sockets, while his dirty torn pants and shirt revealed in various places his hairy skin. He appeared as a savage or a hermit lost in the deepest communities of the jungle. He spoke non-stop; now raising then lowering his voice, but in a fast and intelligent language.

As I stood in the threshold of the door, he raised his eyes, fixed them on me with an expression that made me look away, and he turned around as if looking for some object.

All of a sudden, he bowed down, put his hand on a rock and violently threw it at me, but I saw the movement and hid behind the door, which received the terrible blow, that if reaching me, without a doubt would have done me harm.

I observed him a moment with sincere piety, and I left with a heavy heart.

From that day until his death, I did not return to see him but two or three times.

No one could approach him without being in danger, and his poor family, composed solely of women, suffered cruel punishment in order to attend to his subsistence.

The times when I was passing in the vicinity of his little hut, I listened with emotion for his deep and loud voice, which echoed in the late and silent hours of the night, vibrating at such a long distance and hovering over the sleeping village, and rose to the sky like a painful protest against a society that abandoned him, or like a mysterious prayer permeated by an infinite sadness. Then I wondered why divine justice had not restored reason to that unfortunate one or not ceased his appalling misfortune forever; taking his life, completely insufferable for him, especially since he was not conscious of his state.

They would say he practically never slept; the decline of his strength forced him to keep silent and give way to brief moments of repose.

On different occasions, charitable people tried to send him to the general hospital in Mérida, where if he could not be cured, he would at least be cleaned and better attended to. However, his family was always opposed to this, and entreated one to believe that in spite of the worst, they could attend to him; always being better off than in the hands of strangers.

Deadly misgiving! Fatal mistake that perhaps worsened the situation of that insane unhappy one! For ultimately, he had a disease of the abdomen for some time that was slowly consuming him aggravating his situation (his body was partly devoured by worms anticipating his final situation). Then, on the 13th of the present month, Providence took pity on him, putting a final end to his earthly sufferings.

At that time, he was approximately fifty-two years old and he was insane for thirty-two years.

It is recounted that before he died, that hidden intelligence, like a fateful lightning bolt tearing into the deep darkness of a stormy night, shone on his spirit upon leaving his miserable prison. They said, he pitifully exclaimed in the Mayan language, "Oh, brothers, now the hour of my death has arrived." When death presents itself in that form or in another similar way, I think rather than deplore it, one should give thanks. In these cases, far from being something bad, death has a positive benefit.

Peace to the spirit of Arcadio Góngora! Rest in the abode of the martyrs!

F. Perez Alcala
(Yucatan) Tizimin, December 19, 1882

Ms. Soler:

As our readers will understand, this sad story leaves room for serious and painful reflections because if there is no effect without a cause, the cause of such a deplorable effect should be horrible, dreadful; and unfortunately, we have not deceived ourselves in our assessment because our invisible friend told us in the following communication:

Spirit communication:

"Great remorse weighs heavily upon Old Europe, that has conquered with blood and fire the countries you call the New World and other beautiful continents. Spain has played no small part in those horrible struggles, or rather those many warlords in which they succumbed to fratricidal killings, who were defeated and outnumbered by their opponents; but not by valor or gallantry of the conquistadors, who called themselves civilized (they were wilder and more rebellious than the savages, more depraved and more ferocious than beasts).

"How many crimes have been committed upon these within their virgin forests by those from distant lands? How many victims have been sacrificed for the sake of the crudest, wildest and filthiest passions! It horrifies one to read the history of humans on earth; stained with all the vices, sunk in lust and wickedness.

"Great expiations are being suffered, but if you had to pay eye-for-an-eye and tooth-for-tooth, the centuries would pass the same as your lives, and you would almost believe in eternal suffering upon seeing the continuation of your incessant martyrdom in spite of Divine Mercy. Since the laws of God are immutable and have to be fulfilled, it is that you necessarily have to suffer all the pains, going through all the agonies you have done to others. The only advantage you enjoy and having in your possession when atoning is that no being of Creation lacks someone who loves you. Deceived is he, who says he is alone; all of you are accompanied by a soul who cares for you, more or less relative according to the enormity of your offense. In the absence of rationality, you have an irrational race very friendly to man, you have the dog; a symbol of fidelity, with a slight lacking, it serves to you as a guide, as a companion to take part in your sorrows and your joys, and this in the visible world. Outside the scope of your material life are your protective spirits giving you encouragement and resignation in the hours of cruel agony. Oh, if you were all alone like you say, unhappy ones, what would become of you? Yes; you would fall annihilated, crushed before the terror and the solitude.

"If when your body is laid to rest, your spirit did not find a helping hand to detain it and not hear a loving voice that asked, 'where are you going, poor exiled one? Do you believe you have the strength to reanimate your organism and start the work of another day?' No, the soul needs love like the flowers need the dew, like the birds their wings, and without that essentially divine nourishment, it cannot live. When your faults obligate you to not have a family or a home, or related beings, or to be separated from your peers, then one's reason darkens. Man is a social being par excellence, he is attracted to form a family, like he is a member of the universal family. He remembers his origin, and without the ties of love, of friendship, of relationship, of sympathy he cannot live, visible or invisible. That is why so often the unfortunate say, 'I wish I was always sleeping, because then I don't remember my misadventures.' Yet, it is not because they don't remember; on the contrary, they see them with more clarity. What they have is that they see themselves accompanied by their spirit friends [15] that encourage, fortify and help them carry the weight of their cross. All those who believe they are disinherited upon the Earth have their protectors in the spirit world who care about their future legacy and save their treasures when they are worthy of possessing them.

"There are some spirits so depraved, they make such a bad use of their free will, that for these, isolation lasts longer because they reject with their excesses, all the love and tender care of the souls who want goodness for them. This matter has to do with the spirit that has caused an impression on you with the suffering of his last existence; horrible, but deserved because in Creation, always remember this, everything is just.

"That spirit, in one of its previous existences, was one of those Spanish adventurers that went to Mexican lands to impose his tyrannical laws: reducing to servitude the warring tribes, abusing miserably the innocence of their wives, enriching himself in such a tremendous way with his usurpation and pillage, committing all kinds of abuses, imposing his will on independent villages, and becoming a tyrant, whose cruelty verged on the improbable. It appeared impossible that such a man had received life from the Spirit of God because if it was admitted that there were two powers, one good and the one bad, it seems that this dreadful one would be the favorite son of the prince of darkness, so immense was his perversity. Brutal and lascivious to exaggeration, the most beautiful maidens and the most elegant young men had to accede to his shameless desires; his continued excitement was the eventual martyrdom of his unfortunate slaves. Brave and fearless, he committed the riskiest of enterprises, and only lacked a triumphal chariot to conquer a Mexican virgin, the most beautiful Azora. Lovely as a young woman in the paradise of Mohammed, chaste and pure like the virgins in the Christian heaven, Azora was the

---

[15] While the physical body sleeps, our spirit returns to the spirit world where we can consult with our spirit protectors and loved ones who care about us; this is further explained in Allan Kardec's, *The Spirits' Book*.

darling of her father and her brothers who loved her. Her numerous family members looked up to her as an elected from the Father of Light; and, all respected her as privileged because her big eyes radiated a celestial light, and from her mouth came prophetic words listened to with attentiveness by young and old alike.

"One afternoon she got together with them, and said with a sad voice: 'Great and invisible misfortune will fall upon us; birds of prey spread their black wings and cover with leaden mists our clear skies. Tremble, my companions, not for us that will be the victims, but for the relentless executioners that ignore our sorrowful complaints; for we will depart purified by martyrdom, but, alas, the tormentors!'

"Azora was not deceived, that night one hundred adventurers led by Gonzalo, came looking for her. Azora, considered a perfect beauty, he wanted her to become one of his unfortunate concubines. That beautiful young woman begged Gonzalo to not cause an uprising, and to avoid bloodshed; she would follow him, but he was to respect the life of her father and relatives. Since Azora had an ascendant influence so extraordinary over all the beings of Earth, Gonzalo also felt her magical influence, and for the first time he obeyed the command of that woman. [16]

"Azora had taken precautions and had gathered all of her people in a great council. As they pondered what to do (she went to meet the enemy) telling her relatives that she would place herself in prayer to attract to her head the radiance of eternal light, and that they do not disturb her meditation. Since they were used to her being days in ecstasy, they did not suspect anything. In the meanwhile, she surrendered herself as a sacrificial victim to her executioner, while her imposed conditions were to be respected.

"Gonzalo had feelings for Azora (as much as that depraved being could feel), and he wanted to tarnish her forehead with his unclean lips, but she stopped him with an authoritative gesture, and he stayed petrified which caused him immense astonishment regarding his timidity.

"Upon obtaining the news of what had happened, her relatives swore to die or to avenge the dishonor of the chaste virgin consecrated to the Father of Light. They ignored the magical influence that the young woman

---

[16] Her "magical" influence was nothing more than her moral spiritual superiority which he could sense.

had exerted over them, regarding her abductor. To them, he was defiling the woman who consecrated herself to the divine mysteries and their anger had no limits.

"They marched forward to look for the beast in his lair. Gonzalo (momentarily lulled by the magical influence of Azora) upon seeing them felt reborn with all his bad instincts; the charm was broken. Helped by his wicked henchmen, they imprisoned the assailants, and gagged them cruelly. Azora went mad when she was taken to her father who she idolized, and saw him laden with chains, covered with voracious insects that had been thrown upon his body so as to devour him slowly. Before that martyr of parental love, Gonzalo committed the most infamous of acts which could hurt that unfortunate father the most. He desecrated the body of that poor mad woman, who yielded to his impure desires until the light of her clear intelligence extinguished. Also, for many days the father of Azora suffered the horrible martyrdom of seeing his daughter held within the power of Gonzalo (who took pleasure in tormenting that poor unhappy one) and making him witness acts that cannot be described.

"In the end, Azora died, and Gonzalo continued insulting his unfortunate prisoner; throwing the filth of their horses in the dungeons, spitting on their face, committing all kinds of abuses against those defenders of her honor.

"Azora's father died after cruel sufferings. His children also perished; of that brave tribe, not even one was left. All succumbed to the power of Gonzalo, who continued committing infamy upon infamy, until one of his slaves assassinated him, while he slept in his bed overcome by drunkenness.

"His life was a web of horrific crimes; and as he delighted in evil, as he had the intelligence to know that his conduct was wicked, since he found along his pathway good-hearted men who set out to educate him and he despised them, his expiation must match the gravity of his faults. However, he had already incarnated different times with misfortune being his inheritance. He has done so much wrong!... Therefore, he lacked within all his material existences someone who cared for him. Yet, Azora, spirit of light, has encourages him in all of his excruciating journeys. She went to Earth this last time with the noble purpose of starting Gonzalo's regeneration, but her extreme moral sensibilities could not withstand the violent shock she received when she saw her father in such an unfortunate state; the trial was superior to her efforts, which since only God is infallible, spirits do not always know how to measure the depth of the abyss where they may fall.

"It is very different to see the miseries of the Earth at a great distance [in the spirit world] than to live among them, and many spirits succumb in the midst of their arduous trials and atonements.

"We will never tire of telling you, no matter how criminal a man is seen, one cannot correct him by violence; which that unfortunate one has had enough of with the enormity of his crimes.

"Where is there the most misery then, is it within criminality? What hell can compare to the incessant series of miserable incarnations that a spirit inclined to evil must endure? In some insanity, in others hideous deformity, in that one misery with all its horrors and shameful humiliations, and other sufferings impossible to enumerate. As, there are no numbers enough to summarize all the pain that a spirit can feel in your arithmetic tables to form a total; the imagination gets lost when you want to subject a fixed amount at all, to the infinity of life that surrounds us.

"After those terrible incarnations, came those weary, sad, solitary existences in which life has continual obstacles. The spirit inclines toward goodness, but its love does not find recompense. Spirits, appearing ungrateful, look on with indifference the first steps of that poor sick one that wants to love, and does not find someone to deposit that affection upon, and even the flowers wither with his breath before offering their fragrance. These existences are very painful; expiations of which actually the majority of those on earth suffer; spirits with a long history, strewn with horrors and cruelties.

"In this period, is when man needs to know something of his life, because he now has sufficient knowledge to comprehend the advantages of goodness and the harmfulness of evil. Therefore, since everything reaches its time, that is why we have come to awaken your attention; that is why the tables dance and why the furniture changes places, and the voices of the spirits resounded in different parts of the Earth, because it is necessary that it be understood that you were not all alone in the world.

"We have prevented many suicides and have returned many sick souls to health.

"We have shown a great number of prideful sages that human science is a grain of sand in comparison to the infinite, the universal science; and an immense revolution is being carried out, because the hour of progress has arrived for the generations of this planet.

"You will begin to know the truth, that is now rejected because the light dazzles you, but finally you will acclimate to it, and you will expand the circle of your earthly family and look upon the spirits as members of your universal family.

"You will be more compassionate with criminals when you know, that is what you also have been, and perhaps that tomorrow, you may fall again. A spirit attached to wrongdoing has a hard time deciding to be good. It is like a little one who takes one step forward and then five steps backwards, and goes about repeating the same path many times. In the same way, you also have, for all spirits of Creation have equally done it, with the sole difference that some have more determination than others and more courage to suffer the penalties they have imposed upon themselves.

"What you need to seek in our communications is good advice and useful teachings, make use of the instructions from beyond the grave provided that these will always mark a path of virtue and not flatter your vices or encourage your weaknesses. Always mistrust everything from the spirits that promise a world of glory as you abandon Earth. Study your own history (look at yourself without emotion) and you will see you are full of defects: small ones, very small, even microscopic ones of jealousy, vengeance, envy, avarice. All are very close friends of yours, but with your neighbor, no. So, with such a stained robe, do not expect to sit at the table of your Father; for that, it is necessary to be covered with luminous robes in order to enter the dwellings where life is exempt from penalties. Nevertheless, spirits never cease to provide for the cultivation of science and the noblest works of research, because souls will always have something more to learn.

"We have come to demonstrate to you that the soul never dies and that man is the one who rewards or punishes himself; that the laws of God are those that govern nature and are immutable. We come to give advice, to strengthen you, to teach you to know about universal harmony; to tell you that the story of your mistakes of yesterday are the causes of your misfortunes today. This is the mission of the spirits near you; spurring you on to work, to cultivate your reason, and that is what will lead you to the perfect understanding of God. When you comprehend that all in Creation is just, then that is when you will adore God in spirit in truth. Then you will praise his name in the hosanna promised by religions, which still has not been sung on the earth by the human race; the birds are the only ones that sing when they greet the star of the day in its splendid appearance.

"Remember there is no lamenting without a history behind it, nor good actions unrewarded; work on your progression. When you find one of these unfortunate ones (like the spirit that is the basis of my communication) sympathize with him. After such horrible suffering, for natural reasons many painful existences await him, wherein solitude is his heritage. Although, as I said before, the spirit never is alone. What happens for the sick soul, is as when a man leaves a serious illness; that in its convalescence it is so frail, so impertinent, so willful, that his entire family has to indulge him, caress him and provide him the most tender care. This is the same demand spirits have when they leave the chaos of mistakes and start their rehabilitation. Then, they want the love of family, the sympathy of friends, and social consideration. As they have not earned what they want, and do not deserve it, so they do not have it. Although they do not lack a being that wants them and pities them, that's not enough for them. They want more, and run eagerly after a phantom which man calls happiness, and as the wandering Jew of the legend, they cross the world without finding a hospitable place to rest. [17]

"The majority of incarnated beings on Earth are sick convalescents, and solely with the spirits are found the doctors of the soul that will calm their devouring thirst.

"You are tired and fatigued, you have hunger, you are cold; rest a

---

[17] During this time the Roman Apostolic Catholic Church was very influential and this saying is based on the medieval Christian legend well known in Spain and throughout Europe - about a poor Jewish man condemned to wander the world without resting until the Second Coming of Christ because he mocked Jesus on his way to the Cross. Ms. Soler's use of this was common for the time, but it is not to be construed as her being anti-Semitic. As a firm believer in reincarnation, Ms. Soler was well aware spirits can reincarnate into the body of a family of any religion and all spirits are equal before the Creator regardless of their beliefs or non-belief. In fact, in her book, *Memoirs of Father Germain*, there is a chapter when the Catholic priest Father Germain tells of assisting a persecuted Jew and explains to his parishioners that we are all equally the children of God.

moment, your friends from beyond the grave want to make your journey less painful, demonstrating with undeniable facts that in the infinite life, all is just."

Ms. Soler:

What more can we express after what the spirit has told us? We are completely in accord with his reasonable considerations. Due to very painful experiences, we have to concede to his reason, and repeat with him that the Earth is a hospital of generations of the sick that are passing their convalescence here. Solely with spirits of good intention are those we can receive healthy advice, relief and regeneration.

What we are, we have, due to the study of Spiritism; the purest joys of our life.

We have acquired a profound resignation and an intimate conviction that no one has more than what they deserve. This certainty is true, and the only happiness that the spirit can have amidst his expiations.

We, studying Nature (reading within that book that never ends) admiring the mathematical exactitude that its laws have, we work as much as possible on our progress. When loneliness overwhelms us, when discouragement dominates us, we look to the heavens, we see within it the splendor of eternal life, and we say: all is just in Creation!

CHAPTER FOUR

WITHOUT ARMS AND WITHOUT LEGS

Ms. Soler:

In one of the Roman Catholic prayers, they call this world a "valley of tears," and I believe that it is the best definition that can be said of this penitentiary of the Universe, because in reality, there is not one being that can boast, "I am happy in every sense of the word!"

Many of the monarchs suffer incurable diseases; there are millionaires in the United States that can only nourish themselves with very small quantities of milk; others cannot sleep because they suffocate and have millions in income that don't provide them the slightest enjoyment, with what descends to the poorest. If some poor are strong and robust, they lack the most essential to sustain their vital forces, being watched as they fade as a lamp that goes out in the fullness of their youth. Therefore, happiness is like a cloud of smoke that dissolves at the slightest breath from the hurricane winds of life; like the first rays of sun melts the fog.

However, among so much suffering there are distinct degrees: there is the bearable, and then there is the overwhelming. Speaking just days ago, a friend told me the following:

Some time ago I went to the water reservoir and there I found a family that I will never forget. It was a polite and friendly young married couple, their faces radiating joy. They both loved, with that first love that resembles a flowering tree waiting for much later to become a bunch of beautiful seasoned fruit. They were joined by love, and only love. He was a modest employee, she a humble seamstress. They saw each other and they loved; they loved and they united. Upon uniting and receiving the blessing he thought of the arrival of his first son, and, she contemplated on the baby Jesus and asked God if she could have a son as beautiful as that angelic figure. A year later, the loving couple felt dominated by lively and loving eagerness. Forcefully economizing, they bought everything necessary to dress a newborn; batiste little shirts with precious lace, white dresses with fine embroidery, handsome skullcaps, all the most beautiful, all the most delicate which seemed little enough for a child, that should arrive asking for kisses from their smiles. At last, arrived the supreme moment, Aurea felt the first acute pains of a laborious labor and gave birth to a boy. She wanted to see it immediately, her husband and the persons who surrounded her, sad and quiet, appeared as if they did not understand. They all looked at each other, and whispered.

Aurea yelled alarmingly, "Do you not hear me? I want to embrace my child…Is it dead…?"

"No," responded the husband, "but…"

"But what? What's going on?"

"The child has no arms…or legs!"

"Like that, he will spend more time in my arms," replied Aurea, embracing her son with delirious eagerness.

The child was beautiful; white as snow with blue eyes, abundant blond hair and his large eyes had an expressive look. When I met the child, he was eight or ten months old and gorgeous. His mother was crazy about him. It was the same with the father, but the latter, when his wife could not hear him, would say with deep bitterness, "So much I wanted a son… and he has arrived without arms… and legs!"

Her friend continues:

"How unjust God is! If my son was rich…. but I am so poor! Believe me, Amalia, that child lives in my memories. What could it have done? What role will it have represented in that story?"

Ms. Soler responds:

My friend, I will ask because your testimony has considerably touched me. Night and day, I think of that child; about how much he will suffer if he grows to manhood with no arms and no legs!... What horror! Probably, he will be a being of great intelligence; he will desire to fly with his mind and have no choice but to endure a most painful inaction. My God! My God… it is not vain curiosity that guides me, but I desire if it is possible to know as to the why of such a terrible expiation.

Spirit communication:

"By the fruit one knows the tree, said Jesus. Therefore, all beings that you see in chains from the moment of birth, you can deduce without a doubt that whatever it lacks it has made a wrongful use of, in previous existences. Who has no legs? A sign that when he had them, they served to do all the harm he could; perhaps he was a spy that ran eagerly after some unfortunates to accuse them of crimes that they did not commit, and with his statements, had aborted conspiracies that when discovered early, produced countless victims. Maybe he ran to hasten defenseless beings into an abyss, those that would hinder him realizing his evil plans. He who has no legs has had to have utilized them in tormenting his enemies, he must have been the scourge of those who have surrounded him. A lack of such necessary appendages makes evident cruelty without limits, a cruelty to do evil beyond description, instincts so perverse instincts that testify to the pleasure of doing evil for evil itself. Woe to him who is born without legs…!

"Who has no arms? Perhaps his hands, that are so useful to the human species to do the work of titans and very delicate labor, was the job to sign death sentences that led to innumerable victims sent to the gallows, the majority of them innocent. Perhaps he enjoyed tightening the screws for the horrible torments of the rack, extracting confessions of unhappy accused parties, maddened by pain. Who knows if he wrote horrible slanders that destroyed the tranquility and love of happy families! One can do terrible harm with hands …! They can light the wick of flammable materials, and a devouring fire can occur. They can slap; and strong hands strangle the weak. A most peaceful and honest man can become fierce, and with them the work of many generations is destroyed. They are auxiliaries to man; who with his hands produce wonders or destroy all that exists. When one comes to the Earth without hands, how much damage had been done with them!

"*It is not necessary to be specific with the history of this one, or that one.* All those who come to the Earth without a robust and balanced body are prisoners condemned to life imprisonment, come to serve their sentence because there is no appeal in the course of your life before the verdict that you yourself signed. There are no merciless judges who deny pardon to repentant criminals, there is no other judge than man's own conscience. He could become drunk with the easy triumphs of his crimes. He could not have ears to hear the curses of his victims. He could close his eyes so as not to see the pictures of desolation that he has produced. He could remain stationary millions of centuries, but one day arrives that despite himself, he then awakens and sees, hears, recognizes his smallness, and he himself calls for judgment, and pronounces his own sentence. A final judgment with a sentence that is fulfilled hour by hour, day by day, without exempting the torment of not one second, because all is subject to immutable and fixed laws.

"Do not doubt it; the criminals of yesterday are the crippled of today: the blind, the mute, those with severe mental disabilities, those without legs, and those who do not have hands, the hungry and thirsty, are persecuted by justice.

"You have a saying, "do not trust those crippled by the hand of God." The idea is very badly expressed, but at its root there is a great truth. If you look closely, you will see the many of these unfortunates reveal in their semblance the degradation of their spirits. The right hand of God has not printed ferocity on their face, it is the accumulation of their crimes; they are the wicked and evil instincts which have hardened the lines of their face.[18]

"Yet, for these prisoners, keep all your compassion, guiding them by the best path. Do for them as you would for your children because they are the neediest, the most afflicted, because in the middle of the greatest abundance, there is no water in the fountain, wheat in the fields, fruit in the trees, or heat within the family home. They are as the wandering Jews of the legend, always walking without finding one rock to sit down. How terrible it is to be evil! Goodbye."

Ms. Soler comments:

How well the spirit spoke! By the fruit, the tree is known; and, how awful it is to be evil!

Translator's Note:

This chapter may shock us at first, but it is very important to keep foremost in our minds (after much consideration and careful planning with superior spirit guides in the spirit world) it is the SPIRIT ITSELF that chooses what type of challenges it wishes to undergo in a particular material existence; in this case no limbs. And. the communicating spirit states very bluntly and descriptively the possible acts that could have precipitated such a choice. However, the spirit states very clearly to keep ALL our compassion for the disabled, and "the hungry and the thirsty," so basically ALL people who suffer. Also, keep in mind, looking at this situation through the prism of reincarnation, the SPIRIT of this baby has had a myriad of lives before this one, and will continue in the future to have innumerable lives as well, in many kinds of conditions.

---

[18] In 19th century Spain, the disabled lived with great difficulty, especially the poor; begging for alms in miserable conditions. Even in 1976, in Mexico I saw disabled people without limbs on flattened cardboard boxes begging on the street corners. In our modern age, in affluent countries, some progress has been made and we look upon the disabled much differently; we see many of these individuals with cheerful, positive dispositions accomplishing amazing things, especially as they receive the resources they need. In addition, there are spirits of a certain higher moral quality that may choose illness/disability to undergoing tests of faith and resignation for further soul purification, and to serve as examples of moral courage to others.

Since the dawn of time, Humanity has drenched itself in the blood of its own mutual violence, in innumerable evil acts, many atrocities and wars, even up to the present time. As the communicating spirit states, one day we eventually decide when we want to pay our debts.

On another topic, as translator, I took the liberty to italicize one sentence to make it very clear that the spirit communicating did NOT reveal the specific reason for this baby's situation. The spirit consistently used the words "perhaps" or "maybe" for the possible and various situations of a cause, and also stated it was "not necessary to be specific with the history of this one…".

CHAPTER FIVE

PRIDE IS ALSO A SIN

Ms. Soler:

It has not been very many days since my friend Alicia came to see me; for me a very a sympathetic spirit, a very distinguished woman, truly aristocratic, thoroughly educated, and of vast instruction. A convinced Spiritist, she reads with great achievement all that is written about Spiritism, interpreting and commenting on its best works without her real name coming to light. Yes, she does good things for doing good itself. She works without desiring the laurels of glory, but the glory of the elevation of her sentiments she carries within her being. She is a middle-aged woman but conserves the slender elegance of youth, and there is something within her that attracts, beguiles, that interests one. When speaking with Alicia, one wants to stop time flying by so those brief moments convert into endless hours. Married and a mother, her duty is to her family (who do not carry her ideals), and she, prudent and reserved, hides the valuable treasure of her beliefs and avoids altercations with her relatives. She lives, one can say, in a superior world. She participates in earthly struggles to cry with her daughters if these endure the natural pains of the life of married women. Later, after fulfilling her duties as a loving mother, it appears she enters into another world; she concentrates on herself. It appears she lives on memories; memories that must be very painful because her face acquires a very sad expression, and sadder still because it is not communicative. She is enclosed in silence and avoids very carefully of talking of herself. The way she hides her Spiritist work to avoid disgust by her family, in the same manner she hides her worries, anxieties and her fears. When I speak with her, I understand I am reading from a book where I can only see the first page, the rest are not yet cut.

Therefore, the last time I saw her, upon finding her very talkative, very sociable, she surprised me much. The superior spirit descended from her high pedestal, humanized herself, shortened the distances that undoubtedly existed between her and the majority of mortals, and noticing such a change, my happiness knew no limits. I showed it by saying, "I don't know what I see in you, but I find you much friendlier, and much closer to me."

"Undoubtedly. Don't you see that pain is the great democratizer of the Universe? Those who suffer understand easily (as Campoamor would say). You have been suffering for some time. In these last years, I have suffered great reverses, and by the law of affinity, I put myself to speak with you (as the sailors say) to see if you can clarify what I fail to see. I already know that you have a good relationship with the spirits; that they tell you many stories. I desire that one more time they answer your questions, not to satisfy curiosity, but to study one of the chapters of human history."

"You know that I care about you, that I admire you. I see in you two distinct beings, although there is only one that is true. I have guessed your sorrows, and to give you consolation, I will do everything I can."

"I know it's been a while that your spirit and mine have known each other although this time our destiny separates us, it's not important. Spirits don't need a physical body to have a connection to understand each other, to care for each other, or provide important services. We would be hermits if the humans that populate the worlds could not communicate with each other across vast distances, but we have left the matter that concerns me. I believe you know I was left a widow."

"Yes, I know, and if I didn't know it, the black ribbons that surround you have indicated it to me."

"But my black finery will not tell you the mode of death of my husband, who died of a death so horrible that you cannot imagine."

"How did he die?"

"Of hunger…!"

"Jesus, what a horror! Did he have some cancer in his stomach that blocked him from eating?"

"No, he was very good and very healthy, he knew how to care for

31

himself as few men could. Medical science served him admirably to not suffer physical pain, but a moral pain made him forget all hygienic methods. He delivered himself into the arms of a silent obstinacy, and his life was extinguished, like the light of a lamp which lacks the necessary oil is extinguished."

"He must have suffered immense pain, because as I understand it, your husband was not a man given to sentimentality."

"Certainly not; he was good, but stern. His world was science, his family, the countless sick, and his only joy was restoring sight to the blind. He has cured the blind by the hundreds, within all social classes. In the same way, he attended the rich and the poor; he never entrusted the most difficult operations to his assistants, as do the majority of the free consultation doctors. Him, no; where he saw the most danger there he was. He gave so much that he attended to a repugnant leper as if an aristocrat, clean and perfumed. Science (as he said) is equality in action; for him there were no classes, and a true doctor was a great democratizer, a great leveler. He responded to all appeals; that's the way my husband did it. He never turned a deaf ear when called by the afflicted."

"How well he should be in the spirit world!"

"Undoubtedly, unless his death is an obstacle to his glory; because he was killed, it was carried out by suicide."

"What was the motive of such a violent decision?"

"As I already told you, one of my daughters got married, and became a mother of a precious little girl with such beautiful eyes that they appeared as two stars. From the time she was born, my husband was crazy about her, and the little girl for him. Grandfather and granddaughter were two bodies and one soul, being together they were happy. My husband was rejuvenated, and always was with his granddaughter in his arms, and believe it's useless to tell you that he did not let her feet touch the ground, sparing her the pains of teething and other childhood conditions. However, my dear, smallpox overtook both of my granddaughter's eyes, and all of her body, but especially the eyes. My husband barely ate, nor slept. He was at the side of that poor girl devouring books, looking for a light for those eyes that were his life. Light was given back to the one, but the other came out of its socket."

"My husband was believed mad; he retired to his room, and I heard him exclaim alone, 'Is it possible? I who have given sight to so many of the blind, I who have cured so many with syphilis, yet I have not been able to cure this beautiful angel but only halfway. They will put in one a glass eye, and it will be a marvel... but to see...to not see more than half; and even the eye that I saved is not so beautiful, it does not have that dazzling brightness. For what has science served me for; nothing.'"

"And, he refused to take any type of nourishment. He lived some days...drinking water. All of our pleadings were in vain. He would only tell me, 'It is useless to do as you say; I cannot swallow, even water is difficult for me to consume.'"

"Two days before dying he asked me for very ripe fruit, but...it was too late. He died of hunger without uttering a complaint, just barely muttering, 'where one is useless, one leaves one place for another.'"

"However, he had other grandchildren, and for none of them he showed great interest in, as for his dearest little girl. If you could ask Father Germain what history these two spirits had, because to die in pain as my husband did, so serious a man, so grave, so committed to science, a very powerful reason must have driven him to succumb so tragically."

I told her, "I promise I will take the first opportunity to accommodate her." I kept my word, asking Father Germain what Alicia wanted to know, and the spirit answered with the following:

Spirit communication:

"Just is the desire that drives them both; and a subject of study is what I will give you, listen with the greatest attention.

"The man who died of hunger, who we will call Raul, and his granddaughter, are two spirits that have walked together for many centuries. They have been united by all the earthly ties. In their last existences, they were inseparable friends, rather teacher and disciple. It has been for many ages that Raul has been occupied in curing the sick. Moreover, today who was his granddaughter has formerly been his most outstanding disciple, his most practical assistant. He had fame, almost as much as his master. The two of them were inseparable, the one complemented the other. They were so lucky in their cures that master and assistant became prideful. Their words were prophetic, they were never wrong (neither assuring good nor predicting bad outcomes), and they arrived to such an extent that they persuaded themselves of their own infallibility. They were not content to follow in the footsteps of other learned doctors, but invented their own new methods and specialized procedures. They were not content to do tests on various animals for improved safety in their experiments, as has been the long-standing practice in order to see the results of produced serums and other hypodermic injections. They did their tests in the hospitals and in a shelter for unfortunate children without families. Some died, others were saved, and the two scholars did not feel a bit of remorse for the death of the innocents. What was the death of a child without a family, before the good that the test would bring to mankind? However, besides the good produced, was the universal fame that reached these two imminent doctors, which day-by-day filled them with pride. They believed they were infallible because many of the sick came from distant lands in pilgrimage to regain their lost health. Raul was truly a medical celebrity. His assistant, never separated from him for an instant, and something rare, he did not envy his master as they were united for so many centuries, within intimate and legitimate loves, free from earthly miseries, his admiration bordering on idolatry. His major pleasure was to provide his teacher with homeless children, wherein Raul tested the effectiveness of their daring discoveries. They both believed they were truly gods; pride blinded them. Yet, pride is also a sin, and with all sin, it has its judgment. Raul and his assistant, in this current existence have paid a portion of their long reckoning.

"The loving assistant today is the tender child, whose grandfather (the prideful learned doctor) with all his science was not able to cure but halfway. He who thought his judgment infallible has seen he was impotent to cure his dear angel. Plus, the one who had no compassion for the poor sacrificed children studied in those scientific investigations, today now suffers the consequence of his indifferences of yesterday. It is necessary to suffer pain, that is not sympathized with, to appreciate it at its true value.

"Raul's science was completely eclipsed in this last existence, because in proportion to what he had done, he was nothing more than a vulgar mediocrity. His great medical intelligence made him suffer extraordinarily because he comprehended where the remedy lay, knew the method to apply it, and upon reaching the decisive moment to administer the appropriate medicine to the tenacious disease, he saw that it was wrong. His curative action did not respond to the impulse of his thought, and if he despaired with strangers, his desperation reached its maximum when he saw he was impotent to cure his granddaughter, who was the love of all his loves. He died; as it was necessary that he die, humiliated, convinced of his insignificance, his smallness; he believed himself a god and died persuaded that there are no gods.

"But there is no more than one God, and since the sin of scientific pride up to a certain point is pardonable, and since Raul has not been a sun in the world of science for centuries, today he finds himself in a much better state [in the spirit world]; and he has not lost one iota of his knowledge. However, he has acknowledged a greatness higher than his own [the Creator]; a science [the Divine Laws] for him that is unknown, a marvelous power, a force that sustains the machine of the Universe. Before so much light, before such magnificence, before so many worlds, he has guessed there are great sages, asking God why does the sun shine, and why does not that fire incinerate the Universe. He is considered as one of the many students in the great university of the Infinity. He recognizes great and small at the same time, and pride has not blinded him again. He has his own light, living in the midst of light, and his luminous fluids [19] surrounds his granddaughter now, who is the love of all his loves.

"Carefully study the short story that I have told you; about the death of a proud scholar, for it is not enough to penetrate victorious into the temple of science, one must love, one must be sympathetic.

"You cannot underestimate the outcasts of society, because that abandoned being perhaps has a spirit more advanced than the one who believes he is infallible due to his wisdom. By the mere act of being born, it must be considered it came to Earth on a mission, whether it is of great importance or insignificant. Every human being merits respect, and one needs to strive to protect and love everyone. Science that does not descend to the abandoned, there comes a day when the deserved punishment is received, as you have seen with the learned Raul. Goodbye."

---

[19] An equivalent word in more common usage today is spiritual or magnetic "energy."

Ms. Soler:

The spirit has reason to say it is deserving of further study the story of the death of a man who one day believed he was a god, and so little did he come to value his organism that he stopped feeding himself convinced that his stay on Earth was completely useless.

Fatal error! He could have done yet so much good, even his science could have spread comfort; but, believing he was the master of himself, he disposed of his life ignoring that he committed a crime because he denied benefits to many of the sick.

How necessary is it to know about life beyond the tomb! If Raul had known about it, he would not have given in to despair, destroying his body. On the contrary, he would have redoubled his efforts to give light to the blind, as he knew what it was to suffer an irreparable misfortune.

Only through the study of Spiritism [20] will we do better when in the midst of pain, because knowing that we live forever, we will try to be better today than yesterday, and tomorrow become great benefactors of humanity.

---

[20] Word coined by Allan Kardec to describe "the relation of the material world with spirits" and the moral philosophy and spiritual science which explains who we are, the purpose of material life, why we suffer and what happens when our physical body dies, as explained by the morally high spirits in, *The Spirits' Book*.

CHAPTER SIX

A WISE MAN WITHOUT HEART

A Curious Story: Criminal Exploitation

For some years he had been wandering through the villages and fields of the middays of France with a band of gypsies, living to demonstrate to people a very rare phenomenon.

Thrust into a crate, and exhibited through a glass, it revealed a savage boy, who they say lacked all of his lower limbs, and spoke in a strange barbaric language.

But the boy was not a monster or a savage, and the language he spoke was, neither more nor less than that used out in the countryside of Galicia [Spain].

In effect, the poor boy was more or less a victim of exploitation by gypsies.

They had tied the legs of the child tightly in a very violent and cruel position, and they were hidden by a double bottom drawer, so it seemed he lacked them.

How did this boy from Spain fall under the control of these gypsies?

Very simple; while traveling through the nomadic camps of Galicia, they saw the child, and deceived the parents by getting them to give him up for the promise of compensation after one year. The gypsies stipulated to enrich the Galician family with an amount of thirteen duros [21] upon

---

[21] In Spain, in the 1860's, the "peso duro" was a silver coin worth five pesetas no longer in use.

returning the boy. He was six years old at the time when they took him, and they wandered through Galicia, León, Burgos, Logroño and Navarra, until they penetrated France. At first, the boy was treated as if a king (relatively), but after making such terrible journeys for so long, and straddled on a mule of great height, whose back barely covered the tender little legs of the child, the result was that after some time with this daily grind, in the evening when the boy got down, his limbs were aching and he could not walk. From here, without a doubt, it occurred to the gypsies to completely disable the boy's legs, tying him as stated above, and imprisoning him in the double bottom drawer.

It was ten hard years of torture for the Galician, with varied and always very sad incidents, but not knowing a word of French, it was impossible to make anyone understand that he was an exploited victim, and even less, by the physical condition he was in, he could not escape his tormentors.

Finally, after ten years he became able to understand something in French, and taking advantage of a favorable occasion, he could inform the authorities of his exploitation and martyrdom.

He recovered his liberty, but the forced immobility of the position of his legs for so such a long time, produced in the boy a unique form of paraplegia. Therefore, it was necessary to take him to the hospital in Bordeaux, where he was assisted by doctors Duverjié and Arnozan.

Through mediation of the Spanish consul, he was transferred to Spain and admitted to a hospital in Madrid where he came under the care of Dr. Jaime Vera, who relied on the slow healing of the boy, using an appropriate electrical treatment.

Ms. Soler:

I read the preceding story with deep feelings and came away understanding that the protagonist of this horrible story was undoubtedly a being who had sinned much. There is nothing sadder than to do wrong; since he who sins degrades himself with evil thoughts that precedes the realization of the wrongful work, and later attracts perverse spirits that enjoy and take pleasure in tormenting him. How terrible it is to do wrong...!

Further, it is not only the criminal that falls into the abyss, but with him many others fall.

Desiring to continue my studies, reading within humanity, I asked the spirit guide of my works regarding the past of this unfortunate individual that lived without living for so many years. I obtained the following communication:

Spirit communication:

"By the fruit one knows the tree, said Jesus. In the same manner, in the existence of each being, we can know only a part of their history, at the least the most significant portion, which has produced a turning point in the life of this or that individual. The man that today has been a victim of greed by ill-fated exploiters of humanity, has been for many centuries a heartless learned man. Just as your naturalists and most famous doctors test on various animals the effect of their inventions, inoculating viruses of various ailments that decimate humanity (killing many animals subjected to scientific tests) their death serves as useful instruction to later avoid the torture of men, attacked by an equivalent disease. In the same manner, today's martyr (we will call him Ascaño) in successive existences, did the following study:

"He wanted to see if intelligence tended to expand provided with a healthy and robust body or suffering with paralysis of the lower limbs, condemning men, as well, to a forced quietude. Ascaño has for a long time had many worldly possessions. He had a large number of slaves; and the sons of these, those who had beautiful well-proportioned heads, he fixed his attention on, and began his cruel studies. On some he amputated their legs, others were pressed between iron molds, to others he gave them incurable sores, and all of them were taught to read, write, to paint, model clay, and to sing; to each he noted which showed more inclination. While at the same time, he educated equally other children, healthy and robust, and in that way, he noted the differences that existed between the one group and the other.

"He treated these infidels that submitted to his misguided studies, the same way or worse than your doctors treat their little animals. He did not enjoy watching them suffer, this no; but he cared little about their groans of anguish. What he wanted to observe was if intelligence needed the complete use of the whole body to function and elevate itself, or, if it was enough for it to be impressed by the beauty of Nature with all its harmonies.

"Ascaño searched, without knowing it, for the independent life of the spirit. In those times, the saying "a healthy body, a healthy mind" was not known, nor would it have served for the studies of Ascaño. He searched for something he felt, that he sensed, but he could not find it around him. He looked for intelligence that functioned independent of the body. Therefore, in this he was crushed, diminished, trying at the same time to apply a remedy to a bad cause; to see the direction that intelligence would take, if it flapped its wings toward the ground, or if it soared like eagles searching the immensity of infinity.

"Therefore, like there are men in your day who take the eyes out of specific birds because they say the birds sing better blind, in the same manner, Ascaño mutilated his poor slaves to see if lacking legs their thoughts expanded more.

"Aristotle said that slaves were an animate piece of property. Ascaño believed this, and so he martyred many children because he was a learned man without a heart.

"He did not enjoy the evil that was caused, but in the end, it caused him much pain, and it is just that with his own physical body, he suffers more than one time [22] the torments that he caused others to suffer. Furthermore, do not think that since he is obligated to suffer what he did to others, his own tormentors are any less guilty because I have said many times, it is not always necessary to reveal the role of the tormentor; because each person is his own tormentor, when atonement must be fulfilled.

"You have only to look and see how true it is what I say.

"Many men have sufficient enough to be relatively happy, but if they don't deserve to be, they are not. Vice dominates them, that can do more harm, or they are united with a family without having wrongful tendencies that can mortify them, conflict them and exasperate them. How many are they that say, 'Who was the son of the house of foundlings!' [23] Having a family is a true calamity. Everyone carries within them all the judicial paperwork that is needed to pay for cause: the prosecutor who accuses and

---

[22] Throughout many lifetimes.
[23] Children left in a place for orphans, sometimes abandoned there by their parents who could not afford to keep them.

the lawyer who defends, the judge that dictates sentence and the tormentor that executes it. Man carries everything within him.

"God in his infinite justice could not create beings so that they would be hateful and repulsive; the laws are immutable and eternal. As children play with toys, thereby men play with their laws that last and remain, until that breath which you call death undoes them.

"How many judges (very truly criminals) when so content and satisfied they are with their cruelties, release a cry of anguish, seeing themselves surrounded by their victims and fall as if struck by lightning; and, with all their power, all their authority, they go to hide in a tomb, perhaps of marble and jasper, but a grave nonetheless, a depository of worms that devour that body, which moved solely to produce extermination! [24]

"I repeat, one hundred times a hundred, do not fail to sympathize with the tormentors and the victims; the former, because they will prepare to be sacrificed in the tomorrow, and the second, because they have sown bad seed and their crop is being harvested and watered by their tears. Have love and sympathy, because love and compassion are needed for the victims and the tormentors. Goodbye." [25]

Ms. Soler:

How beautiful are these teachings! How much one can learn by these truly rational instructions, stripped of all mysticism!...

How harmonious they are with my mode of thinking! I have always believed that God is very much more elevated than our miseries and our blunders.

When they say: God punishes his rebellious children and rewards the just; this appears to me that it profanes the grandeur of God. I consider God as Soul of the Universe radiating onto the worlds, not converted into a schoolteacher guarding over the actions of his pupils.

I adore God in Nature, but I do not tremble at his anger, and I have confidence in his clemency. God is just, immutable, eternal, superior to

---

[24] They lived solely to abuse their power and unduly punish and/or sentence others to death.

[25] Compassion is needed for both victims and wrongdoers alike.

all properties and all mercies; there is no need to be lenient because God is just; because the law of love has to be achieved and when the law of God is fulfilled, there will be no sunset on the day of universal happiness. [26]

---

[26] Based on spirit teachings, the Creator is not anthropomorphic or pantheistic. God is not as has been portrayed, an old man with human qualities personally or arbitrarily deciding people's fate. The Creator and all creation are not the same thing. We are not able to fully comprehend the Creator, but as we progress, we will. Yet, we may see and contemplate the grandeur of the works of the Supreme Intelligence by admiring the Cosmos, especially those spectacular awe-inspiring images, taken by our telescopes of space. Our technology has only scratched the surface of what further discoveries await us.

CHAPTER SEVEN

THE PUNISHMENT IS
BASED ON THE SIN

Ms. Soler:

Leafing through the paper I read a news item that strongly caught my attention:

Beggars by Trade

Some days ago, an individual that was dedicated to publicly imploring charity from the public, was picked up by the resultant night watch, and had in their possession 7,500 pesetas in notes and coins of different countries.

Last night a ragged homeless woman, on whom they found titles and obligations valuing 8,392 pesetas, was conducted to Asylum Park.

Ms. Soler continues:

What a terrible history these two must have had! When they both have to go about the world laden with gold and begging; a torture like Tantalus! According to the mythological story, Tantalus was cast into hell to suffer a horrible punishment that consisted in remaining in the middle of a lake, where water reached his beard but escaped his mouth, whenever he wanted to drink, while possessed by an ardent thirst, and, he was surrounded by fruit trees which elevated towards the sky every time he raised his hand to pick fruit, though devoured by hunger. The two unfortunates above also had *water* and ripened *fruit* and were dying of hunger and thirst. What had they done in their yesterdays?

Spirit communication:

"What did you want them to do? (a spirit tells me) They fell short concerning the divine and human laws, and today they reap the harvest of the seeds for the bad hours they sowed. The beggar of today imploring public charity in one of his past existences, was a Prior of an immensely rich religious community. The convent was situated in the countryside, surrounded by many villages, whose inhabitants came obligated to give to the Prior of the convent ripe fruit, an abundance of all their crops and best livestock. Oh, and from those who did not! Then, he excommunicated and threatened them with the eternal punishment of hell. So, those unhappy ones, very frightened to not fall into mortal sin, humbly offered all they possessed to the Prior to attain eternal glory; a promise he made to them whenever they brought him the best from their estates. He abused his power so much, that man (whose avarice knew no limits) became the scourge of the poor; who gullible and naïve, considered him as if a saint. However, everything has its end, and finally the Prior left the Earth, leaving considerable assets, and entering into the spirit world so poor that he had not even one atom of virtues. He had nothing but vices, incorrigible vices, inasmuch as his guide made plain the errors in the way he had lived, and it was necessary that he retrace his path. He has returned to Earth repeated times, always eager for money, and even though his expiation did not permit him to enjoy his riches, he was always seeking treasure. He goes crossing the Earth without ever having a house or home, sometimes begging and other times through theft or deception, always afraid that his valuables will be snatched by the authorities, but always living in a most miserable way.

"He has been going like that through various existences and many are still left because he knows well the wrongfulness he has committed, but gold for him (the serpent that curls around his neck) does not let him breathe. He has done much harm through the acquisition of gold, that gold is his executioner. Unfortunate one! Sympathize with the beggars that among their rags, they carry water and ripe fruit that neither calms their thirst or hunger!

"Regarding the woman beggar that possessed a small fortune, she started her current existence with a settlement of her balance. In her previous existence, she was a beautiful young girl, a daughter of the town, who dreamed of becoming a great lady. She met an elderly millionaire, and she employed all her arts to enter his service. She was very sympathetic, appealing, so loving and expressive that she captured the affection of the elderly gentleman completely, who doted on her lavishly. However, she was still not content with this, so she got him to prepare a will, leaving his abundant fortune to her. Later on, in *gratitude* [italicized, the spirit being sarcastic], fearful that he would go back on his word, she bought at a good price, a medical doctor so poor of material goods as well as humanitarian sentiments. This one gave the man a poison that slowly killed without leaving visible marks on the patient. So, it was in this state, a sick man who was languishing and losing lucidity of intelligence, when she took him traveling far away from their homeland, and left him abandoned in a hotel, leaving a wallet with a small amount of money. Furthermore, since the old man was completely incompetent, he could not explain or say anything, and was put into an asylum for the elderly where he died without noticing anything. Meanwhile, she returned to her homeland, and there found the start of her punishment, because the millionaire's family filed a lawsuit, and the courts ate the fruits of her crime.

"She died nearly destitute, and upon arriving in the spirit world found her victim, who generously pardoned her. He advised her not to continue undertaking that path. Going further, she decided to settle her enormous debts, because it was not the first time, she had committed such abuses. She continued with his advice, and in this existence, she found the means to possess a handful of gold, but she did not enjoy it; it did not serve any useful purpose. She was a slave to a few coins, and she lived without living. She did not deserve to live tranquilly because she made a wretched payment of ingratitude of the generosity and truly paternal affection offered by her protector (who was a noble and elevated soul).

"Reason dictates that when one lives begging, and one has with them a sufficient means to satisfy the primary necessities of life and one cannot satisfy them, there has to have been much sin.

"Understand these unfortunates who suffer the worst of sentences."

"Goodbye."

Ms. Soler:

Indeed, living unsheltered, lacking everything and eagerly guarding what could save one from suffering, is to be one's own tormenter. So, we must live within the strictest morality for us not to become deserving to be outcasts, degenerate helots[27] that no one is interested in, living in the shadows, here and there. "How true it is that the punishment is based on the sin."

---

[27] One deprived of the rights and privileges of a citizen; serf or slave, as in ancient Greece.

CHAPTER EIGHT

DREADFUL REVENGE

Ms. Soler discusses her spiritual work:

I am continually receiving letters begging me to ask the spirits *the why* of many truly interesting events and many of them terrible. I can't always accommodate my friends or fellow brothers/sisters. Sometimes, it is because I do not want to abuse the communications so I can conserve them for what I need, which is for my literary works. I do not want the spirits as dispatchers, to see and tell, bothering them with impertinent questions to satisfy the mere curiosity of the ignorant. No; when I converse with the spirits, it is to benefit by their narratives and transfer them to paper to publish them in Spiritist newspapers; and, in this way, my work is truly productive because there are many who read my writings and learn from them; how to suffer and to have hope.

At other times, I have to reply with nothing, because the guide of my literary work simply tells me that one cannot always get close to the fire (metaphorically speaking). There are spirits with histories so terrible, such is their inferiority and degradation that they are wrapped within a thick mist and their fluids [28], not to say that it causes death, but produces an indefinable bad feeling, an unnamed anguish, and in reality, they have to be that way. Upon the Earth, I have experienced painful sensations when

---

[28] Spiritual energies, vibrations, and/or spiritual atmosphere; quality of the ethereal, astral, aura or biofield – the surroundings around individuals and/or spirits, which corresponds to their level of morality and intellect.

by chance circumstances, I have had to go to certain places where inferior beings assemble, or I have crossed the street whose neighborhood consists of lost women and degraded men.

What fatigue! What uneasiness! What repulsion! I believe that a spirit also feels nauseous when they encounter in their path a malevolent being or beings. One is able, after the first impression to control oneself and feel compassion for the culpable, but in the first moment one draws back in horror before such inferior beings. [29]

Ms. Soler relays an experience she had:

I remember perfectly, though many years ago, I visited a prison in Barcelona accompanied by the warden and a clerk. When we arrived at the courtyard of the prison and stopped in front of a fence, I was horrified to see a crowd of pitiful men, many of them half-way unclad, who approaching the fence and smiling, stupidly asked me for cigarettes. What lowered heads! What looks! What gestures! I turned my head, and addressing the warden, I murmured bitterly, these are men?

"Well, note this prisoner I am going to present to you, and see what sensation you experience," he said.

We continued walking, and we entered a clean kitchen; all the utensils were very well situated and the pans shined as if they had had a bath in gold. A small stocky man was sharpening a knife. Upon seeing the warden, he stood at attention, smiling humbly. I looked at him and I experienced a very painful feeling; it seemed as if sharp spines were stuck to my body and hot hammers struck in my temples. The warden (without a doubt, on purpose) spoke to him, asked him several questions so I had time to contemplate him, but I felt so bad that I rapidly left the kitchen, while asking for some water because I was choking, and with a very vivid curiosity, I asked the warden:

"What did that man do? Why is he here?"

"He violated his three daughters, and each one had a son. That father and grandfather wanted to strangle them, but the three babies were saved. He will march to the Ceuta penitentiary within a few days."

---

[29] People of low morality; with thoughts and feelings involving vices of all kinds.

48

"What horror! Now that explains to me why I could not be next to that man." [30]

Well, the same thing that happens with criminals on Earth, must happen the same to the criminals in the spirit world. What I know is that, they want me to ask questions which cannot be answered, because as my spirit guide says, "They suffer very much, let the dead bury their dead."

Ms. Soler:

Ultimately, a Spiritist from Mexico wrote to me very interested in knowing the cause of a tragedy that occurred in the insane asylum of San Hipólito in Mexico. In that house of healing, a sick man named Ambrosio Sámano entered it on September of the year 1894. The doctors said he was intoxicated with marijuana, had an impulsive mania and was homicidal; of strong constitution, very muscular, he had herculean strength and he had dominated (without exaggeration) three men. He came from a family that had nervous conditions. His mother was prone to hysteria, his father had neurasthenia [31], and their oldest son of this marriage was also sick. Ambrosio gave himself the nickname "the god of the Earth." In the hospital, he made himself notorious for his ferocity; he would hit himself brutally, tear his clothes, and yell, "Who's like me?"

Not long afterwards, a young sick man, Mr. Antonio Marrón entered the hospital, but not for insanity. However, due to an unexplained negligence, Marrón entered the courtyard where Ambrosio was walking (wearing a straitjacket) accompanied by two caretakers, but these two were called away by someone. Marrón was left alone with the insane man, who said to him, "Give me my freedom." Marrón untied the bonds that held the straitjacket, and that insane man was free and master of the courtyard. He, without losing any time, put the straitjacket on Marrón, took him into his arms, carried him to his cell, closed the door and was alone with his

---

[30] Here clearly, Ms. Soler was quite sensitive to spiritual/moral vibrations; she felt actual physical pain, and also note she felt like she was choking, which is what the criminal had wanted to do to the tiny victims. Mediums can at times feel the pain a spirit is perceiving.

[31] A term not generally used now, to describe a general condition of chronic fatigue, depression and mental distress.

victim. Nobody knows how terrible the drama was of what happened in the darkness of that cell, but the screams of the other inmates attracted the caretakers. Those who saw, were horrified that Marrón was on the floor with the straitjacket on and his feet tied up. Ambrosio, kneeling before the body, struggled to extract a huge spike which he had for the fourth time embedded into the skull of Marrón, and with such a force that it perforated the skull of that unfortunate man, penetrating into the pavement.

They subjected Ambrosio to an interrogation, asking him: "Did you kill a man?"

"Yes, I did."

"Why?"

"Because you have me tied up, and I am tired of this life; I want you to send me to Bethlehem."

"But you are here because they found you crazy."

"I am not sick."

"Yes, you are insane."

"No sir. No sir."

"Why are you so bad?"

"Because you have me tied up."

"If we let you go, would you be good?"

"Yes, sir. Yes, sir."

Much longer and more explicit, is the story published by *El Imparcial* [*The Impartial*] in Mexico on the 8th of last June, but with an extract it is sufficient to understand the terrible event that occurred at the mental hospital of San Hipólito.

The epilogue of a history of crimes has to be the death of the unfortunate Marrón that by a series of unexplained circumstances, was left at the mercy of a terrifying insane man (who never walked about alone) and was always accompanied by two caretakers, and this young man who went into that courtyard (solely intended for recreation of the mentally ill). A young man, that was very well recommended there by his brother (the director of the hospital) which his pension splendidly paid because he was very rich. The two brothers having lately inherited one hundred thousand duros. Then, one to precisely enter the courtyard with the insane man left alone by the caretakers (confident that he could not make use of his arms or be able to move), obeyed the insane man, and with extraordinary speed a terrible tragedy unfolded...this is not the product of chance. There is a causality, a frightening causality; one does not die so cruelly and tormented without having had committed a similar offense. When did Marrón commit this; in what epoch? The shadows of the centuries have erased the written pages in a book whose sheets no longer exist. Futile question! The acts of men are never erased; for on the blackboard of the infinite are written the quantities of all our vices, our atrocities, and of all our crimes. Those indelible ciphers are waiting that God prepare a total of them, but God will never add them up, because one single sum would mean the absolute perfection of a spirit, and solely God possesses perfection.

Spirit communication:

"Well said (a spirit tells me) there will always be men among the world and souls in the spirit world, with one heaven more to ascend, and one more abyss where to fall; progress has no limits, time has no end. Spirits are eternal explorers, tireless workers, miners of the Universe, space travelers of Creation; the day of a universal life never sets, a night of rest does not exist.

"However, in the histories of humankind, of whose first page is not known with certainty and in what epoch it was written, terrifying episodes abound on par with charming scenes. Each spirit, the owner in the use of its time, according to its own aspirations and desires, is delivered to all kinds of excesses, sometimes mortifying its flesh and at other times degrading its intelligence.

"This epilogue of a story, as you call the incident in the mental asylum, you are right to say that it is the outcome of a drama. So many have taken part; it has been a long time they have been struggling together! There are four actors who have played a part in that final scene; three that were on Earth and one in the spirit world. In broad strokes, I will lay out one chapter of the tale of these unfortunates. You are not in a position to penetrate very deeply into the intimate lives of four beings that have acquired great responsibilities for allowing themselves to be dominated by their untamable passions.

"In a not too distant, past existence, he that is today nicknamed, "the god of the Earth," was a fierce and indomitable man. Satisfying his lewd desires, he stained the honor of many women, and killed treacherously (face-to-face as the occasion presented itself) more than one deceived husband, and more than one desperate father (by the dishonoring of their daughter). Among the men who died by his hands was a Count; who had his honor washed away by the death of his wife and of his only daughter. The Count, dishonored by his killer, swore upon dying to eternally pursue the man who had taken away his happiness. Ambrosio Sámano incarnated upon the earth, and his enemy took ahold of him, still not having left him.

"You say, that to die such a cruel tormented death, one has had to have committed a similar crime, and in this you are right to assert so. The young man who died, having his cranium perforated, did not commit by his own hand such a crime (but he was a joyful witness to such martyrdom, suffered by a commander he conquered by his disloyalty and betrayal). The executor of that crime was the spirit [the Count] that swore to never abandon the one who today is called "the god of the Earth."[32] A chain of crimes unites these three spirits, whose links have been forged in different existences. He who is today dead (seemingly an innocent) has many pages written with blood in the book of his history. The spirit that obsessed "the god of the Earth" has avenged the killer and the victim, for the two, in other times, have taken away honor, fortune and happiness.

"Even the brother of the victim of today has contributed to the realization of such vengeance, taking that poor sick one to the hospital where he would die. It was he who opened the door of such sad a place, because in another lifetime he was the governor of a fortress by religious mandate where male and female prisoners moaned. Unfortunate women that did not want to disavow their religion and wanted at the same time to retain their virginity, those poor ones had to succumb to the threats of wealthy men forcing their way into their cells, drunk and wild. The governor was complicit in such infamous outrages, letting in several tycoons, one of them being who today was killed by the hands of "the god of the Earth." Yesterday, he opened the doors of a prison, so that he could satisfy his brutal appetites dishonoring defenseless women, and later he opened the doors of a hospital so that one would be killed as he had made another die with a perforated skull. He laughed yesterday at the moments passed by his victim upon dying, enjoying his agony. The executioner [the

---

[32] Influence and/or obsession by a spirit with a violent nature.

spirit] of that horrible death today, lifted the arm of who is believed crazy, avenging both of them. All of them had written the sentence realized today.

"You ask, 'This being the case; was it written?' Yes, it was written; not by fatality, it was written by the series of crimes committed by them all. He who has passed as crazy is not; he was the victim of an invisible enemy. Science was assured that he belonged to an unbalanced family, which he himself was. However, he has hours, has days, has nights that he sees clearly, very clearly and says, 'I am not crazy! No! I am not. I feel that through my veins flows molten lead. I feel my brain exploding, that some iron hands press my throat, that I have a thirst for blood; and, at the same time I want to flee far away, far away from here in order to live tranquilly within the arms of a loving woman.'

"Have compassion for the victims of invisible enemies; they suffer the most horrible of all the torments, they struggle with actual titans, whose force is so powerful that the most powerful on Earth fall defeated. [33]

"I understand you suffer on my recounting so many horrors, but all is useful; as anatomists do an autopsy on dead bodies to study diseases and organic defects that so torment the majority of men, it is also convenient to speak of the invisible, of the unknown. Don't you look with a telescope into the sea of space where innumerable suns navigate? Well, the mysteries of the afterlife also deserve to be studied, because without knowing the unknown you live blind, one arrives at a serious crime without remorse. Now it is time that men know that hell and heavenly bliss exist, that it is not above or below, but that we carry it within ourselves, that each spirit constructs his or her own paradise or hell."

"Goodbye." [34]

---

[33] *The Mediums' Book* by Allan Kardec discusses obsession in great detail. In addition, the book *Fundamentals of Spiritism* written and published Jon Aizpurua in 2000 in Spanish, but translated into English and published in 2013, contains a comprehensive explanation on spirit influence and spirit obsession.

[34] We have enemies in the material world and may have invisible ones in the spirit world from past lives, but we each have our free will and will power to try to resist their influences by being a good moral person and soliciting help from our spirit protectors.

Ms. Soler:

The spirit speaks very well; it is of great utility to lift the veil that covers the lives of yesterday. It is true that one suffers, revealing crimes, but if the wounds of the body are cured by cauterization, we apply the cauterization of beyond the grave revelations about incorrigible vices, about the passions, about hatred, about vengeance. Let us make manifest how wrong it is to be evil, and how good it is to be good, and if with our writings one man stops at the impending start of his vices, blessed be this utilized work! A soul that wakes up and sees the light, is a new sun, radiating in the universe!

Translator's Note: To clarify, the four characters in this drama, they are: **1) "the god of the Earth"** - the womanizer and murderer; **2) Marrón** - the vengeful and traitorous military soldier; **3) spirit of the Count** (in the spirit world) who vowed to take revenge; and, **4) the brother/hospital director** previously a governor of a fortress for religious prisoners and who allowed them to be abused. All had violent past lives!

CHAPTER NINE

THE GREATEST OF THE SUFFERINGS

"It is the small body of water that creates mud,
fast moving water leaves no trace where it has passed.
The small sufferings are the ones that do us the most harm;
because the major ones kill us swiftly, or go straight past."

Augusto Ferrán
19th Century Poet from Spain

Ms. Soler:

The poet speaks very well! The small sufferings are those that hurt the most; consequently, they are the worst because they are the ones that most torment us; those that go consuming our lives over a long period of time. For we have known many persons that, in a brief period of time have lost all the members of their family, and some time afterwards, have smiled, and within their agreeable countenance show flashes of happiness.

We remember a young woman that within fifteen days lost her husband and her only son, being left in a miserable state; and, some months afterwards, there was no reflection of pain on her face. Another woman, within three months, lost her husband and three children, and today she lives as if she never had a family. Another one watched, as the chosen one of her heart and five children died within a year. This last one quickly became as if unresponsive, but today smiles happily, consoled in great part by a new love that offers a promising future. Also, we know of many families, as regards death, that when one of the members of their family is suddenly taken, but due to the advanced age of the individual or by chronic illness, it is such that their absence does not give occasion to that terrible pain that could drive one mad.

Also, they have what they need to live, they don't know the horrors of hunger or the persecution of the creditors. They can sometimes satisfy on occasion even their whims. However, despite these favorable conditions, they have little annoyances that all being counted, make them laugh and sufferings that make them cry.

We heard a story told by a little girl, that contained a profound lesson. This is what the pretty child said:

"There was a poor man, so poor, that he did not have a bed to sleep on. He slept on a piece of a mat just in front of a low narrow corner, where nearby lived a well-off family. Every day they placed all their bed mattresses on their balconies, and the unhappy beggar would look at them with such envy that it would devour his heart. He suffered so much that he came to confess that sadly he accused that envy poisoned all the hours of his day, and that those accursed mattresses were his nightmare.

"A good priest, pitied his misfortune, and told him, 'Come to my house, I will give you a bed better than the angels have, with one condition, that you don't leave the house. You will have a view of the garden, you will eat sumptuously, you will not suffer of hunger, cold, or depression, and in fifteen days I will go see you and you can tell me how you are.'

"Ah! I warn you, do not leave your corner or toss away that piece of mat who knows what can happen.

"The beggar, intoxicated with joy, went after the good priest to his new room and his joy knew no bounds, when he laid down on a bed with three mattresses, so soft, they appeared as cushions, and also some sheets, disputing its whiteness to the snow, and feather pillows.

"The first night the beggar slept with total pleasure, and the next day he woke up with a good appetite. He ate how much he wanted, and afterwards he peeked out the window and looked out at the garden for a long while. He returned to lie down to enjoy his bed awake, and that is how it was for five days; eating, sleeping and looking out the window at the gardeners working in the garden and the horticulturist who arranged the garden.

"On the sixth day, with a strange longing, he woke up thinking about his low narrow corner and his piece of mat. He remembered with relish his long wanderings throughout the city and the country and the complete freedom that he enjoyed when he slept at his corner. It is certain that he fasted many days, but he recounted his sorrows to others and was consoled. He stayed struggling with his memories for three days, until he asked to see the good priest. That one came quickly upon his being summoned, and the beggar told him,

"'Sir, I am very grateful for all your goodness, but I plead that you let me return to my poor corner where I was happy, because now I do not envy the mattresses of my neighbor. These last days I am now convinced that it is not abundance that provides happiness; here I lack for nothing, and yet, since I live discontented, I need everything.'

"This is what I wanted to demonstrate to you,' said the priest smiling, 'that it is an illusion, that it is all a fantasy. When one envies another, because the one who envies almost always, in reality, has very little to envy. Live tranquilly in your poverty, one is never poor when one is content with their lot in life.

"The beggar returned to his narrow corner, contemplated his little mat with cheerful satisfaction, he laid down on it and smiled joyfully because his mind was no longer gripped by that serpent *envy*."

Commentary by Ms. Soler:

The moral basis of this story is of profound instruction because it demonstrates that small vexations can poison lives to the point that one prefers misery rather than enjoy abundance. Amid the hardships that so mortify us, and yet, pass completely unnoticed for many beings, many generally believe that with their basic needs of life being covered, everything else creates havoc within the heart of being. It's not like that in reality, for there are delicacies that are more bitter than bile, and there is stale bread much sweeter to the taste than honey.

To us [speaking of herself], due to the special circumstances of our lives, by not having family and other causes, we have had to live without our own home for natural reasons, it has provided us with more chances than others to know and suffer those little annoyances, that at times so much influence the events in our lives, that with a distinct twist they usually give us our determination.

Upon the earth, as is logical, are an abundance of inferior spirits of instincts at odds with good inclinations; they are vulgar beings, and when one of them unites with a more distinguished spirit, one more delicate, more sensible (even though it is far from being good) there is such a distance between vulgarity and that distinction, it is as if a whole world is between them.

Many of us have studied within society, not precisely those beings that have surrounded us too close, but those who have appeared happier. Covetous of happiness, like all unfortunates, we have observed the beggar that envied those mattresses. We have always looked with enthusiastic desire upon the faces of those beings where contentment is radiated, and we have tried to come into relations with them to see if their happiness was complete, and in those studies, we have learned much! In those profound observations is where we have found a series of small contrarieties, that form an unbearable whole.

How many times has it happened, believing ourselves deeply unfortunate, that we go to relay our sorrows to one of the happy ones of the Earth, and to begin with the lucky one enumerates all the mishaps that surround them. Then, upon having heard their story, we compare their sorrows with our own and believe ourselves happy; and us, as being rich, very rich, compared to them as one of the many beggars that abound in the world!

One observes on this sad planet such disunion and animosity between spirits, the same within marriages, parents and children in intimate struggles, and one is saddened to see this dismal war that divides the majority of families.

What selfishness so deep! What self-love so exaggerated! Everyone wants all to be perfect; all believe the right to have such lives and estates!...

So much bitterness is locked up within intimate personal lives! Inferior spirits...how they torment! Some out of ignorance, and others by their refined malice; they do not waste one sole occasion to bother anyone around them. Women! You that live continually within the house are responsible for the domestic home; with your warmth, small children develop and grow. Listen to our voice, friend, we love you very much, at the least because we are of the same gender. We see clearly that you could be the angels of the earth. However, you engage many times in being a torch for discord; you dedicate yourself to work and sacrifice for your family, but in such a way that does not awaken appreciation, but foments annoyance and boredom.

We have said it in many other articles, but we never tire of repeating it: some upper-class women have a fatal habit, and we notice it more with these beings among whom we have most dealt with it, and in reality, they suffer as well, which so mortifies those who suffer the consequences of this defect, and it is their getting up in a bad mood.

We have seen many women in a town, countless of them, going to the river carrying a great bundle of clothes on their head, a child in one arm and holding another one's hand while talking happily with their children. While those women that can afford to stay in their homes, that don't have to pass through those tough times, they wake up many times bickering and looking for occasions to hurt people with their words.

During dinner time, it is fearful in some homes; all the unpleasantness and annoying questions, and at that moment of the reunion of the family is nothing but to dispute one with another, and this terrible habit is at the base of great domestic conflicts.

Some say what we are noticing is petty, and not true. However, unfortunate is the family that when individuals come together, they don't exchange a smile. Those who are millionaires are poor, the poorest upon the Earth, they are the ones who suffer the greatest sorrows; those who drink honey all their lives.

We see inferior spirits always miserable, discontent, subject to misfortunes; on the other hand, one sees smiling a loving spirit of progress, and a smiling face is so beautiful! We love these women, and they exist; on their lips is drawn the sweetest of smiles, and on their forehead is a divine glow like those mystical painters put on the heads of their saints; staying by the side of these beings that bless us as they speak, one can support all the bitterness of life, because their sweetness encourages us.

However, next to these are malicious people who always talk with ulterior motives, which run counter to our more concealed thoughts, and do not know to be grateful for the benefits they enjoy. They even get bored with our affection, and to live next to these beings that unfortunately abound, is to live dying.

We are thinking of writing a series of articles classifying the great sufferings that undoubtedly are found among the smallest of troubles, that when combined form a whole that is unbearable.

A study of Spiritism is lacking for the development of life, and we want more than ever to popularize it when we look at those families whose members live together but are more separated than the two poles of the Earth.

We see these inferior spirits pleasuring in fomenting discord, stationary in their ignorance, without caring about taking one step forward; and the same beings usually have virtues, and some of great value, like small roses surrounded by thorny brambles, that before inhaling in their essence, one has to lament the pain that one receives from its sharp thorns. Having knowledge of Spiritism, before mankind, is to open up such new and expansive horizons that necessarily the spirit begins to progress because before an infinite future, the spirit's aspirations aggrandizes; and, we are entirely convinced that when the Spiritist school has letters of credence in all social circles, the small contrarieties that are the basis of the greatest sufferings will slowly disappear.

In successive articles, we will be developing our theme; today we solely repeat the old adage, "Lord, deliver me from the calm, I will liberate myself from the rough waters." That is, we prefer the suffering that overwhelms us with its enormous weight, instead of those dull disappointments that seem like the torments of the Inquisition, killing us slowly.

CHAPTER TEN

THE DEATH OF A BODY
GAVE LIFE TO A SOUL

Ms. Soler:

Among the many letters I receive daily, one that was sent from Mayaguez (Puerto Rico) signed by Rosendo Terrens moved me very much, in which after praising my writings for the solace that it produced, she said the following:

"On February 18, 1905, Miss Eloísa Castro was very enthusiastic with the next festival of carnival, because she knew that she was going to be proclaimed queen of the festivities in the nearby town of Cabo Rojo. So, with that motive she dressed with her best dress and adorned herself with all of her jewelry, to go with her mother to Mayaguez to buy the crown, and because of such dedication to adorn and beautify herself, her amazed mother asked her, 'But, Eloísa, why do you adorn yourself with so much eagerness? Do you think we are going to a reception?' And, the mother had motives more than just surprise to wonder at the strange whims of her daughter to dress herself with such luxury, because she had never had the desire to look beautiful, for she would go to the theatre and the social club dressed with the utmost simplicity, but that day, she was adorned as if she was going to get married.

"She got up into a carriage with her mother, and they headed to the city. Unfortunately, the road crossed a railroad crossing. The mother saw a train coming and yelled for the driver to stop, but Eloísa yelled in turn, 'No, mother, no, no, mother, there is no time, and...' There was time for the train to destroy the carriage, and the unfortunate Eloísa died in pieces. Meanwhile, her mother was saved, to lament with great distress the tragic death of her daughter. Even Nature seemed to cry before such misfortune, for it rained in torrents when the train destroyed the carriage where went the gentle Eloísa. Her poor mother cried into the heavens saying, 'What I don't understand, what I cannot explain, is how my daughter who carried so many relics upon her, so many relics with images of saints, had not been saved so well accompanied. Is it a lie the protection of the saints?'

"Can the spirits tell me something about such a sad event? Write to Amalia, tell her that an inconsolable mother begs her, that she ask the guide of her works as to why my daughter had to die such an unhappy death; it's not curiosity, it is the pain of a mother without consolation who asks for a ray of light, to not end up going mad.

"This is what the mother of the unfortunate Eloísa asks, if you can, to the invisible ones, because she, a young girl so loved, has died by a means so tragic; who had no enemies, as she had done no harm to anyone. Ask, Amalia; ask, for a mother awaits your response, as one who is thirsty awaits a drop of water to wet dry lips, and also with her, wait many Spiritists."

Ms. Soler continues:

This letter by sister Rosendo Torrens moved me very much, but there are not always mediums available to make use of. I had to wait quite a while, more than I wanted to in order to ask regarding the past of that beautiful girl (who dressed with such great care to then die). She, who had contemplated herself with all her jewels before a mirror, something she was not accustomed to doing. Finally, my desires were fulfilled and a spirit dictated the following communication:

Spirit communication:

"The pain of a mother is sacred, and to provide her comfort is a work of charity; she laments that her daughter could not be saved from death, carrying on her chest so many blessed scapulars.[35] Poor mother!... When a spirit decides to pay a debt, there is no saint or Christ that can save her, nor the virgin that can separate her from the abyss. The law is fulfilled whether believing in all the religious legends or denying the existence of God. Eternal justice is superior to all beliefs and negations, and Eloísa died in the manner that she wanted to die.

"In one of her previous existences, she belonged to the stronger sex and was a handsome young man of gentile bearing, very boastful of his physical beauty because he was what you would say a handsome young man, but...he had no heart. He wooed woman with pride, to see them submissive at his feet, and enjoyed dishonoring the women with the most virtues, planting discord in the most tranquil of houses. Many mothers of families were despised by their husbands and their children by having failed in their duties, victims of the wiles of this son of Mars [36], because he was an irresistible seducer who (of the military with his gold embroidered uniform and hat decorated with white plumage) was so attractive and an interesting a figure, that he won victory in all the battles of love; to be conquered, it was enough to look just upon him.

"He was a longtime in a populous city surrounded by enemy forces, and to entertain himself during this spare time he attempted to seduce a young girl from a family of high lineage. The young woman yielded to all his affectionate demands; she was the submissive slave to all his caprices, she did not live for anything but to love him, she was mad for him. When things were more favorable, the hostile forces raised the place, a peace agreement was signed, and the troops that had defended the besieged city received orders to leave the plaza. The seducer harshly told his victim with considerable frankness, 'I have consecrated more time to you than I dedicate to my gallant adventures. I take from you a very agreeable memory, but as I am a bird of passage, do not expect to see me return. Goodbye.'

"The young woman did not respond with a single word. However, the next day she dressed-up in her best clothes, she adorned herself with her most precious jewelry and knowing where the column of troops

---

[35] Originally a cloth worn by monks, later on patches of cloth with holy relics attached.

[36] Referring to the Greek God of War.

commanded by her lover would pass, she went up to the tower of a church on the outskirts of town, and, when she saw those sons of Mars coming, she threw herself his way, falling precisely at the foot of her seducer. This moved him so deeply; he felt such profound remorse upon seeing that shattered body (caused by him). Mad with terror, he ran swiftly to flee from the dead body in pieces. However, his rapidity did not release him, she was tightly clinging to him; and they both ran together, climbing the mountains and descending into the abysses. That son of Mars feeling such remorse, the image of that young suicidal girl was engraved in his mind, of that woman who had loved him so much and had so pleased him with her passionate caresses, that on the very first occasion that he had, he caused himself to be killed by his enemy to flee from himself. However, on arriving in the spirit world, he found his victim even more in love with him than ever before. She told him, 'Yesterday, I loved your body, today I love your soul; and I will save you and regenerate you, because to save you and reform you, I threw myself at your feet in order to impress you and awaken your feelings; to drown your passions and raise them to the sincerest repentance. I will never leave you, not in your dreams, not in your wakefulness, not in the heights of pleasure, nor in the depths of pain. You will keep paying your debts, for you have contracted many, and while settling them all, my spiritual arms will always be your refuge and your door of salvation.'

"That son of Mars incarnated various times upon the Earth, always discontented with himself, always sad; his remorse was a slow fire that never extinguished, until he decided to suffer the same fate that his victim had, due to his indifference, and that is why relics and reliquaries nor amulets could not save him [37] ; for when a spirit signs its death sentence, no salvation is possible. Tell that inconsolable mother that the spirit of her daughter is now tranquil and is accompanied by its good angel [38], that with its sacrifices obtained the redemption of a rebellious spirit.

"Blessed are the sweet feelings of love! Through love, souls are purified! Through love, cities are exalted! Through love, universal progress is realized! Goodbye."

---

[37] His spirit was the daughter who died in the carriage accident.
[38] A spirit protector.

Ms. Soler:

There is a great teaching within this communication that I have received; it serves as consolation for the grieving mother and is of study for Spiritists. The history of humanity is the best textbook to study the whys of things, to provide a solution to the greatest social problems, for those who are so preoccupied and are so desirous that love with all its sweetness, and justice with all its rights, reign upon the Earth. I dream that it can be realized when the truth of Spiritism is known; when all men are convinced that we have lived yesterday and will live tomorrow, and that it is dependent upon us, to live in either heaven or in hell. As the election is not in doubt, that one day will arrive, and the Spiritists will make the Earth an oasis, a paradise, a mansion of peace inhabited by wise and good men.

CHAPTER ELEVEN

EVERYTHING HAS TO BE PAID

Ms. Soler:

It's been thirty years that I have known Carlos and Luisa. He was a pale young man, sickly, with a sweet but melancholy look. She was practically a child, still did not know how to wear a long dress. She appeared a symbol of modesty and humility, and she gazed steadfastly at the chosen one of her heart. It seems that I still see them, she sitting on an old sofa and he seated on the arm of the same couch. He looked at her intensely, and she with her head tilted and eyes halfway closed, appeared as if hypnotized. Neither of them pronounced one word, because when the heart speaks there are no interpreters for that divine language. In that way, they isolated themselves, although they were surrounded by her family and various friends. They did not mix in with the general conversation, and no one dared to disturb their loving ecstasy. Those two beings, that appeared to be not of this Earth, inspired respect and admiration and were silent, tranquil, reserved and so humble that they did not dare formulate the least request.

Luisa had no mother, and this added to her timidity. One could see that in her home she was as a plant without roots, and Carlos was a ray of sun that invigorated her fragile existence.

They kept in touch for years and years, and although he adored Luisa, to avoid serious dissatisfactions from his family (especially from his mother who wanted to unite him with a rich heiress and did not want Luisa because she was poor), Carlos (who was extremely compliant), consulted with Luisa.

She then told him, "I don't want you to be the cause of annoyance to your mother because of me. I want your soul, not your body. I will always love you, whether you stay a bachelor or if you give your name to another woman. I know your soul is mine, later your body will later be possessed by the worms. Anyway, I will have to lose you years before or years afterwards; what is of the earth returns to it. I know that souls live forever, therefore living always, our union will be eternal." Carlos, encouraged by these words and remembering the words of Dumas (the father) who said, 'The science of life is to trust and wait.'[39] So, having confidence in the justice of God, and awaiting the fulfillment of the eternal laws, he consecrated himself to his mother, while continuing to stay in contact with Luisa. Daily, he wrote affectionate letters to her, for they lived far away from each other, transmitting via telegraph their troubles if some illness prevented them from writing. This is how they passed thirty years, the letters of both, being as passionate as in their youth.

As Carlos's mother reached ninety years of age, and when least expected, Luisa fell gravely ill. Feeling she was about to die, she asked that Carlos be telegraphed regarding her alarming state and he attended to her call to receive her last breath. Afterwards, he devoutly closed the eyes of Luisa, those eyes that so lovingly had looked upon him. He then received a new telegraph to come to the side of his elderly mother, who awaited him so she could die. Her mission had concluded on Earth; Luisa was dead, so she no longer needed to be an obstacle to the happiness of anyone.

The death of the elderly woman greatly affected me to the point that towards a useful study, I asked the guide of my works what ties or what history existed between Luisa and that woman. She always negated the entreaties of her son (who she greatly loved) and was never softened by his pleadings, but allowed him to be sad and somber. She firmly repeated, "What is to be, is while I live, you will not marry her." Why such opposition, being that Luisa was from a nice family, beloved by all who knew her, because she was a model of virtues? What abyss was there

---

[39] French author Alexandre Dumas who wrote *The Count of Monte Cristo, The Three Musketeers*, etc. His name was written as *Alexandre Dumas père* (meaning "father" in French); his son of the same name and an author as well, used *fils* (son) at the end of his name, to differentiate themselves.

between these two spirits that separated them, causing such misfortune between such good souls?

Spirit communication:

"I see that you forgot (says my guide) what one should not forget, and that is, every cause produces an effect, and nothing can impede or prevent it, once the cause is produced. No one can elude that law, no matter how high a step one occupies on the interminable scale of evolution. What is above, is what is below, and the law is one.

"Carlos and Luisa are two spirits linked together many centuries by a powerful love; that is why for them there are no earthly obstacles that can diminish their affection. They love each other! And, that word says it all.

"In their past incarnation, they united before the altar, and a little girl came to add to their happiness; one who was sincere and good, sweet and reflective, sensitive and passionate. A young man of the town, a humble worker managed to attract her attention and the two loved each other with ecstasy, because love is the great equalizer of the Universe, it is the one thing that shortens all distances.

"However, Carlos and Luisa wanted for their daughter [to marry], a sovereign, a noble who wore a ducal crown around his temples. Therefore, their wishes were satisfied because a noble with many parchments and a genealogical tree full of shields of nobility offered his palaces, treasures and an enviable social position, to the girl in love. She replied resolutely, 'Do not unite me with anyone, but the love of my heart. I would die than be unfaithful to him.' Thus, she faithfully kept her word. The humble worker was deported as a traitor of his country, dying in exile. She, faithful as promised, lived some time without exhaling a complaint. Their parents were inflexible before her pain, and the girl died forgiving them for their blindness.

"Did Carlos and Luisa deserve in this existence to enjoy the delights of a love match? No; their suffering has been just, and the mother of Carlos was the instrument of their torment, and she could not die before Luisa, because it was necessary that the law be fulfilled. For it was by them, in the previous existence, where as an innocent being died alone in exile, for the humble worker of yesterday was the inflexible mother of today.

Carlos and Luisa continued loving each other, they conquered the Promised Land. They purified themselves through suffering, and do not exercise tyranny with the spirits that ask them for shelter in their home.

"There is only one law; who tramples over someone, will be later trampled over. One who abuses authority, will be a victim of their same abuse. The ignorant and proud laugh over this. The facts will convince them in due time, since one cannot be happy, he who has caused the unhappiness of another. Goodbye."

Ms. Soler:

The spirit says it well. Many do not support Spiritism because they do not want to know their smallness and moral misery. However, before the truth it is not enough to say: I don't want to believe that you have to incline one's head before a sentence is pronounced by oneself, as Carlos and Luisa did; both being very good persons, long-suffering, very spiritual. They had to live separately without the power to liberate themselves from a mysterious spell that made them suffer perpetual disappointment, waiting for thirty years, the pardon for a crime that they did not know that they had committed.

There is so much to study in the bible of humanity! By it, we know that everything has to be paid.

Translator's Note: People and spirits have freewill. Therefore, all three spirits chose to be reborn together in the above lifetime. The mother acted out of her own freewill in insisting on keeping the couple separated because she felt Luisa was too poor. Also, her son Carlos voluntarily complied with his mother's wishes as Luisa advised him to do. Preordained was when the two women would die, their spirits returning to the spirit world. Yet, spirits can retain an intuition when alive, of their feelings (good, bad or indifferent) of those people around them that they have known in previous existences, which can influence and play a role in their decision-making. In conclusion, with Luisa and Carlos, the Divine Law was fulfilled by all their choices. As for the decision made by Carlos's mother (previously the humble worker) in keeping the loving couple apart, that spirit will receive whatever consequences it deserves for its actions in future existence(s).

CHAPTER TWELVE

WHAT WE GIVE IS WHAT WE RECEIVE

Ms. Soler:

"Our life is what we make it; the world does not return more than what we give it." – an American saying.

Nothing is so true. We reap what we have sown, and what bad seeds has humanity planted, because the majority of the inhabitants of Earth collect no more than sharp thorns! On reading the newspaper one is saddened, anguished and anxious because there does not occur one day where there is not a description of horrible shipwrecks, train crashes, bridge collapses, devastating cyclones, volcanic eruptions pulling down flourishing cities, violent fires that destroy entire towns, and explosions in the mines where they are buried hundreds of miners.

It's extremely sad considering the manner in which one lives upon the Earth. For those who are not the victims due to a mass loss of lives, there are those who seemingly live with relative tranquility, but if one penetrates within their homes and if one lifts one corner of the veil that covers up their intimate lives, what sad scenes are to be contemplated on! Families formed by irreconcilable enemies, make affection a ritual of mutual tolerance. They try to control their inexplicable hatreds, mysterious aversions, but don't always succeed. More than not, an unextinguished spark of hate catches on fire, and quarrels, jealousies, differences of character burn like a pile of straw. There, it develops into those tragedies which produces the eternal story of Cain and Abel.[40]And, if it does not reach to such a sad finality, some live dying under the tyranny of a despotic father, a tyrannical mother, a selfish sibling, being the abuses of some and others, the currency in the great marketplace of life.

Is this living? No! This is payment, an eye-for-an-eye and a tooth-for-a-tooth, to continually drink honey and vinegar that according to tradition they gave to Christ. It is to receive wound after wound, caused by relentless disappointments; and if this is what life is reduced to, it is not worth having been born.

Spirit communication:

"What you say is true (a spirit tells me), if there were no other scenes to represent the eternal drama of life of the Earth that you inhabit, God would be injustice personified and the last serpent of the Earth would be happier than the king of Creation (vulgar man). For man is subjected to innumerable calamities, starting with incurable diseases, pains that conduct one to desperation, the way wars are, paralysis, and that lack of necessary [body] members such as arms, hands, legs and feet, and [loss] of the tongue, hearing and of understanding. Man suffers torments so varied and multiple that if he did not have a past life and a tomorrow that did not await him, he would have to renounce having been born. However, fortunately, in the night of time, without being able to specify a fixed date, man found himself king of the jungles. He looked at the sky and felt budding forth from his thought, the intangible flame of desire. He contemplated his nude body and experienced the necessity of covering it. He saw himself strong, and used his strength to acquire the most indispensable, to meet the most pressing needs of life, and went conquering palm by palm the land sufficient to raise his tents, and to surround himself with submissive servants, with families that satisfied his thirst of reproduction. During the course of the centuries, the ancient patriarchs left the Earth, returned once again to populate it, but now they were not content living between the harshness of the forest and the roughness of the mountains. They raised up cities, and they asked the

---

[40] Brother killing brother; the story in the Bible.

magicians and soothsayers of the secrets of their science, to destroy the darkness of the night.

"They understood that the law of Nature, as one of their thinkers said, is that of 'work or die.'

"If one walks away from work, then one dies morally, intellectually and physically, and death has always been rejected by men with lucidity of understanding. Only those who are unbalanced commit suicide; solely those who do not comprehend the immense value of life look for complete destruction. That is why work has been, is and shall be, the eternal law by which men shall be eternally governed. For all the actual inhabitants of the Earth, all have their history, all have lived yesterday and will live again tomorrow.[41] Everyone has worked to create a means to live; utilizing their intelligence and passions, their vices and virtues, each one planting a seed that appeared the best in the circumstances provided, but many times a step incorrectly taken causes one to slip and fall. Since the slope of vice is so slippery, man descends down it without being able to stop because being the *first* step, the fall is inevitable. Because knowing so, sometimes, the error that encompasses the fall, or whether a relapse of the transgression, it comes to the point the spirit grows accustomed to wrongful works. Each vice acquired is like an insatiable drunkenness, and much more than your habits and your evil so-called laws. Small is the circle your crimes orbit in, all the doors close and solely are open the arms of vice, of the most humiliating degradation.

"I always read within your thoughts this eternal question: Why does God, that can do anything, not turn away man from the border of the abyss and tell him, 'Wake up, for I love you...' And I will answer you: what merit would there be for the regeneration of man? None; absolutely none. Your struggles would not have the least importance because they would not have served as a lesson. A saint and a wrongdoer would have the same worth, if at the end of the journey God said, 'Enter my kingdom because that is my will.' Mankind has been created to climb all the heights, to affront all dangers, to discover all the secrets that the worlds hide, to know all the properties of the material, to put to use all the Natural forces available, to be wise, to be good; and, to arrive to possess the virtue and the science that a man knows for himself, the hurt of the wounds of the body

---

[41] Past and future lifetimes.

and the wounds of the soul, and the humiliation that ignorance, cruelty, and the persistence of a crime carries. Without the pain of the fall, it is not possible for man to appreciate the superior pleasure compared to human corruptness and human miseries.

"The work of God is perfect, but perfection is the work of titans, and to perfect a spirit it needs the incessant struggle of the centuries. What you call disasters, calamities, mass killings, horrific events, do you know what they serve as? To clean the atmosphere of your world, to liberate humanity of insatiable monsters, which puts in manifest its inferiority and separate from you the many Cains disposed to continue to sacrifice their brothers/ sisters. When you receive notice that a city has disappeared, annihilated by a fire or the fury of a hurricane, or by geological trembling, do not believe that God is unjust snatching up your home the same as the elder or a baby dependent on its mother's breast. The advancement of the spirit is not revealed by the material covering; it is its past history, in its present aspiration, that puts manifest its inferiority or its elevation.

"It is not a capricious coincidence that a village is devastated, it is the law of compensation that is fulfilled. The cruelest conquistadores, those who have enjoyed destroying cities where the defeated ones were staying, have to suffer the pain that they caused others, they have to wake up terrorized and stunned, they have to wander around the smoky ruins of their homes without realizing why in less than a second, they have lost all they possessed. In the eternal laws all is just, unknown is no oversight or forgetfulness, all arrives at its time. No one gathers one atom more that does not belong to them, nobody takes no more of a load than what justly corresponds to them, and however great that is, its weight will not overwhelm them because the spirit has a deposit of forces to resist all that justly corresponds to what they carry. If this were not so, God would be unjust and its justice would alter the march of the worlds, because it would create obstacles that would make the immense spheres jump out of their orbits that carry other civilizations in their bosoms.

"What we give, is what we receive;" that is the law. There is no need for subterfuge or compromises, there are no worthy religions or philosophies that can alter the order of that created. With the divine work all is immutable, the mines of the infinite always have their deep holes open so that through them all peoples can descend and take out the precious metal of progress and of truth.

So, be good miners, look in the mountains of the Earth for the weak and the conquered ones, give them what they need, light for their souls and bread for their bodies, for from the blind and the hungry come the Cains of humanity.

"Goodbye!"

Ms. Soler:

How many considerations are provided by this communication I have obtained! So many truths! Heart-breaking truths, bitter, but undeniable truths, and this is what must be sought out in spirit communications; the truth without veils, rational teachings, faithful advice to incline one towards the practicing of the virtues. The conviction that without the improvement of the individual, the common people will never be free, or progress or aggrandize, or have their names recorded in the history of their native home, appearing as heroes, as redeemers, as inspired sailors taking their ships to safe port.

How blessed are the communications of the spirits! They guide us, they encourage us and they oblige us to learn the grandeur and justice of God.

Translator's Note: The spirit understands from its perspective in the spirit world, that to choose those existences full of challenges, provides more opportunities for their souls to progress further, which then leads to sooner reaching a much happier future state of existence.

CHAPTER THIRTEEN

PREMONITIONS

I don't know which poet said, "It is evident; there is no prophet like our heart."

And in truth, he who said such a thing was right because undoubtedly many times we have hunches. We sense an inner voice that warns us that danger is near us, and we don't pay attention in the majority of occasions; we do not attend to the warnings that our relatives give us from beyond the grave. I believe we make ourselves deaf, because when we have to pass through the gallows, it's despite all the warnings and reminders given. In proof of this I copied some sections, or rather, I will try to sum up from an extensive letter that was sent to me by a Spiritist from Minas (Montevideo, Mexico) telling me about the disastrous death of her daughter Maria, that from very young, she had the premonition that her death would be very painful.

Young Maria was beautiful, good, sensible, affectionate and loving of her family, especially of her father, whom she felt true idolatry.

At the early age of sixteen years old, a handsome king's page courted her love. She responded to his wooing happy to see herself attended to and given presents. The suitor wanted to carry out the matter as soon as possible and put the deadline of four months to effectuate the marriage, but her father asked to wait for a year, and he had to concede to him. During that year, their heated love cooled down, until their relationship ended much to the contentment of Maria who remained calm. Three years afterwards, a second admirer offered Maria his name and love. She expressed lively satisfaction, but when she got to the day to buy a basket for the wedding, she embraced her father and told him sobbing:

"My betrothed is very good. I don't have one complaint regarding his behavior towards me, but I am overcome by the horrible foreboding that I am going to be very unhappy in my marriage. I completely regret my determination. I do not want to separate from you, my father."

"But woman, "he replied, "Why did you not think about this before giving your word, and I of mine?"

"Because before, I didn't feel like I feel today."

"But you love him?"

"Yes, very much, but now I do not want him, it's as if I had never considered him."

"In the end, daughter, everything is for God! It's worth more you back down now, at this time, then later."

Don't think, Amalia, (my friend tells me), that my daughter is a flirt, or had bad judgment. She was a model of a girl, loved by everyone, because she was all sweetness.

At two or three years of what had happened, another new suitor fell madly in love with Maria, and she reciprocated. Distrustful of the previous events, her father interrogated his daughter and told her to think about it before deciding. She assured him that she was sure of having no regrets with this one. The relationship lasted two years, without any minor annoyances. When the time arrived to prepare everything for the wedding, one morning Maria called her father and told him with horror, "My Father, what a horrible dream I had last night! I dreamt that I had married and on that same day I had died. I saw myself dead and my husband by the side of a cadaver. Forgive me for this new annoyance I am going to give you, because I am not going to marry. Since last night my fiancé inspires in me the most profound aversion; it does not serve for me to be married. It is clear I should stay a single woman." To all this, Maria cried with the greatest of distress, her father did not know what to say, and the groom upon finding out, fell gravely ill, saved only by a miracle.

Maria reached thirty years old, and a young man of twenty summers went crazy for her. Her father gave an account to him and his family, about the past grooms of his daughter. But his narrative did not prove to be an obstacle, so the relationship continued forward, and eventually the marriage was planned. Although Maria told her most intimate friends, "I will regret my marriage. I sense a great misfortune, a most painful event. I know I will suffer horribly. It seems I am already tormented by the sufferings, but I do not want to disgust my father anew."

They married and after two months, she and her husband returned to Minas and took up residence in the house of her parents. Upon recognizing that she was going to become a mother, Maria told her whole family (except her father), that in the act of delivering a child she would die. Eight days before giving birth, she called for her husband, her mother and her siblings, and to all of these she pleaded with them to faithfully carry out her last wishes. She wished to be buried in her wedding dress, and to give all that she possessed among her sisters-in-law and closest relatives, giving the major portion of her most precious objects to the poorest, and the neediest. Every one of them asked: "But, are you crazy?" She repeated herself, smiling sadly, "Soon you will see how my presentiment will be fulfilled. I do not feel more than that you will not be left with my last portrait, but I only ask that you fulfill my last wishes."

Her mother and her siblings felt that fear dominated her, but she told them, "I will die, I will die, and of a dreadful death. All these years I have avoided paying this debt! Finally, I will pay a part more than I owe. God have mercy on me."

Maria's father ignored what was going on in his house, while everyone stayed quiet so as not to torment him before time, because in reality, they believed that Maria was delirious or seeing visions. However, the day of birth arrived and her father, an excellent operator, realized the situation and believing he was losing his senses, left his daughter's room crying like a child.

The family anxiously surrounded him, and everyone asked simultaneously:

"What is there to do?"

"That she dies, and there is no remedy for her."

"Nonsense," said others.

"Science has not had the final word."

"I say it," answered the father sobbing, "Do not torment her, everything is useless!"

"Impossible," yelled the husband.

"Love blinds," the children said, "Here come the doctors."

There went in the doctors; they operated five times. As Maria was dying, she reassured her father saying, "I knew what awaited me, now you understand my aversion to marriage. Fulfilling my presentiment, I have one less debt. Be happy, my father."

Ms. Soler continues:

Being happy isn't possible before the dead body of a loved one. My good friend was left profoundly shocked by the tragic end of her daughter. Thanks that he is a convinced Spiritist, because in his long life he has had irreproachable proofs of the eternal life of the spirits.

One year before the death of Maria, a child of two years old died, also leaving him with deep desperation for the following reason:

Years ago, my friend went to see his elderly mother, that lived very far from Buenos Aires (Argentina). She demonstrated great persistence to go there (with her son) to Minas. He, considering her advanced age, did not think it prudent to expose her to such a long trip, and he promised her that following year he would return to see her. However, she then told him:

"Next year will be too late. I'll be dead, and being dead without you to close my eyes, being this is the desire of my life, after which you will have embraced me in your arms." And the old lady caressed him as if he was a young boy, and repeated: "Take me with you, I want you to close my eyes."

My friend did not fulfill his mother's desires, and she died far away from the son that she adored. Well, two months after leaving her body, her spirit presented itself to her son, who during the night (particularly at dawn) one is put in contact with disincarnated relatives to speak with them and interchange impressions.

His mother presented herself very affectionately as she always did, and every two or three nights he saw her. Various months passed, and the wife of my friend gave birth to a beautiful baby girl; and after that his mother never appeared to my friend. Yet, upon seeing the daughter that was just born, he felt an extraordinary shudder. He steadfastly looked at the child, and told his wife, "My mother is with us, I am sure it is her."

At six months old, the little girl started to speak hesitatingly certain phrases, and towards her father, she called him "child" never saying "papa."

"Child" is what he was always called by his mother never by his name, and she would caress his cheek with her little hands as when he was her son.

When she reached two years of age, she became sick with convulsions, and twenty-four hours before dying she caressed her father most tenderly. Later, she extended her right hand with her finger pointed to the sky and she stayed like that for a few moments. Afterwards, lowering her hand, with her finger she touched his forehead and closed her eyes tenderly. She later opened them, and did not stop looking at her father until she died; with kisses and expressive gestures, all bid her farewell, but in particular her father gave her impassioned caresses. My friend closed the eyes of his daughter, completely convinced that it was the spirit of his mother who had returned to reclaim that last act of affection.

It is very significant that a little girl of two years old would touch her finger to her eyes and close them, to later reopen them; who called her father "child" and never "papa" and to express affection towards him in the same manner as previously. Finally, he would say to his friend that the spirit of his mother had come from the spirit world, since he had not wanted to please her, even when she had asked with such insistence.

Ms. Soler:

When one lives so closely identified with the beings from the beyond the tomb, [42] unforeseen disasters are supported with more strength. Death disappears with all its horrors, because we are in touch with the reality of the immortal soul, and before undeniable facts one has to believe in the survival of the spirit; for if it wasn't for this, one would feel the violent shudder that one can experience before the dead body of a loved one. But the pain of a convinced Spiritist does not reach the violent expression of desperation because next to the inert body of the being one cries for, stands the solemn and serious spirit that once animated that body.

Life and death are joined, tomorrow and today, the known, what we have tried and the unknown, the mysterious, the inexplicable, the spirit is not afraid. Surprise and dread do not take possession of us, and the

---

[42] Through spirit communications and visions from the spirits in the spirit world (afterlife).

fountain of tears dries before a new eagerness, before a new hope. One always lives! The beings who have loved us, have not abandoned us! We can count on their inspiration, counsels and their moral support! There is so much to think about regarding this! ... And when one thinks, the pain loses its power, it does not tyrannize us, it does not sink us into the abyss of desperation; life moves forward and leaves it well behind. Blessed is Spiritism![43] You are the best friend of man. You tell us with irrefutable proofs, "The spirit never dies!"

---

[43] In 19th century Spain, the concepts of spirits, mediumship and reincarnation was known mostly through the principles received by the spirits and documented and compiled in the books of French educator and paranormal researcher Allan Kardec in a spiritual science he called Spiritism.

CHAPTER FOURTEEN

—————

BAD HARVEST

A friend relays an incident to Ms. Soler:

Luisa says to me, "Hey, you are a storehouse of stories and narratives, like the blind ones that sell romances in Andalucía. Let's see if you can tell me why they had to kill a poor boy infected by rabies. Joking aside, and although I don't believe in what you do, and never will, this has affected me greatly to see that black boy defiled, surrounded by his family crying without consolation. Involuntarily, and without wanting to, I thought of you and said, 'What has this creature done in order to have died this way?' I have come so that you can ask those people from the Beyond why this great misfortune has happened. Imagine this, that child was playing in the street with other children in front of his house, and becoming the one playing dead, he laid on the ground. When all of a sudden, a homeless dog boldly attacked, and gave him a terrible bite on the nose, then disappeared as fast as lightening. No one took care to look for it, because all those there, were surrounding that desperately screaming wounded boy. They took him to the laboratory of Ferran. They said, 'If the dog was rabid, the boy would die, because he has drunk a lot of the blood that was dripping from his wound, and there is no remedy for him. However, for whatever it's worth, we will use every means to save him. Then, the boy's house was converted into a department of medicine. Doctors came to him in droves, from the most famous to the less known, due to their youth. It was all in vain!'"

"At last, the father had to give authorization to the eldest doctor, so that he could give the boy a sedative that would induce death. This is horrible.

To order the death of his son! … Ask them, and see what they tell you. Don't believe I will laugh; no. This is no laughing matter to see a family completely desperate."

Ms. Soler:

She has reason. I will ask to see if some spirit can answer me, and that they do not think that we are hurling nonsense to receive communications from beyond the grave. It is not enough to ask; one has to consider the motive of the questions and the use one makes of the revelations.

Luisa:

"Puerile curiosity does not drive me; it is that it has affected me so much, and I am not the only one. Among the doctors that visited him, there was a man that, upon entering, looked at the child and burst into tears with such disconsolation; and I had to accompany him to his house as he could hardly walk."

Ms. Soler:

Ok, well, I will ask. I will return in two to three days. Let's see if my medium has received some communication.

Luisa:

In three days, Luisa came to see me, not laughing as was her usual way, but very serious and worried. She calmly asked me, "Well, what do you have? I want to believe you did not forget about that poor boy."

Ms. Soler:

True pain is not a laughing matter and enclosed within the death of that child is a very sad lesson. The medium had obtained the following:

Spirit communication:

"We are always willing to respond to those who ask for the truth.

"In very distant epochs, the child that today suffered so much dying, belonged to a very proud noble family, by fact of its genealogical family tree. This boy attained ten years of age, and with a self-possession inappropriate for his years, he felt such profound antipathy towards his older brother (one who is what you call now a true democrat [a supporter of social equality] and did not give one straw regarding his titles of nobility. He loved the town, he attracted the humble, so much so, that he blindly fell in love with a young shepherdess, a daughter of one of the servants of his father.

"One day he left the house with his younger brother (and not suspecting anything of him and in front of him) spoke a long time about the elected one of his heart and making plans for the future. It was within no time when this youngest arrived at his house to relay to his father about his brother's love, telling him with embellishment what he was going to do, and suggesting to him that the best thing would be for the country girl to disappear so the young man in love would not dishonor the family with such an unequal match.

"The father was in much agreement with his son's plan, and as if all the circumstances helped towards the realization of this crime, the first born went on a hunt. During his absence, they took possession of the young girl he adored, and locked her up far from where she lived. When they did not know how to kill her, they locked up the young girl and threw in a hungry dog that had the symptoms of rabies; that young innocent that had committed no wrong other than to fall in love with a noble. Two days afterwards, the killer and its victim presented a terrifying scene; they were both unrecognizable. The rabid dog devoured its prey, then later devoured itself. Such a horrible crime was a mystery. No one suspected that beautiful young boy, the baby of the family that always went around with his older brother, and even less, that within that head crowned with blond curls had concocted that truly diabolical plan, carried out so secretly that no one ever knew who its author was. The conjectures that were made were so wrong, and as the victim was a young girl of the village (in that epoch servants were the property of their masters), it wasn't worth it to make an investigation for the fate of one peasant woman keeping a herd for her master, destroyed by a dog, probably defending the sheep entrusted to her care.

"A veil of the most profound indifference covered that sad criminal act. Solely one man, who was advanced for his time, the beloved of the victim, for it was he who could not be consoled having lost the love of his life. A profound sadness overcame his soul, he closed his eyes from his understanding to know the story of that sudden death; he had a horrible intuition of something horrible, but he kept silent. He entrusted to nobody the terrible suspicions that he harbored in his mind. He blamed his father, but not his brother; a soul so noble could not conceive that a young boy could be a murderer. He disowned his noble lineage, he convinced himself that instead of being a feudal master he would be a sad commoner. Their love had had a greatly beautiful complement, with dreams of equality, fraternity and of liberty; and it went consuming him slowly. Tuberculosis consumed his body, and one year after the death of his beloved, he died very happy to leave the Earth. This caused great happiness to his brother who inherited his older brother's noble titles, but not his noble sentiments; and at so young an age he could cause harm in the shadows, afterwards more indiscretions were committed with impunity. He was the master of lives and estates and could kill without compassion.

"His first crime stayed covered in the shadows. On Earth, no one accused him, but he accused himself, when reading the story of his crimes upon return to the spirit world. He horrified himself when he saw that for him there did not exist a childhood of innocence and goodness; that he had committed premeditated murder of that unhappy one in such an ingenious manner as to avoid suspicion. What a more natural a thing, that a shepherdess taking care of her flock, be devoured by a rabid dog?... That cruel boy was so proud of his ingenuity! What precociousness so horrible! ...Of all his crimes (and he committed many) none horrified him as much as the one he committed in his youth, enjoying his crime, and seeing his brother die slowly later on. Upon seeing him consumed, he would say to himself, 'All this was my work! ...'

"His joy later turned into frightful despair, and strong and animated, he dedicated himself to suffer as a martyr, as he had caused the young peasant girl to endure [suffering] and die devoured by a rabid dog. He returned to Earth accompanied by his father from that epoch. It was just that he who allowed an innocent girl to be killed without compassion, would be there to see his desperate and rabid son dying, and who had to speed up his death to stop him his suffering.

"What came to pass you already know; a sentence was discharged without any judge on Earth to pronounce the sentence; the crime that the both of them committed (that no one knew about). Furthermore, nobody suspected them because the lover of the victim did not confide his suspicions to anyone. However, nothing remains hidden in the eternal life of the spirit, and one pays for all the wrongdoing that one commits; when they enjoy doing harm, when they enjoy the agony of their victims.

"It is not unusual that your friend was so upset contemplating the body of that boy; because that dead child symbolized the eternal justice of God, the immutability of its laws, because God neither rewards nor punishes. The law is fulfilled, and each one reaps what they sow. What did that boy sow? Horrors, infamy and wickedness! That is why in his last existence he received a bad harvest.

"Many more bad harvests are left to be reaped, but the sun will also shine for him because he is loved. His father of today loved him very much, and he has spirits that love him. The last doctor who saw him, cried like a child upon seeing him suffer so much; it was the spirit of his mother (when he was the murderer of the young peasant girl). How far away was the comprehension of that doctor in understanding that centuries before, the child had been her son! ... He cried, without knowing why he cried so much, because generally doctors are used to seeing suffering. Strangely, he asked himself, 'Why did I cry?' One sees so many effects, ignorant of the causes!

"Tell your friend, to go on thinking about what the spirits say, to not laugh about the past, and do not throw at the roof of the future. Goodbye."

Ms. Soler:

"This is what the spirit said to the medium. What do you think of this communication? Does it make you laugh?"

Luisa:

"No, no," Luisa said, "Much to the contrary, it gives me much to think about. Although I do not believe I will ever become a Spiritist, I swear that I will never laugh regarding your stories from the world beyond the tomb."

Ms. Soler:

"You will do well: do not throw stones on the roof of the future." [44]

---

[44] My personal interpretation: Besides, do not judge of what you may not fully understand or know about; when we see a person or people undergoing something terrible, we cannot make a judgement of the matter because we do not usually know what a person's actions (in their present life or in a past life) was the cause of the consequences (the effect) of what they are now undergoing based on their previous acts.

CHAPTER FIFTEEN

VENGEANCE

Ms. Soler:

We are continually receiving letters in which our brothers and sisters, the Spiritists, asking the why of many times truly dramatic events, and some of them more than dramatic, tragic, frightening and horrible.

As in this world according to an old saying, it never rains to the likes of everyone, our writings have their adversaries, also are criticized and censured harshly, which in honor of the truth does not cause us surprise. It is impossible to please everyone for the simple reason that each spirit (person) has its own way of thinking and in appreciating things.

The true proponent of an ideal, writes for all and for none. They throw seeds convinced that a minimum amount will be the ones that will germinate, that most of the grains will slip through the hardened earth, and others will sprout among thorny brambles whose thorns will not let them grow. However, since the Truth is like the Sun that always shines and always illuminates its splendid light, may our writings solely reflect the truth of eternal life; if rejected and anathematized by some, they are commented on, studied and analyzed by others. [45]

The communications that we are given by the spirits serve as teachings, and more than teachings, as consolation. A comfort of which humanity

---

[45] Anathematized – to be detested, shunned or cursed; a formal condemnation, especially by the Catholic Church. As an example, Ms. Soler's magazine *La Luz del Porvenir* [*Light of the Future*] was condemned and its publication was suspended for forty-two weeks for an article she wrote regarding the Creator.

is thirsty! Since there are many afflicted ones, many incarnated [humans living on earth] as well as disincarnated ones [as spirits in the spirit world], who have reported to us the good that our writings have produced. We continue to write not to receive applause from those who are happy, but to be useful to the unfortunates, whose number is incalculable.

Ms. Soler:

From Rosario de Santa Fe (Argentina), they sent us the attached story, published on March 24th in a newspaper from that city called *La Capital* [The Capital]. We have read and reread that sad narrative, and as a useful study we have asked a spirit, who gave strength to a child's arm to strike as sure as it says here.

In continuation, I copied what the daily newspaper *The Capital* stated:

> *"The crime of a child. The mother beheaded by the son. A difficult process. Confession before justice. Painful details. The law of Talion was fulfilled.[46] The heroism of a mother. Reports complete."*

A feeling of strange piety, as its confused origin sprung from many emotions found, weighs on my pen upon initiating this account that by the nature of its motives should present exceptional characteristics, and perhaps, convey itself to be rare in the annals of crime.

The imagination feels small in this case because the events are so obvious, so veridical and deep, that one of its most minute details speak with a definitively painful eloquence.

The spirit that is accustomed to the investigation speculates about the insignificances and about the ideas, in the presence of a phenomenon of human nature one is plunged into despair, concentrates one's mind, and from deduction to deduction loses oneself in immense chaos.

In the brief time of a few minutes, listening to the astonishing revelation of a soul born yesterday to the life of the flesh and that, nonetheless,

---

[46] Talion law - a system or legal principle where the punishment specifically corresponds to the type of crime.

appears to have immense black wings[47] ; we have gone from the tender and simple emotions that produce the spontaneous tears of a child, to the astonishment that shrinks the heart and puts a tight knot in the throat.

The scale of feelings has been traversed in all its extension, and since the journey is too distressing to offer it to the public with all its barren sadness, we will try in this account to lessen it of some very strong notes, without for which the truth would be distorted.

Background information:

On the occasion of the last visit of the jailing made on February 25th of this year,

in the detailed chronicle that then we by preference for a fact to which he was the first to call our interest: Dr. Bravo, the judge of court proceedings of the investigation, felt by the words of the presumed innocent, was given the idea of having a high and generous confidence, with the noble yearnings of repairing a tremendous injustice.

In the detailed chronicle that we then made, a preference for a fact to which this was the first to call our interest: Dr. Bravo, the examining magistrate gave suggestion (as we did later) because of the heartfelt words of the presumed innocent, given uplifting and generous conviction, noble aspirations to repair a tremendous injustice.

Reminding the readers of this newspaper, that a boy of twelve years old was in jail called Juan Muja, accused by the authorities of Carmen del Sauce of having caused the death to his own mother, Ana de Muja, by beheading.

We could not believe the truth of this crime attributed to a puny, sickly child of twelve years old, whose appearance inspired pity and compassion, and suggested the concept of a being physically unfit for any action of medium effort. In order to confirm these doubts, we interviewed him, and the next day he informed us about what happened between sighs and tears, according to which he had nothing to do with the horrible crime that was charged to him.

---

[47] A figurative analogy of the boy as the Devil. Ms. Soler, a Spiritist, did not except the existence of the Devil.

We have already said, that the judge believed in the cause of this child at first, also in his innocence based on the all the details that he had so far.

Workings of the Law:

The investigation was carried forward in spite of this, patiently working with perseverance, recording dates of one part and another, statements, documents; comparing words and attitudes. Finally, everything that could serve to illustrate the criterion of justice, in a matter shrouded in shadows, demonstrated an honorable laboriousness that was crowned by complete results.

The file threatened to grow, indefinitely by the day, for at times, events and sinister conjectures became related to each other by amazing connections, which forced new and endless actions.

The court of instruction was exclusively re-energized with this single cause of a typical court, and it was a matter of despair in order to find the end.

A little one, a child, gave this tiring haste to the law, despairing the judge and the secretaries, sometimes with his tears and at other times with his energetic and serene negations, and all, as seen later, involuntarily, with an astonishing calculation that could fit into the head of a twelve-year-old.

The judge, Dr. Bravo, had repeatedly interviewed the Muja boy, eager to establish the true face of things, but he always found tears followed by precocious energies that were not advancing towards a summary.

Confession of the crime:

At last, he decided to make a last attempt by calling Muja to his office; and for long hours was closed up with him and the secretary Mr. Villalon. Immediately after this conference was over, we learned that something extraordinary had taken place. We wanted to find out in detail, right there, but we found strict silence that the secret of the summary imposes.

At all costs, it was necessary to clarify what happened and without loss of time we went to the Penitentiary, to where the small indicted one had been returned.

Finally, attended by the warden, we requested to speak with the child Muja and we were immediately accommodated.

We found ourselves in the presence of the little one, who recognizing us from our previous visit, obstinately lowered his eyes, costing us much work to get him to look at us.

In those somewhat sunken small eyes there were tears, and his face did not show the pallor of strong impressions, but the quick blush that can be observed in one who has been discovered in the crime of a lie.

A small pair of briefs suspended by an ordinary strap over a rough gray shirt, old espadrilles and a discolored cap in his hand, such was the costume with which presented the terrible accused, three cubits high [about 4 feet, 6 inches].

We called him benevolently by his name. We produced in his mind the caress of friendly words, and we saw him conquered.

"Do you remember our first visit?"

"Yes, sir, but..."

"Speak, have confidence in us. Were you with the judge today?"

"Yes, sir, it was for a long time, this morning and the afternoon."

"Were you treated well?"

"Oh, the judge is very good; very good!"

"He has told that you have finally confessed the whole truth. We do not wish you any trouble, but tell us all that you told the judge."

He looked at us for a moment in silence, and as he twirled his cap in his hands, we noticed that an indefinable tremor agitated the sides of his small nose and the back of his knee.

We brought him a chair and now comfortably seated, he slowly, with the fragility of one sick, asked this question,

"Who are all of you?"

"Well, your friends. Your friends, and defenders."

"Are you sure?"

"Why so much distrust? We are not going to cause any harm. What did you tell the judge?"

"I told him...don't look at me! ...I told him that I was the one who killed my mother. I could not lie to that man anymore. They treat me so well, with so much affection, and they spoke of such beautiful things of heaven, that here in the heart and here in the head, it appeared a strong sounding voice told me not to lie."

"Poor thing! You, when you murdered your mother did not know what you were doing, we are sure of it. Tell us all that occurred that day."

"Yes, I will tell you, but don't hold me down. My mother would hit me a lot. Almost every day she would get drunk since my father went far away, and when she was like that, she would grab a broomstick or a whip that she had at the house and would hit me hard."

"What reasons did you give her?"

"None. None. At times, I would entertain myself outside of the house with the driver Ailana, and on return she would not give me food and would hit me hard."

"What did you say to her when she was punishing you?"

"I cried and sometimes she made me very angry, but nothing else."

"While your father was in the house, she never beat you?"

"Sometimes too, and I remember that my father would get mad at me, and saying that he should throw me out of the house."

"The day before the death of my mom, a boy threw a rock at my head and blood came out. I went home crying and with my clothes stained, and then my mama hit me. That day I felt more anger than ever, and I left the house staying overnight in the countryside. The next day, I arrived early and this time my mama did not hit me; but yes, she said, threatening me with a knife, that she would kill me if I again gave her cause to get angry. I stayed quiet and left for the countryside. My body hurt a lot, and in the evening, I returned to the house."

"Was it that very day that you killed her?"

"Yes, Sir. Upon entering I saw my mama on the bed. I got close to her slowly and she was sleeping. I do not know why my hands and legs shook, nor why I grabbed that knife she threatened me with. Oh! I don't know what happened… my eyes dazed my head. I gripped the knife, the knife with the white handle, moving closer. I slowly reached a drawer to the bed that was high, but at that moment I thought my mama had awoken and I crouched so that she would not see me. I passed some time trembling. Squeezing the knife until my hand hurt, I put one knee on the bed and…

"Don't cry, little one, continue."

Supreme Moment:

"I saw I would not have the strength to do it with one hand. I grasped the knife blade with two hands, to lower the cut and press it very much against the neck. Hot blood came out, mom sat down suddenly on the bed, and wanted to scream but she could not. She raised her arms and rolled to the ground, remaining still."

This time the thin, angular face of that child who now appeared as a great criminal was very pale. There were no tears in those little gray eyes, nor did his feeble body tremble. There was in all his being the calm of an unconscious one that relays a story without feeling the emotions it produces.

We asked him, "What did you do next?"

"I threw the knife and got close to my mama; she had her eyes very open, staring at the ceiling, but she did not move. She was dead and blood squirted from her neck. Scared, I opened the door and swiftly went out into the countryside. When it was starting to become night, I saw that my bag was stained with blood. I thought this would make people suspicious, and to avoid this, I went back again into the house. Still on the floor was my mom with legs and arms open. I pulled a sack out of my trunk, wrapped in it the one that was stained, and jumped out of the window after closing the door."

"Did you not say that the handle was white?"

"Yes, sir, it was."

"The one found stuck in your mother's neck was of a black handle."

"That was another one. When I went to jump out the window, I threw the knife with the white handle under the bed and grabbed the other with the black handle that was on the dinner table, and I put it in her neck."

"Why did you do this?"

"Because I believed they would place blame on another."

"You see how you were wrong."

"God had wanted it."

"Do you believe in God?"

"Before, my mama used to teach me to pray."

"And, didn't she say that God punished those who were bad?"

"Yes, she would tell me, but she would still hit me, and no one punished her. You see that!"

"Do you know that what you have done the law will punish you?"

"The law? I don't know what that is, but if the law is like the sheriff over there, it must be very bad."

"What did the sheriff do to you?"

"He beat me so that I would say that I killed my mother."

"Why did you cry and deny yourself here?"

"Because they taught me that inside."

"Inside? Who?"

"The prisoners, all the prisoners. They said that if I denied it, they would not be able to punish me."

"Are you repentant of what you did?"

"Yes, very sorry. Do you know if my mamita will forgive me in heaven?"

"Yes, she will forgive you."

"The other crime. Will they pardon her too?"

"Her? She did not do anything."

"Nothing? Well then, the judge did not say everything!"

"Let's see, what's left?"

"My mama also killed a person."

"What are you saying, boy?"

"It's true, but it's been a long time and far away, in Austria. One time, when my father was here, he got mad with mama, and told her that she would have been better off captured for having killed her first husband. I told all this to my older brother and he knew everything that happened long ago. He told me that my mama Ana, drank too much in Austria, and that being her way, she killed her husband with a knife."

"How was it they did not capture her?"

"The mother of my mama, my grandma, to save her, told the judges it was she who did it, and they locked her up in jail."

"Are you certain of what you are saying?"

"I am certain of what I am saying."

"The judge knows this! Ask him, and you'll see I have told the truth."

This unexpected revelation ends with the painful interview that we have tried to reflect with all fidelity without altering the simple language with which it was made.

By means of information and not without great efforts, we corroborated yesterday the veracity of everything related by the child Muja, as far as the crime of which the author confessed, and the violent death of Ana de Muja's first husband.

In fact, from the investigations carried out, it appears that some years ago, without being able to specify the date, Ana committed a murder. The mother of this one, a brave one, was charged as the perpetrator of the crime and was convicted.

Maybe this even purged the pain that corresponded to the daughter. If so, the representative of Austria in Argentina would have a sacred duty to fulfill, contributing to the liberty of an innocent mother who did not hesitate to sacrifice herself for her daughter, obeying the eternal laws of the heart and of blood.

Heart and blood! Perhaps in these tragic dramas of life, especially in this one that a red stain has necessarily been given to the chronicle, psychiatry has an elucidating mission. The Lombrosian theory, in which the transmission of a morbid source is a first-line argument of strength, has been fulfilled many times. [48] The sick mother, the mother predisposed to delinquency, and that delinquency, the same criminal tendency transmitted by their blood to the son. Then a terrible sentence is usually fulfilled; who kills by iron dies by iron! Precisely as is reported in this case.

Autopsy:

Now, a few words to conclude. The examining magistrate doctor Bravo, in the said manner, ended a very burdensome process that has been hampered in his investigation by many circumstances.

Among these, not the smallest measure is as it relates to the certificate of the doctor in [the city of] Carmen de Sauce who recognized the corpse of Ana de Muja. He said that the deceased had her head completely separated from the trunk, which according to the statement of local police

---

[48] In the 19th century, Italian criminologist, psychiatrist and medical doctor Cesare Lombroso (1835-1909) hypothesized theories that criminality is inherited biologically. In modern times, scientists know that environment and other factors also play a role; not all children of criminals grow up to be one.

and many neighbors is not true. Yesterday, the judge ordered the autopsy of the corpse, and left it to the same (authorities) at Carmen de Sauce to complete other interesting formalities.

Spirit communication:

"You ask me (a spirit tells me) who gave force to the arm of a child to give such a blow so certain? It was the spirit of the first husband of his mother from the spirit world. It put into practice the saying of 'that such who did, is such who pays,' dominated by the desire for revenge. Since I know it is not puerile curiosity that guides you in your investigations, I will tell you the truth of the case, so that it serves as teachings who want to study the writings of the Spiritists.

"The unfortunate woman, which at a bad time killed her first husband (though she had an angel savior in her mother), in appearance she was clean of sin, but was not free from the persecution of her victim. The man, cowardly murdered, without having committed no other transgression than to serve as an obstacle to his unfaithful companion who sought comfort with illicit lovers; upon separating from his covering (his physical body), he swore vengeance on that woman who so vilely deceived him. For him, he was not in the spirit world (he did not hear the voices of his guide and other spirits). He remained beside that woman, who he hated and loved at the same time, with the firm purpose of changing her home into a hell. Plus, to later on carry out the law of talion, he penetrated into the innermost recesses of who had been his wife, and returned to Earth without realizing that he was in the spirit world, so attached he was to the material world with his hatred and his passions. [49]

"The birth of Juan Muja gave no happiness to his parents. These ignored who was a traveler from the infinite (spirit world) who had asked for hospitableness, but the little one appeared to carry a torch of discord in his hands. There was an incomprehensible uneasiness in the house, but

---

[49] At spirit seances/sessions, numerous spirits communicate still convinced, and in denial of that fact, that they are spirits without a physical body and are leading a spiritual existence. In this case, the spirit was totally fixated and obsessed with hatred to get revenge.

it ruled without a doubt. The quarrels were continuous, the intolerance was empowered in absolute by those (in reality) guilty spirits, because if Ana killed her first husband it was not long, when she would commit the murder of her second husband. They accused each other of such, without speaking; and after so long, it became a mutual annoyance that he went far away, running from home where it seemed that he was stepping over hot irons. Thenceforth, she surrendered herself completely over to the vice of drunkenness to forget her crime. When least expected, her victim of yesterday (her first husband as a spirit) stuck a murderous weapon in the same spot where she had plunged it years ago. [50]

The heroism and abnegation of her mother, delayed the fulfillment of the law of talion, but Ana undoubtedly had to die a victim of her own treachery. The avenger did not separate himself from her for one second, so much as he penetrated into her innermost recesses, tormenting her when he could with his unrelenting hate and in the end, he carried out his wicked objective.

"It's horrible! Right? Many say these communications are the tales of old women. I wish they were! There would not be so many unhappy families living in a hell because they cannot tolerate one another, but it is sadly true. Hatred is not erased by death, but on the contrary is increased; and there are premeditated vengeances over the course of many centuries, because time is not measured in the spirit world like on Earth. 'If you don't do it, you don't have to fear it,' says an adage and it is the truth.

"Flee from crimes, mistakes, impatience, work on your moral and intellectual improvement, and do everything in your power to be useful to others, and in this way, you will be able to live in sweet calmness surrounded by spirit friends who are the true family on Earth, and on the other worlds where you will live later on.

"Goodbye."

---

[50] This was partly a case of spirit obsession and influence by the first husband towards the boy. However, the boy was also angry at his mother who mistreated and abused him, making him an easy target for the influence of spirits of ill intent.

Ms. Soler:

We have obtained so many lessons from this communication! There is no debt that is not paid, or a payment that is not fulfilled! Woe to those who want to lay the foundation of their happiness at the tomb of another!...

In one way or another, a debt contracted will be paid. Some allowing their body to be used by the hands of an avenger; others living without living, surrounded by spirits that try to work out their misfortune.

Father Germain says it well, 'How good it is to be good, and how bad it is to be bad!'

CHAPTER SIXTEEN

CRIME BRINGS CRIME

Carmen Ayala y Ayala - A child of ten to twelve years old murders her crippled sister.

Carmen Ayala y Ayala - Abandoned orphan murders her younger sister Teresa, perhaps believing to lessen her suffering.

(Cause of the Court of Maricao, year of 1901)

Background - Carmen and her younger crippled sister Teresa, were found orphaned by their mother and father in a solitary shack in the deserts of Maricao (Puerto Rico), in the hazy days of 1901, "days much hazier than the present."

Carmen sought protection in the house of her Uncle Pablo, man without a conscience, of bad temperament, who ill-treated these two poor beings. So, Carmen saw herself forced to go to other neighbors; the house of Mrs. Denizar, who welcomed them. But lacking resources, Carmen had to abandon the hut and go to another home; the house of Alejo García, whose charitable wife gave them a motherly reception.

The Acts - Declaration by Carmen Ayala y Ayala. [51]

It said: "After the death of their parents, they were taken in by the charitable neighbors Alejo García and his wife, and in their house were given to do small chores, with the greater part of the day to take care of

---

[51] Spanish last names can include the mother's and father's last name. The Spanish word "y" means "and," so therefore, it appears the parents were relatives with the same last names. Marriage to cousins was not unusual.

the smaller sister. Yesterday, the Garcia couple left in the morning for the river, she staying alone in the house with her sister. The honorable woman charged them to entertaining themselves by collecting some coffee beans from the ground and she attend to the little girl, until they returned at dark. Those having left, the declarant went to the coffee plantations, and there came the bad idea to murder Teresa (an idea that was for three days compelling her, she resisting it); and, she had this suggestion with such a force on that day, she ran to the house where she [Teresa] was, and when the declarant arrived, she regretfully burst into tears. She returned to the coffee plantations, and the idea of killing her sister returned to disturb her mind to the extreme of impelling her to, catch and throw her into the water pond near the house. Meanwhile, she hurriedly ran to make a pit to bury her that way she would suffocate. The excavation made, she went to find the corpse, took it and buried it in the hole she made, using a forked pole to take the body out of the pond provided by Mr. Ayala's machete to make the pit. Later, when she killed her sister, she wasn't in her right senses, for afterwards she went running away from that place until she reached the house of Segunda (a woman of a certain Justino), where Alejo García met up with her at one in the afternoon. The declarant, before that woman, stated what she had committed, and was advised to stay there until they went to look for Teresa. She did not hate or dislike her sister (that before that she felt tenderness and thoughtfulness) despite having to take care of her and attend to her day and night, and having to carry her on the shoulder since she was crippled, which is all she can declare."

Ms. Soler:

The Court of this city, tells our reporter who knows the case, it had done a job that honors it to a great degree. It tried by so many skillful means it could, to put the unfortunate little girl in the Asylum of the Beneficence, since there are not any appropriate establishments on the island for these cases. They could not do it, and entrusted the little one to the sisters of the city's Sanctuary of the Poor, where Carmen died last February 2nd.

Our reporter desires to entrust the case to the thinkers, in particular Spiritists, to give an explanation to the public so hungry for light.

Ms. Soler:

A writer from Ponce (Puerto Rico) sent me the message that precedes these lines, begging me very earnestly if it was possible to ask if the misfortune of Carmen de Ayala was the victim of a spiritual suggestion, or if she was the sole author of such a horrendous crime. Following my desire to serve mankind, I asked Father Germain for the cause of such a disastrous outcome, and here is his reply:

Spirit communication:

"I have told you repeated times that when a spirit does not want to be dominated it rejects all influence, because if it did not have free will to reject it, it would have been born with the stigma of servant, with the infamous mark of slave, with the passive humility of outcast, and spirits by patrimony do not have blind meekness nor stupid obedience. All spirits are free to exercise the desires of their will. What occurs is that many are compliant and satisfied to continue to receive instructions from another spirit. They are too lazy to think; if another spirit thinks for them and tells them, 'You already have your path laid out', they continue the same route that is indicated without looking where they are going. Although these unfortunate ones obey the suggestions, they obey because they want to obey; because it is too much work to think. They are slaves because they themselves forge their chains and lift up the walls of their prison. It is not because there exists a power superior to enslave them, because if it existed, God would be unjust and with God there is no room for injustice; because He symbolizes equality.

"The little girl who killed her sister, committed the crime by her will and with another invisible being [a spirit]. Teresa and Carmen were rivals in another time [past life]; they hated each other with true cruelty. The crippled girl, when in that other time had a strong and robust body, she employed her herculean force to hurt without mercy, killing more than once her terrible enemy; who was ultimately her murderer. Frequently quarrelsome, a routine traitor, she had many enemies created by her bad behavior, enemies who have pursued her without compassion. One of them was the invisible being who lifted Carmen's arm to kill the crippled girl. However, Carmen was satisfied with this act because she hated her sister, without her being able to explain why. When she came into this lifetime, she knew that her rival would suffer the torment of not being able to have full use of her body, and she said the following, 'I will give start to my regeneration by materially caring for my enemy. The occasion cannot be more favorable. The trial will give me excellent results. Hands to work!' However, theory is one thing and another is putting it into practice and since hatred is the plant most rooted within the human heart, and Carmen had been a victim of her sister many times, the trial of loving her incarnated enemy offered her many difficulties. These were increased by the deceitful advice of the invisible being [a spirit] who hated the two sisters (this hate was justified because from the two, it had received grave offenses), and so it took advantage of Carmen's confusion to take revenge on the two, killing the one and making a murderer of the other. Therefore, Carmen was not the sole author of the crime, but if her spirit had been more inclined toward goodness, she would have rejected the advice of the invisible being that pushed her to the abyss and triumphed over her evil intentions.

"This new fall has caused much harm, since returning to the spirit world, she has seen that her own intentions of amendment have been crushed and pulverized by her new crime, but she is determined to take a new course. She has been convinced that crime begets crime, and the satisfaction of vengeance resembles a venom that tastes sweet, but then later burns our insides. To destroy a body, is to put in our way a small block of granite that obstructs the path, and one does not know how to lift or to destroy it. Woe to those spirits who, upon returning to the spirit world, find corpses in their path! The dungeons of your prisons are delightful gardens compared to the shadows surrounding murderers.

"On the other hand, when an offense has been forgiven, when one has become as a 'guardian angel' of the being one most hated, what pleasure is experienced when the traces of blood and fire are erased, that on another day, we had left in our way! Create love! Awaken sentiments! Soften harshness! Shorten immense distances! Do good, for the sake of goodness! ...What a productive work this is for the spirit! However great your explanation, however long your account, in the midst of your sufferings you will have hours of rest. If you have to feel the horrors of hunger, you will find bread in the most arid desert. If a fiery thirst has to torment you, from the hardest rock will sprout a trickle of water for you. In your hours of greatest distress, you will hear a harmonious voice that will tell you with tenderness: Love, and wait!... Goodbye."

Ms. Soler:

Thank you, good spirit! For you, I love and wait! Bless you! How much consolation I owe you! How much light have you have spread around me! I am less than an atom and today I have a great family. I did not have a place on the Earth, and through you, I know that I have an inheritance in the spirit world. I did not have one penny and because of you, I have my savings bank in those who are poorer than me. Bless you, blessed are you! [52]

---

[52] We know from Ms. Soler's biography, after her mother died, she was left alone, ran out of her inheritance and basically left destitute. She says she suffered hunger, poverty and homelessness, and many things that come with living like that. She went blind many times as her eyesight was always a problem. She found consolation in the information from the spirits that gave logical answers as to why people suffer, reasons for resignation as well as an understanding that there is hope for a better future.

CHAPTER SEVENTEEN

THIRTY-TWO YEARS

Ms. Soler:

Some days ago, many newspapers published articles referring to an attack of catalepsy, a prolonged attack that had lasted thirty-two years. The sleep of an unhappy woman who had suffered much during thirty-years of torment. According to the confessions of some unfortunates that have been the victims of such a horrible illness, they hear perfectly when one speaks around them, and they learn all of the what relatives and friends say around them. Some have felt being placed in a coffin and were being prepared for performance of the burial of the supposed corpse, until with superhuman effort, they had broken their chains of immobility. The newspaper item in question said this:

ATTACK OF CATALEPSY: EXTRAORDINARY CASE

The newspapers of Burgos report the following facts:

More than thirty-two years ago, the neighbor of Villavicencio, Benita de la Fuente, suffered an attack of catalepsy.

The patient lay prostrate in bed, unmoving and unconscious since 1874, without having for a long time spoken a word, limited to only exhaling from time to time some inarticulate moaning. Her only food has been water, and at times taking small amounts of broth and milk. A multitude of doctors, some of great reputation, could not scientifically explain such an extraordinary case.

Well then, last Thursday the sick one opened her eyes, and suddenly recovering speech expressed her desire to leave the bed.

The following Sunday, the family lifted her up and since then she has been recovering quickly her lost health, being desperate that very soon she will recover the normality of her physiological functions, even though she has not been given anything to eat fearful that her stomach would not tolerate it.

Benita de la Fuente already knows all the members of her family, but the case is extraordinary as she does not remember anything that happened to her, and she stubbornly refuses to believe that she has been asleep and without eating for more than thirty years.

She is actually seventy-two years old.

A sister of the sick woman, whom all hold as a serious and trustworthy person, has communicated this news, which is an extraordinary case, worthy of being studied by eminent physicians.

Ms. Soler:

I believe that this case, truly extraordinary, should not only be studied by doctors (and there are those who are of the same opinion as me); many Spiritists have written to me pleading with me to ask the spirit guide of my work, the "why" of such a horrible sentence. Hence, to live thirty-two years without moving, without speaking, without taking part in the struggles of life, there has to be a powerful reason. The spirit so punished must have committed one of those crimes without precedent. One of those crimes that if it were not as they say, we never pay all what we owe, the condemnation would last millions of centuries; all the agonies that we have caused to suffer one or various victims, and if only applying the minimum of a deserved punishment, thirty-two years of martyrdom, how many crimes does that represent?

Spirit Communication:

"Not as many as you think (the spirit tells me); that as a general rule, those who think you are most inspired are so far from the true cause that produces such evil effects, as is the light from the shadow, the fire from the snow, love from hatred, virtue from vice, and selfishness from self-sacrifice. Do not judge from appearances, that from a hundred times that you pronounce a condemnatory judgment, ninety-nine will be dominated by error and you will be turning into unjust judges, when by your own defects you should not judge, but be judged.

"In the case of the cataleptic that has caught so much of your attention, and in which medical science has not found a satisfactory explanation, there is effectively much to study and much to learn to recognize the energetic will of a spirit, which has subjected its body to such a painful test. Those who deny the existence of the soul because they do not find it when they amputate an arm or a leg or extract a fetus, or open up a head to remove a tumor (since science cannot tell the history of the spirit that animates that organism) have to cross their arms and be silent, before the cause of facts they do not understand. For Spiritists, those who know that the present is intimately linked with the past, and that the spirit is an eternal farmer who sows today to gather up tomorrow, and on seeing that some farmers gather up such a bad crop, one asks with terror, 'what has this unfortunate one done to deserve such a cruel punishment? What role has been represented in universal history? Has it utilized science to be an executioner of mankind? Has it been an insatiable conquistador? ...' And, you go accumulating question upon question, and the more you ask, the farther away you are from the truth. Now as it happens, with this poor cataleptic woman, which you piled horrible crimes on her, and in fact, it is not so. She is an unbalanced spirit who has loved much, but with that earthly love: selfish, possessive, domineering, overwhelming, and one who prefers the death of her beloved one rather than seeing him happy within the arms of another being.

"This woman, who today belongs to a humble class, and except for her illness would have completely passed unnoticed on Earth. In another time, her seat was a throne, and although her reign was small, she made it great by the severity of her laws; and her being the judge, she was the one who dictated the sentences. She seemed insensitive to the charms of love. Married for reasons of state, without succession, she was a woman of ice, intolerant of sins committed for love. Her court seemed more like a community of nuns and friars without votes, such was the rigidity of the customs and faithful observance of duties in all respects. That is how Ermesinda lived, without enjoyment, and without letting others enjoy themselves.

"Until one day, they introduced her to a young military man (almost a boy) highly recommended by one of her closest relatives, who put him under her royal protection, who was expected to make himself worthy to at least honor his illustrious surname. Ermesinda upon seeing him, felt what she had never felt before, to the extent, that she fell into a chair because she lost her consciousness; and the young Ezequiel was greatly disturbed to see the ill effect that his presence had caused on his sovereign, and he retired fearful from something unknown.

"Ermesinda, from that day, felt an unexplained uneasiness and anxiety. Well yes good, she soon realized that her heart had awakened too late, and understood that she loved Ezequiel with all her soul, and tried to make him understand. However, Ezequiel was so young, and had been educated in such a manner that for him, Ermesinda was not a woman of flesh and blood, she was a saint whom he had to worship on his knees, but at a great distance, so that human breath did not stain her purity. So, while she shortened the way to meet with him sooner, he moved away from her dominated by the fear of offending her; and when one does not want, two are not found. Ezequiel kept distancing himself from Ermesinda; this one was convinced that the youth was fleeing from her. She then felt jealousy; from who? All the woman of the court. She did not have enough courage to say, 'Come to me, I love you.' The austerity of her principles prevented it. Proud of her lineage and virtues, she did not want to descend from her high pedestal to fall into the arms of a child, who did not feel the slightest attraction to her, who on the contrary was inspired with an inexplicable fear. Ermesinda managed to dominate her feelings, she covered them up with her mask of ice, she won in the struggle of her passions. However, she did nothing but be cold and stern with Ezequiel, who was the pampered child of the Court for his gentleness, by his distinction, his nobility and by his valor. Seeing him so beloved and so full of attention, her jealousy increased in such a way that one night she had him arrested as a traitor to his country; a spy paid by enemy hosts. Ezequiel was locked in a tower that looked like a nest of eagles, it was so high, based upon a promontory of rocks where raging waves crashed. It seemed that at that site the storm was continuous, so strong was the surge of the roaring waves that raged, crashing against that watchtower, a structure reaching the clouds.

"When she had him locked up there, Ermesinda calmed down, saying to herself, 'Not seeing him, I do not descend from my high pedestal. I did not tell him I cannot live without him, and I will not suffer the atrocious martyrdom of seeing him in the arms of another woman; great evils, great remedies. I have committed a crime accusing an innocent, but I avoid my dishonor before the world and before him, and am stopped from suffering a pain that would lead me to madness, because the pain of jealousy is madness in action.'

"During a few days there was talk of Ezequiel, but afterwards everyone fell silent for fear of being punished like the young spy; upon him were accumulated such horrible accusations, that it was assured it was he who had sold many strong fortresses to enemy legions. Ermesinda weaved in secret the cloth of so many fake stories and soon Ezequiel was given up to oblivion. Although many women mourned his absence lamenting his unfortunate fate, but everyone in silence. No one had the courage to defend that innocent, and Ezequiel was locked up thirty-two years without speaking even to his jailor, because he could not see him. His food was delivered by a mechanism that did not allow him to see who furnished it. He had no more comfort than to contemplate the sky through the thick iron bars of a skylight that gave light to his confined prison. Hence, he lived like that for thirty-two years. During that time, the strong handsome young man transformed into an ailing old man, his blond hair lost its golden color turning yellow, and then finally white as snow. When least expected, the doors of his prison were opened and he regained his freedom, ignoring why he had lost it. He returned to his home, and everyone in his family had died. Then he learnt of the slander that had dishonored him and he asked to see the sovereign. He asked for an audience, but it was not granted because Ermesinda was already in agony. Upon comprehending that she was going to die, she wanted to free the man who she loved so much. She died peacefully, because a lady confidante told her that she had seen Ezequiel and that he was unrecognizable, with his body doubled over with the weight of his years and of pain.

"Ezequiel was not slow in following her. When they saw each other in the spirit world they felt mutual sympathy, and he forgave her because she had sinned for love. Ezequiel's forgiveness achieved such goodness for Ermesinda that she asked to be his most loving mother, since the love of the mothers on Earth is the most willing towards self-abnegation and sacrifice. Yet, before becoming his mother, many, many times she asked to suffer the torment that he suffered as a victim due to her love and jealousy. She wanted to suffer the worst of all ailments: the cataleptic sleep. She wanted her prison to be the most horrible one, without irons and chains holding her to the rack of torment. Since, cataleptics hear everything spoken around them. They are present when the family gathers, are measured by those who hear the affection of their relatives, the interested views of ones and the selfishness of others; for them the truth (which is always bitter) is presented without veils! Oh, those who live without illusions! In her prolonged agony, she has had the consolation of Ezequiel at her side, that very often murmured in her ear pledges of love, but not of earthly love, a love superior to humans. The two spirits linked by one of those affections that are not known on Earth, will join later to never separate. Her willing to be his mother, his guardian angel. He, grateful (appreciating what was worth in the ardor of the passion of Ermesinda) is willing to return to her and be faithful forever.

"You see how beautiful a future awaits those two spirits who have suffered so much as victims of love, of earthly love and of divine love. Ezequiel lived imprisoned for thirty-two years, the cause being his undeserved captivity of the love and jealousy of a woman who enjoyed thinking that no one would see him, that no one would receive his caresses nor hear his promises of love. She had taken him from society, he belonged to her; he belonged to her because she adored him. And now, Ermesinda has suffered another prison more horrible to be made worthy by her martyrdom to adore her beloved Ezequiel, sanctified by sacrifice. Yesterday, she could not say that she loved him. Tomorrow, she will present her son to the whole world, and say, 'He's mine! I held him at my breast! I heard his first cries before seeing him! My arms have been his cradle! His first smile was for me! Mother mine! He is my son! Isn't it true that he is beautiful...!' Ermesinda will be of those passionate mothers who will follow her son everywhere, even to the gallows if it was necessary; all her love will appear too little to make Ezekiel forget the torment that her crazed passion caused him during thirty-two years.

"Goodbye."

Ms. Soler:

How many considerations does the previous communication provide! How true it is that appearances deceive! One hundred times, ninety-nine we judged wrong!

Generally, how wrong are our judgments, given that we are always ready to increase the blame of others, and to diminish, if possible, our own!

How much do our thoughts sin! For with just an intention that suffices; as some believers say, by our wrongful intentions, we, the majority on Earth, deserve life imprisonment. And, in truth, how we deserve it; we carry it hanging on our necks, which surrounds the shackle of our many defects, and only the communications of the spirits will in due time make us reflect regarding our smallness.

Blessed is Spiritism! Blessed are the spirit communications because through them people will be redeemed!

CHAPTER EIGHTEEN

FOR PEACE, JUSTICE

Ms. Soler:

How good it is to love!

The spirits tell me that if I remain on Earth, despite my advanced age, my continual ailments, and my incessant struggle to be able to live under a roof and feed my sickly body, is because I have to write much still; to comfort and accommodate all those that address questions to me, in which I understand that they have a thirst for truth, those who ask for advice and spiritual light.

Some days ago, a lady Spiritist wrote me telling me the following:

"Dear Amalia: By an inhuman act, unfortunately very common within humanity, has been placed in my hands a newborn child, which I am raising with bottles. They left it at the door of my house on the coldest day of last winter. Emotional by such a transcendental finding, I do not care to find out anything that is spiritually related to it. However, calmer and reflecting on the case, it induces me to ask you, if you have the goodness to investigate it, because I love him so much!...

"When I believed myself alone and infertile, this being came with its smiles to illuminate my home, and to close with its kisses the deep wounds of my heart, wounds produced by the rough blows of life. The child has come so timely, to ask me for my care and my love, that I would like one of the glimpses of Father Germain to guide me, without it being my desire to satisfy childish curiosity, but for the good purpose of redoubling more my love for this being. For I am willing to sacrifice myself, until I can raise it and instill in it the consoling principles that you and I are encouraged and sustained by, in the rough battle of life.

"Is this child's spirit a test? If so, it is welcome, therefore it comes to purify its spirit and mine.

"Does it come to fulfill some order of the Supreme Law? Blessed be God that gives me this grace, and if we are united by previous existences, and sympathy has brought him to my lap, I will be the most devoted mother; since in my heart I have felt the imperative necessity of externalizing the pure and maternal sentiments of which all women are possessed with, except for some unhappy ones of which we must sympathize.

"The mother who has separated this child from her side, deprived of her maternal warmth, inspires within me a deep compassion and with respect to the secrets which may have forced her to part from her son.

"I wait for you anxiously, and I repeat to you it is not curiosity that guides me, it seems to me that this child is mine. Yes, I love him so much! ...."

Ms. Soler continues:

As is natural, I was very interested in the content of this previous letter, and when I had an opportune occasion, I asked a spirit about the matter, obtaining the following communication:

Spirit Communication:

"I see that you are continually being asked questions on interesting matters, and you, with the best of desires question us, thus establishing a direct communication between the living and the dead. A relationship that has existed from all eternity, but that now has become more in general use thanks to the progress made in all social classes. This has caused the initiates to have lost their preponderance to the divine mysteries, those great priests who descending from their high pedestals, kept the revelations of the spirits in their temples; those who have always communicated with earthlings, because that direct relationship is necessary between those who you believe are alive and those whom you call dead.

"It is not yet the otherworldly communication that it will be with the course of the passing of centuries; it is still very defective, to have to make various transmissions, because at times the communicating spirit transmits the communication that it gives to another, and when repeating it to the medium, this one, when it gives an account of what was said it is already the third transmission, but something is something. The great beginning began by the union of the atoms, as it happens with the worlds. In the same way, the communications between the inhabitants of Earth and the residents in the spirit world has had its start with manifestations of little importance (to all appearances) with knocks, movements of objects, strange noises, moving lights, that have necessarily had to draw the attention of the most indifferent, causing rational men to think. They have had to look at those phenomena and say: nothing produces nothing. However, these noises, these knocks, these luminous flashes which spring up at various points, are the effects of some cause, and of an intelligent cause; and they have asked, investigated, inquired, until they obtained what they already had: sustained conversations with spirits. Some of them very interesting, some very instructive, although the means that you now have are very imperfect, very deficient, but the epoch will come when mediators will not be needed between all of you and us. Each one will speak with his relatives, with his disciples directly. How? In what manner? Speaking? Writing? Appearing with the last covering they used upon the Earth? The details are the least, the positive fact is the most we should occupy ourselves with; but, until that happy epoch arrives of direct communication, it is necessary that you conform to the current transmissions. One of your celebrated writers said that a translated work looks like a papyrus of Flemish turned upside down. This can also apply to a major part of the communications that you receive from beyond the tomb, but every thing needs your work and your time to be appreciated at its just value. Therefore, continue asking the spirits 'the why' of many events that surprise and awaken your most active interest, and lend comfort to many who cry in the dark.

"A woman who dreamed of being a mother asks you if the child left at the door of her house has ever been at one time hers; you can tell her, yes. He has been, flesh of her flesh, and bone of her bones. In her last incarnation, she belonged to the nobility, was deceived and seduced by a baron who could not give his name to her, because he had already given it to another woman. Upon realizing she was going to become a mother, she confided to her brother the secret of her dishonor. This one, having pity on her misfortune took her far away from their homeland, and in a little place hidden within the mountains, attended the delivery. He took the newborn away to a charitable asylum, casting him among the groups of children without names; while the young mother, as much as she asked him, begging futilely on her knees that her son be returned to her (even if he left her alone in the middle of the street).

"She returned to her palace, with her heart in pieces. She could not see a small child without having an attack of horrible convulsions; and all the time that she remained on the Earth she wept for her son and died calling him. When in the spirit world, she came to realize that he lived. She found her lost son, and with his caresses forgot all that she had suffered. She promised to be his guide, and that as a reward of her constant memory [of him], she would later on have that lost child in her arms (who in fulfillment of his own atonement already had in many incarnations been taken from a maternal womb). He had to be loved with charity, compassion; but he was not worthy by his past actions to repose tranquilly in the loving arms of a mother. That is why in his present existence he had been left abandoned, without recommendations, and, she was deserving to be a mother not more than at the time during his gestation. Today, they delivered her son of yesterday, so that her soul may enjoy the ineffable delights of motherhood. She deserves to be a mother, that is why she has recovered her son, because many years she called for him in her sleep and in her waking hours. In memory of him, she visited many orphans and sheltered innumerable helpless men; she gathered the harvest of her sowing of yesterday. May she love that orphan; that by loving him, she guides him, educates him and instructs him, they have delivered him to her. May she enjoy these good hours; protecting orphans is the most meritorious action that can elevate the spirit.

"Goodbye."

Ms. Soler:

What a touching and interesting story! Happy will be that generous woman who has gathered in her arms the little castaway; that in the sea of life, at the mercy of the waves (if not but for her) would be dead before the rocks of official charity (as Eusebio Blasco said) left to die of hunger. [53]

Happy are the good souls who know how to love!

---

[53] Journalist, poet and playwright from Spain (1844-1903)

CHAPTER NINETEEN

SORROW CURES THE PAIN

Ms. Soler:

When grief overwhelms, when misery oppresses, when loneliness throws us into the arms of desperation, it is necessary to look for an alleviation to the suffering, and for a thinking soul, for there is no place more appropriate to console and lighten the weight of sorrow but to visit the sick who moan in the hospitals. When one looks at various sick people who do not have by their bedside a living soul, and one sees, as they look at all those who pass by with that anxious look, and with that sadly ironic smile, as if to say, 'Even here fatality pursues me! ... Even in this mansion where the equality of misfortune reigns, I am more unhappy than others! ... Nobody remembers me! ... And, then they say that there is a God!...

I, who have complained so many times of my expiation, when I found myself the most discouraged, I hurried to the Hospital of the Holy Cross. There is where I made a true examination of conscience. And, how small I found myself after inner contemplation! ... How discontented my spirit was! ... So, demanding! ... How obstinate! ... How ignorant! How completely ignorant of the just laws of life! ... Asking for joys! ... Asking for love! ... Asking for the warmth of sentiments, when you have not thought of someone else's pain!... When one has fled from the gloomy mansions of the indigent!... And, not having to abandon one's home, being able to resist the onslaught of misery, to complain and to deny having been born, is to commit a great crime; not thinking, not remembering that there are so many poor, who are more unfortunate than us, and suffering the cruelest of torture in a hospital bed.

These and many other reflections gathered in my mind, as I contemplated on the sick who looked at the multitude, some pleading for mercy with their mournful eyes, and others with their menacing smile, at those who passed by without a word of consolation.

In my visits to the hospitals, I have learned to know the justice of God and I have become convinced of the inferiority of my spirit. There, I saw myself very small, and very great at the same time. What a countersense! Is it not true…? There is no possible explanation in the human language what I have felt, of what I have progressed, sitting next to the bed of a sick one in the dark room of a hospital.

Spirit of Aureliano communicates:

"It's true (a spirit tells me). I know, because many times you have kept me company in my bitter hours of pain. Do you remember Aureliano? Do you remember when you kept me company at the Hospital of the Holy Cross? What good you did for me accompanied by the most beautiful Filomena, a soul full of love, always ready to sacrifice! Many times, I go to said hospital, because there I paid a minimal part of my many debts, and there I received the unequivocal proofs of your loving compassion. How much good you did for me!... You sympathized with me so sincerely!... You, were so interested in my well-being!... You, prayed to God with such intimate feelings to put an end to my torture!... You took such an active possession of your motherly role; as if a being that you had carried in your womb, or you would not have lavished so much attention and so much effort.

"Did I match your tender and spiritual solicitude? No; with stinginess and selfish calculations, I imagined a love that I was incapable of feeling. I brought disturbance to your spirit, doubt and anxiety, and thanks to your firm sense of purpose of being a 'priestess' of Spiritism, your vocation could do more than the praise of my deceptive love, and you rejected (although with pity) all my offers of marriage. You struggled a lot, but at last you won, for your good and for mine; because you avoided a most cruel disappointment, and I, another new crime. Your refusal elevated you in my eyes. I saw myself in all my smallness. We parted, and through the distance your spirit grew more extraordinary before me, and more than once, dominated by my incurable disease, I asked your pardon for disturbing the melancholy tranquility of your life. During my nights of insomnia, how much I thought of you!... The impurities of my mind were withdrawn, and I came to regard you as a liberated spirit. I saw you far from me, far away!... I left the Earth, and I have remained for a long time (neither alone nor abandoned because we all have affinity with a family of spirits). However, yes, at a great distance from you, a distance so immense that I have not seen you or sensed you. I have remembered you many times, like one remembers a happy dream when one only retains a vague impression, something that has no name, that caresses like a gust of perfumed wind that stirs the tops of the trees in whose shadow we sit to rest.

"Why did you get so close to me in my last hours of tribulation? Did you owe me those attentions that were the expression of all loves? Did I serve as an instrument to torment you, and make you struggle between your duties and your desires? I do not know and you do not know either, but we both have an imperishable memory of our confidences in a hospital. The two of us, at those moments, shortened the distance that separated us. You descended to me!... I ascended up to you!... It would not have been very good of me to mix the divine with the human, because the love of the spirits is divine; selfish calculations do not have the slightest sublimity.

"Today, I see more clearly and when least expected, I have seen you overwhelmed by pain. I was by your side when you gave the last farewell to the companion of your works, and since then I have been with you. [54] You're so lonely!... You find yourself among ruins!... You are disoriented, looking around you, you see only pending accounts. What surrounds you, affects and hurts you. You are surrounded by ancient creditors, and all present you their letters saying: Pay! ... Now you cannot go to the hospital, your pain cannot be cured with another pain, but the pains of others come to you in another form. The book of life does not close for you, it always presents you its pages full of sad stories, you already know how to read in the manuscript of the book of errors, and you will study without rest until your last moments.

---

[54] This could mean the transition (the death) of Euldaldo, the unconscious medium Amalia mostly worked with to receive the spirit communications.

"I am very happy to be near you. I am much better than before. There is so much I want to tell you! However, they do not let me.

"Goodbye."

Ms. Soler:

What a surprise I had with the preceding communication! ... Satisfying, yes, agreeable. The memory of a good work is always gratifying, and on that occasion, I served as aid for an unhappy spirit who was a poor man of solemnity. How beautiful it is to remember an hour of Sun! And, the Sun shines always for the soul, whenever it wants to live bestowing comfort and love.

CHAPTER TWENTY

WHAT IS NOT EARNED,
IS NOT OBTAINED

Since the study of Spiritism has convinced us that it is an axiomatic truth "that what is not earned, is not obtained," when we see a being overwhelmed under the enormous weight of a horrible expiation, we look at them with deep compassion, and we say with indefinable anguish, "what did you do yesterday? How many miserable ones have you condemned to death? How many families did you leave in misery? How many years of your life did you consecrate to the consummation of dreadful crimes? Great must have been your crimes, when you have not achieved a day of rest, nor an hour of solace."

These or similar reflections, we made a few days ago when visiting for the first time a family that occupies a good social position, possesses sufficient wealth, and yet however a lot is missing for them to be happy.

The family is composed of a married couple and three children. The eldest [César] is twenty years old, thin and of medium stature, white and blond, with the head of an artist, countenance of a thinker and eyes that tell a story of tears; the expression on his face is melancholy. When he is sitting, his bearing is distinguished, his figure aristocratic. When he stretches his white hands, fine and delicate, it appears that they grasp like the hands of a child, so soft is their touch. He speaks very well, expresses himself with ease, reveals a clear intelligence and a deep knowledge of the arts that immortalizes Murillo, Velázquez, Juan Juanes and of Rafael. However, when he arises, when he takes his first steps, an extreme weakness in his lower limbs causes him to bend his knees and forces him to lean and balance his body; his sympathetic figure losing all its slenderness and distinction, for he resembles a man dominated by drunkenness, walking awkwardly, taking unsteady steps in opposite directions.

What a painful impression we feel, when we contemplate on him! Our compassion increased when we talked with him for a long time, when we saw that he possessed (as we said before) a fine intelligence; yet feeling, as it were, the influence of youthful passions; life is overflowing within his being, his voice vibrates, his glare glistens, his manner is passionate and…everything has to be drowned within himself. His imperfections, his physical disability, separates him from love and the relationships of life; for to be loved upon the Earth, to be preferred by others, it is not enough to possess a great and passionate soul, it is necessary to have an aesthetically configured body. The hunchback, the crippled, the maimed, the epileptic, the bow-legged, and all those who have a thousand other physical imperfections, *it seems* that they have only come to the Earth to inspire laughter for the many, and compassion for the least. Although sometimes they become loved, as said before, they are generally disdained. [55] This disdain has infiltrated his soul and has been forming in his heart a deposit of bitter irony, that deep distrust that is such a pity; that hurts, humiliates, that mortifies so much and that it ferments in the soul like sour yeast, forming an emptiness. In spite of him being a genius, in spite of him being a great man, he flees society as if he had committed a crime. He is ashamed of himself, he is repulsed by his form, and has to live united to his greatest enemy, he must be bound to the instrument of his torture, and not one day, not for a year, but all of his life. Oh, that is horrible! It is a prisoner's life sentence! How great the crime must have been, when the chain is so horrible! [56]

---

[55] This is the perspective of someone in Spain in the 1870s. Ms. Soler always had fragile health and poor eyesight (and went completely blind many times throughout her life). She had first-hand experiences in Spain with her disability and was around many who were also disabled, especially among the poor during that time period.

[56] During the 19th century, a crippled generally could not work, there were inadequate diagnoses, no specific medicines or special prostheses as there are now, and of course, no disability benefits.

This is what we thought looking at César, after asking with maternal affection, how many times he had seen the almond trees bloom.

César:

"I am twenty years old, Madam!... Twenty years!"

Ms. Soler:

How much was said with such few words! He told us his whole story, his ambitions and his desires, disappointments and deceptions; and in them the bitterness that fills to the edge the fragile cup of his existence.

Poor César! He is immensely miserable! Young, with a nice face, clear talent, nice in social relations, and nevertheless...he has no friends and no one who loves him. He cannot run about like his fellow students; these do not have the patience to accompany him on his short and fatiguing walks. He has no amorous illusions. He is not promised to any charming girl. His family has not been able to arrange for him a liaison with any of his young relatives [57] and he is condemned to celibacy, despite having a sensitive heart and a passionate soul. His body is very weak, he is almost always sick, and until a few months ago he has always gone out with his tutor. His childhood, without playing! His youth, without romance!... Having within him all the seeds of life, but in a latent state, without development. Giant of spirit that only has at his disposal the body of a pygmy [58] ; and for greater mockery he is rich, but his wealth is not sufficient to strengthen his body. The last beggar of the Earth is much happier than him, since his agile limbs allow him to go where he wishes, while César lives a prisoner within himself.

To live without wings, he who was born with genius, it is a torment that is understood, but it is not explained. There is no language that faithfully describes that continuing agony; the awfulness of the cause is judged by its painful effects.

---

[57] Not uncommon at the time.

[58] In Spanish, directly translated word - common usage meaning inferior, unimpressive, etc.

We knew before meeting César that he was incredulous of religious matters. In naming God, it was always with apostrophes, to rebuke him hard, for giving him life.

Hundreds and hundreds of times, he had said to his parents, 'for what was I put upon the Earth? What harm have I done to you that it please you to form me of clay so brittle and despicable? What curse weighs on us to legitimize your love; that you give life to a rickety being that cannot live and enjoy it, like other men? What luxury of cruelty do you have to display, that you called upon an intelligent and sound soul who loves beauty and grandeur, to offer it a weak and sickly body which cannot sustain itself and which instead of being a helper of its spirit, is an executioner tormenting it incessantly with helplessness and weakness?'

César:

"They say the mission of parents is a divine mission. It has not been one for me. No! Why did they awaken me, if I was asleep in the universal cosmos, if my intelligence had not individualized? Why did they ask Nature to divide up some of its atoms so that they could form the first fruit of their ill-fated love? Why did they meet? Why did they love? Why did they reproduce? Were you not enough for each other?

"I, as a child, waited. I believed that gold was a mysterious amulet with which everything could be obtained on the Earth, and I was told my rich parents could call for and pay splendidly for wise doctors that would invigorate my body. So, I waited on science, on riches, and on my youth. However, the doctors would look at me and gave me ineffective remedies. The years passed, the child of yesterday is the man of today, and my legs falter, my body oscillates like a sapling without roots under the power of mischievous children. The ridicule of some and the compassion of others irritates and humiliates me at the same time. I want to aspire and the evil ones have closed the pathway. I want to love, and I cannot find out who loves me. I want to wander the universe and yet I can barely leave my home.

"Tell me, what did I do to you? ... Answer me. If every effect corresponds to a cause, I want to know why you have made me so immensely miserable! ..."

Ms. Soler continues:

His parents, as is easily understood, suffered with their son in all his sorrows, in all his anguish, and when they saw him so desperate, his poor mother wept bitterly. His father became enraged drowning his furor with philosophical reflections that only succeeded in increasing more often than not the exasperations of César.

As there are no disinherited upon the Earth, as all pain finds its relief, César, when he least expected, has seen new and expansive horizons before his eyes. Among his friends in infancy was a sweet and affectionate girl named Angela, who associated herself with his games with the docility that characterized the weaker sex in childhood. [59] Cesar did not know how to appreciate the sweetness of his innocent companion, and he repelled her more times than he accepted her childhood caresses. During one of those times that they were angry [with each other], Angela died. And, César cried for the absence of the beautiful teenager who when making her entrance into the great beyond (spirit world), she brought her hands to her heart, gave a sigh and fled the Earth because she felt nostalgic for the infinite.

Among the numerous friends of César's family, there were one or two who were Spiritists. After heated discussions, mocking on one side and serious reflections on the other on magnetism, and all that was needed to carry to conviction new ideas to stubborn spirits, and each one of them believed that their belief was the best adding to this a great confidence that almost totally rejected the authenticity of Spiritist phenomena. After struggling with so many and such diverse setbacks, an intimate friend of César's mother (a woman completely devoted to religious practices, a good Christian to the fullest extent of the word, incapable of lying, fearful of spirits and doubtful of experimenting at Spiritist sessions, with opposition, fear and all that was necessary to ward off the influences of invisible

---

[59] A common phrase, although Ms. Soler was a believer in equality of the sexes.

beings), was subdued by a good magnetizer, [60] and she slept with the sleep of a somnambulist.

Before César and his family, from the beginning, she gave some sessions of great importance because by means of the somnambulist, spirit communications were obtained from several relatives of the parents of César, to which the medium had not known, describing their form with perfect likeness. César observed attentively; and, as he could not distrust the somnambulist nor the magnetizer, because both were respectable persons unable to omit the truth, his skepticism began to falter. Even more so, when he himself saw a kind of whitish smoke arising at points indicated by the somnambulist, as well as the smell of aromatic flowers that the medium described with enough lucidity, increasing his interest.

When the somnambulist said elatedly, "Oh! What a beautiful apparition! What a young enchanting lady! I want to know her, but she is wrapped in a long veil of snowy chiffon! What did I say?... No, it is gauze, it is another fabric more impalpable, her dress is of wool or of gauze, but transparent. It gets close to César, picks up one point of its veil, wraps it around him. It leans over and it almost touches his forehead, looking at him with immense tenderness, it asks that he discovers well, and it removes the folds of its veil. My God!... Yes, it is Angela, but much more beautiful than when she was on Earth. Do you not feel its fluid, César? You are wrapped in its floating veil; it looks at you as mothers look at their sick children. It speaks, do you not hear it?"

César confessed that he felt a sweet emotion that he had never felt, and since that memorable day his existence has not been so bitter.

Angela, by means of the somnambulist, has told César that she exists in space (in the spirit world) and that she approaches the Earth to console him and to make him comprehend that life is eternal. In a series of the sweetest communications, she has helped him to recognize the error of living in denying the immortality of the soul and the unlimited progress of the spirit. The atheist, the desperate patient, the genius imprisoned in a useless

---

[60] In Spiritism, magnetism deals with spiritual/magnetic energy (mediums may feel it). A magnetizer can assist in producing a somnambulist (for Spiritists, a variety of medium); mediumship for spirit communications. For the non- Spiritist, a magnetizer is – a hypnotist, and, for others a somnambulist is known as a sleepwalker.

body, today smiles sweetly and speaks of the spirits with natural simplicity; showing eagerness to read the communications and in recounting all the details of the sessions, not forgetting the most insignificant ones.

What a development must have been verified in the mind of César! How surprised he was upon encountering in his path the companion of his childhood now converted to a loving mother; counseling him to completely consecrate himself to the divine art of Apelles [61] by which César has a determined predilection, and urging him to study the spiritualist philosophy to find out the reason for what appears to be an anomaly, in order to convince him that existences such as his, have at their root total forgetfulness of duties and a complete abuse of rights.

César cannot be happy on the Earth, but he can be much less miserable, rationally studying Spiritism.

Ms. Soler:

Not for curiosity, but solely for study, to know the cause that has produced such painful effects, have we tried to procure to see the roots of the tree that has produced such bitter fruits, and a spirit told us the following…

Spirit communication:

"You ask who César was, with that painful anxiety of all who are interested in the misfortunes of his fellowman. By the type of atonement, it is possible to infer what crime was committed. So, since solely with your reason alone you cannot with all clarity deduce what you desire, I will tell you in a broad stroke what César did in that world, in his previous existence.

"It is not a spirit in whose history is recorded with horrific crimes. No; in his last incarnation, he chose a noble birth, great wealth, a beautiful figure and adventurous genius, but not to use in profitable enterprises

---

[61] Apelles was a famous painter of ancient Greece, even painting portraits of Alexander the Great. His paintings have not survived, but are described by writers of the times.

for him and his country, very much to the contrary. He only thought of enjoying what he possessed, without taking care of little else or much of the growth of his hacienda. Much given to love affairs, he wasted the best years of his life taking advantage of the ephemeral advantages that his physical beauty gave him, his distinction and his goods to be attended and given away wherever he appeared. So, from the woman born in the gardens of a throne, to the unhappy woman who (by hunger or vice) surrenders to the best buyer, he lied and lavished caresses, under purple pavilions and in the nauseating corners of the last brothel of the Earth.

"For those evildoers, for those outlaws who enter an honest house, without exposing themselves in the least, steal the treasure of most value, he that is once lost is never recovered. For those bandits without a heart there is no penitentiary on that planet, and more so if the thief of honor is immensely rich; his wealth makes him inviolate. He who today calls himself César, abused his social position so much, that with impunity he brought disgrace on many families, and, more than one enamored woman in her desperation, died cursing his memory. He was so handsome and had such a powerful look of attraction that he just had to look, to benefit. He was a philanderer by trade, always with luck. He considered women to be worthless goods since he found no ungrateful beauty who despised his flattery. He did damage, much damage, without measuring the consequences, without looking for a second at the total sum of his victims. For him, a woman was living property; slaves, as one of your sages called them. He believed that they were born beautiful to satisfy the whims of their master. Their tears would make him laugh; their furor excited his anger. He granted women but one obligation, that of dressing and embellishing themselves to be agreeable to a man, denying them all their rights, and that is all. Furthermore, just as a mailed envelope from a cabinet does not worry about the post horses breaking down to arrive sooner at the end of their day, similarly, the one you call César, did not give a straw that the women died poisoned by his caresses. Women deserved no more consideration than being looked at, and caressed in a night of orgy.

"A woman who was a mother did not get any respect either. As for the rest, he was neither miserly, envious, nor treacherous and his servants loved him dearly. He had only one vice that dominated him completely, a sexual appetite. This attracted (as we have said before) upon his head, many curses because there were many women who loved him and had to curse this deviance.

"He died alone, and abandoned by all. When he was more intoxicated in his lucid memories, he misjudged the path and fell into precipice where he remained for some hours suffering in great pain until he uttered his last sigh; without a pious hand closing his large eyes, without a kiss of tenderness to seal his lips. For his remains, there was no burial, and there is still the tradition in his country that his body and his soul was taken by the devil. No one found his remains, so deep was the abyss where he fell; and, as if that were not enough, there was a detachment of rocks, that fell on his corpse, crushing him.

"When that spirit came to see the picture of his life, his pain was immense, indescribable... He did not lack loving beings who gave him consolation, but he had enough intelligence to understand that he had sinned much. Although in some of his acts, he had been powerfully influenced by the debased education he received from his teachers, all ministers of God. [62]

"One of his victims who succumbed under the weight of her shame and of her pain was the one that influenced his spirit to ask for the atonement he suffers today. César himself [while in the spirit world when his spirit was more lucid] asked for a loving mother, so that in her arms he could begin to love and respect woman. He asked for riches, a defective body and to be animated by a clear intelligence. Also, a nascent feeling to desire love and not be able to obtain it, because on the Earth defective organisms only inspire laughter at the most and compassion at the least. The irresistible seducer of yesterday, he who at each step sowed pain and shameful remorse, today can barely leave his palace. He is rich, he is loved by his family, much loved, but his body is his relentless executioner. He is practically always sick, surrounded by innumerable cares that sometimes increases his feelings, because they awaken in him the purest desires of creating a family. He dreams of a wife, with tender children, but ... will he find one who will love him? Can he resist the horrible torment of jealousy that he will necessarily have to suffer, if you associate his existence with another existence? Oh! His expiation is terrible! He is a soul awakened from life, imprisoned behind thick bars. He loves the fine arts, loves everything that

---

[62] priests

is grand, loves everything he despised in his past incarnation. He did not think that those who were deformed were rational, and that is why today, on observing himself, he convinces himself of his error and his injustice.

"You do well to pity all those whom you see overwhelmed under the weight of their atonement. Woe to oppressors, because later on they will be the oppressed!

"It is not tiresome to relay the stories in whose sad pages humanity encounters useful teachings that remove it from the unfathomable abyss of shameful vices. Say it, repeat it in a very loud voice, that the cripples of today are those who were in a hurry to commit blunders. Say that the arm that does not move, yesterday [past lives] moved to handle a murder weapon and hastily sign death sentences. Say that the eyes that today have no sight, yesterday were pleased to look at impurities, also contemplating with delight the contradictions of the condemned when on the rack of torment declared lies or truths to avoid suffering. Say that the greatest sufferings are the result of great crimes, and do not worry that your words do not find an echo within humanity; if a single being hears you, you have the recompense of your work, as with a blind man who recovers his sight, you can say that you have conquered a world. [63]

"Goodbye."

Ms. Soler:

We believe the same thing that the spirit says, that has been kind enough to give us some explanations about César's past. We believe that a being that awakens from the lethargy of ignorance, is a world within himself which starts all the germs of life to begin to develop. A single thinker is sufficient in many occasions to give different directions to the

---

[63] Here the communicating spirit lists various types of wrongdoings and various possible consequences. And, although a person who suffers may not know the reason why they suffer now, when they return to the spirit world after physical death, they come to realize they selected the challenges they underwent for specific and just purposes having to do with the evolution of their soul, which involves many times facing the consequences of their actions in past lives. Many communicating spirits through mediumship encourage the spreading of this information because it has provided consolation to many, of which I can personally attest to.

philosophical and religious schools that have ruled millions of centuries. A single artist with a wonderful genius can make a true revolution in art. A single poet serves to awaken the feelings of a hundred generations. A community of people serve to grow the innovations of progress. However, when the time comes for the redemption of a people, it is one sole man who pronounces the magic words, "Let there be light!"

Let us say, to conclude, that each day we are convinced more and more that the rational study of Spiritism [or in other words, the teachings of the spirits] is the Promised Land of all unfortunates.

César, since he has become convinced that the communications from beyond the tomb are an undeniable truth, he seeks with eagerness to put himself in contact with the spirits, consulting with them his doubts and misgivings about his advancement in the illustrated arts. [64]

When a disappointment hurts him and deeply impresses him, he evokes his spirit friend, and if this one comes, he hears sweet advice and sensible reflections, his face lights up with the glow of immense satisfaction. He has those who love him, who advise him, who watch over him, and these are not individuals of the family. No; they are other affections. He is no longer alone in the small circle of his home. He has friends; friends who do not envy him for his advances in the arts, but, quite the contrary, they say, for geniuses there are no distances or heights. Rise up! Move forward, the future is yours!

We will never forget César. His expiation makes us look at him with maternal affection, and it has never seemed so useful to us the communications of the spirits on seeing Cesar listening eagerly for the advice he receives from the beyond the tomb.

For her, he as a martyr, smiles at himself! Blessed be the light of Truth!

Translator's Note: Firstly, whatever condition a person chooses to be reborn as is for its spirit to progress, and it has a responsibility to better its own situation to the best of its abilities. There are many examples of people born under terrible circumstances, or with extreme disabilities or undergone terrible traumas who have thrived and are great successes in life. However, there are still many who are depressed, desperate

---

[64] This knowledge of the spirits and their teachings have provided consolation and hope to this individual. The knowledge he acquired in past lives is never lost. He will have opportunities to pursue the arts or whatever other interests he may have in another time and place, in many future lives!

and suffer greatly. These wonder why they arbitrarily suffer so much, while other people do not. The three major religions have no answer why their **one lifetime** is so miserable compared to others, except it is God's Will. The process of reincarnation offers some reasons for suffering and for some, this knowledge has saved them from committing suicide. We have as many lifetimes as is needed to make better choices each time.

Secondly, morally superior spirits teach that whatever a spirit has done in a previous lifetime, or going through in the present life, ALL people deserve to be treated equally with respect, kindness and charity; we are all spiritual brothers and sisters to be helped as much as possible. We are all upon the earth to help each other. It is our moral responsibility! We need to treat everyone with compassion and love, as Jesus would have, for he taught, "Love others as yourselves."

CHAPTER TWENTY-ONE

WHAT A FORTUNE CAN DO

Ms. Soler:

Leafing through a variety of newspapers, we read in *The New Athenaeum* [*El Nuevo Ateneo*] the following news item:

"Although these comparisons are odious, we are going to make one that makes clear the differential product of the wealth of the three richest men on Earth.

Mackey, wealth: 55,000,000 pounds; a year, 2,750,000; a month, 200,000; a day, 7,000; an hour, 300; per minute, 5.

Duke of Westminster, wealth: 16,000,000 pounds; a year, 800,000; a month, 60,000; a day, 2,000.

Senator Jones of Nevada, wealth: 20,000,000 pounds; a year, 1,000,000; a month, 80,000; a day, 3,000; an hour, 120; per minute, 2.

The richest man in the world is Mr. Mackey, whose fortune increases by five pounds per minute.

About twenty years ago, he traveled throughout the United States as a wandering salesman, and sixteen years ago he was a poor devil with no room. Today, at the age of forty-five he owns three-eighths part of the great "Bonanza," the Argentina mine located in Nevada, the richest that is known, and produces an annual income of 2,750,000 pounds at five percent. Mr. Mackey has a magnificent hotel in Paris where his family lives, meanwhile he passes his time close to where his interests are." [65]

Ms. Soler:

The following question occurred to us: What will he do with his fortune? Or better yet: what will his fortune do for him?

This is a deeply philosophical question: What will he do with the fortune of a millionaire? How many things can he do?...

It can make him an agent of Providence, and an executioner of humanity! Relief for the afflicted, and a tyrant of the poor! Hope for the sad, and despair for the needy! The purest light of dawn, and the gloom of night! All this, and much more, a rich man's fortune can do.

A rich man can do much good and much wrong!... Unfortunately, the wealthy of this world (for the most part) are weak to resist the test of wealth, since the test is a great one, to be the owner of immense treasures. It provides multiple pleasures that form an atmosphere of continual adulation, given a rich man, for the many defects they may have, nobody dares to tell him face-to-face that he is despicable. They often kill him with treachery, but in front of him they all smile, for gold has a special power over the multitudes. That is why for the rich man it is so difficult to progress, because alone he has to do all the work of his regeneration.

He has to let go of the desire for treasure. He has to think of the poor even if he cannot conceive what poverty is. He must feel sorry for the unfortunate, without knowing the unfortunate luck of the disadvantaged, and there is nothing more difficult than taking on suffering that one has never felt.

Ms. Soler:

A friend of ours told us (a very unhappy man) who when small, occupied a good position. Every night he went out with his mother, and

---

[65] Starting in the 1850s, silver ore was discovered in Nevada, U.S.A (the Comstock Lode) and many fortunes were made when several "bonanzas" (or rich veins of metal) were discovered.

passed in front of a church where in the doorway, a few beggars of both sexes slept outdoors.

The mother of our friend stayed staring at that sad scene, and said, shaking her son's arm, "Oh, Antonio, we give much thanks to God that he has given us a good bed!" The child shrugged, as he said to himself, "My mother is a fool, why thank God that we have a bed when it is something that the whole world has." The years went by, and the boy became a man, lost his parents and suffered difficult changes of fortune. There came a time that he had to sleep a whole summer sitting in a chair by the Prado of Madrid. When after many deprivations, he was able to make money to live, and the first thing that he did was to buy a cot, a mattress and rent a small private room on the fifth floor. When night came, and when for the first time he saw himself alone in a room, he fell to his knees, thinking of his good mother, and exclaiming with intimate expression, "Oh, my mother! I called you a fool in my innocence, because you gave thanks to God for having a bed where to sleep. Today, I too believe myself blessed because I have a poor bed where I can rest. My God, thank you, for I have been granted of what I looked so indifferently upon in my childhood!" The poor young man told us that there is not a single night he has stopped giving thanks to God before going to bed. Deeply sorry for the beggars who sleep on the hard ground, he has pitied them after he has known what it is, to live without a house or home.

In the same way, the rich look with indifference on the suffering of the poor because they do not know what poverty is. This is why we say that wealth is the most difficult test to which the spirit can be submitted to, and that it has worse consequences. Many of those beggars with twisted bodies, of deformed bodies that have to drag themselves on a cart were the rich who did no good, and denied, even the breadcrumbs their dogs left, to the hungry beggars (looking for compassion with bitter tears) who asked for them.

Recently, we have seen a girl, who they say is six years old, and is lead around in three feet long and two feet wide cart. The girl, we do not know how she is configured, but her desiccated arms, and her legs that look like two strips of parchment are crossed in a strange way in front of her face, whose expression was one of extreme idiocy.[66] On her round face of good color, is drawn a vague smile, and that small heap of flesh and rags inspired compassion and repugnance at the same time. A poorly dressed young woman pulled a rope tied to the cart, and a swarm of street children surrounded that vehicle of misery. We, painfully affected, contemplated some moments on that disinherited of the Earth. We repeatedly asked ourselves, within our thoughts, what did you do yesterday? Did the Earth shudder under the weight of your crimes? Did the enslaved multitudes moan, lashed by your terrible whip? How horrible must your past have been, when your present is so dreadful!"

Absorbed in our thoughts on (that girl who lived that way) continuing on our way, deliberating on the intentional question that *The New Athenaeum* made, referring to the first millionaire of the Earth. What will he do with his fortune, or better yet, what will his fortune make of him? Immediately, we are reminded of the unhappy cripple, to that poor being who would look at her, and were it not for the head, one would doubt whether a person or an irrational being was inside that cart. And, we said with such profound sadness, what did fortune do to you?

And a voice, a clear intuition, a repeated shaking that agitated our being, has indicated that one of our friends from the afterlife wanted to get in touch with us, and obeying the influence we relay the following:

Spirit Communication:

"I thank you, poor being of the Earth, that you pity those who are even poorer than you. Look always at the poor! Especially those who the common people say are marked by the Hand of God, for those are marked by the iniquity of their own works. God, all love, beauty and harmony, cannot create anything inharmonious. The spirit after being created, is the sculptor who molds his own covering, and the work corresponds to the wisdom of the spirit.

"The vulgar, in the midst of ignorance, see something in those great

---

[66] Inappropriate now, during the 19th century it was commonly used, even by the medical establishment to diagnose someone with serious mental and/or emotional conditions, or someone not of sound mind.

victims. They do not know how to explain it and unconsciously they say, 'A crippled man cannot do good things, if he carries God's anger!' Yet, what he actually carries is his terrible condition, the perversity of its spirit. It is the rebellion of its unyielding character (that even being overwhelmed by the weight of its chains and confessing it is conquered), but no, on the contrary, it is irascible, violent, enraged and hates humanity. Although he looks at it with a hypocritical smile to inspire more compassion; at the depths of his soul is kept the germ of its past errors, which would like to have sufficient strength to keep practicing evil.

"You do well in looking with interest upon those with great misfortunes, because in these beings one sees the epilogue of the horrific stories that humanity hides. You don't understand by this epilogue the final point of life, because this has no end; the stages of the progress of spirits are divided into epochs, and these involve several incarnations, being the end of such of these existences of pain what I call epilogue.

"If you saw how much she has made me suffer, that girl that you were so affected by! If you had seen her some centuries ago; she was beautiful as the Graces of your Olympus, she was as discreet as your Goddess Minerva. [67]

"She was honest as your chaste Susanna![68] But, alas! Tempting vices seized that weak spirit, even to resist the test of happiness. And, she fell, she fell to the bottom of the abyss! And, it took hundreds of centuries before leaving the quagmire of her restlessness!

"Poor deluded of the Earth, how much pity you stir within me, to hear your words making plans for happiness! Not one of you say, 'I want to be good.' All in chorus exclaim, 'I want to be rich.' That is, I want to fight the most formidable enemy. I want to be exposed to losing the affection of the soul; the hardening of my spirit and I want to get drunk with the opium of adulation. I want to be greatest among the worms of the Earth, to live forgotten tomorrow and unnoticed among the regenerating spirits.

"That poor young girl inspires compassion. Today, she is fortunate in proportion to her yesterday, because yesterday she inspired hate and contempt. Today, she wants to awaken compassion.

---

[67] The Graces were the three daughters of the Greek Gods, Zeus and Hera. Minerva was known mainly as the Roman goddess of wisdom.
[68] Bible story in Book of Daniel.

"These rebellious spirits are more wretched still in the spirit world because they are alone with their lewdness, and the same darkness that envelops them does not allow them to see the friendly souls who want to comfort them in their grief. They only see all the crimes of their existences, and only hear the lost voices that accuse them, as they have accused for some centuries that poor crippled one of the Earth.

"Yes, that unhappy spirit climbed and arrived to the pinnacle of all the greatness of human life. However, because she was not content with being beautiful, wise, and pure; she wanted power, she wanted wealth, but fabulous wealth. She wanted the sovereignty of seduction (she wanted to struggle with all the enemies of the soul) and she gave in to the deceitful compliments of strong sexual desire, staining the bridal chamber; profaning family ties with incestuous concubines, and showered the path of her life with blood to erase the trace of her crimes, which led her to the abyss, and after taking the first step, she hastened to the bottom. Have compassion. Yes, pity these disinherited of the Earth, perhaps yesterday [past life] your soul was one of those beings of frenzied rapture, and to obtain one of their looks, you lost an existence amongst the brazen pleasures of lust.

"Run, run as you do after the unfortunate; read within these books more eloquent than all your treatises of philosophy. Neither your Socrates, nor your Plato, nor your Seneca, nor your Aristotle, nor your Thomas Aquinas, nor any of your great sages will give you the useful lessons that these deformed beings give you, surrounded by all their humiliations and all their sorrows.

"Study, yes, study in those terrible misfortunates, all the degradations to which the spirit submits itself, which solely wants to satisfy the gross appetites of the flesh.

"When a poor one calls at your door, not only give him alms, talk to him, do not do it for charity, do it out of self-interest. Look at his repugnant figure well, in his filthy rags, and put your thoughts back to some centuries ago, and you will see (if you want to see) the same one in front of you, clothed with purple and ermine, bearing in his right hand the scepter of power.

"Beggars are the vibrating memories of the life of yesterday; pity them, love them, protect them. If you look at them indifferently, tomorrow you'll be in their company, for earthly beings are much closer to the condition of beggars than those on the worlds of light."

Ms. Soler:

You are right, good spirit, men are closer to pain than of pleasure. They are perfectly confused by the mere fact of being on Earth; where there are so many beings who live homeless, who spend the day in the streets, and at night go to those unhealthy places called sleeping houses where for twenty-five cents, [69] they allow them to lie down on a little straw and there the great oppressors of yesterday sleep. Beggars are the remnants of past greatness, they are the complement of universal history, they are an index of human failures. They testify to the crimes of the past, for this we must be intimate with them; first to comfort them, and secondly, to discover closely the consequences of the abuses, and learn to prevent ourselves from falling again. As the spirit says very appropriately, most of the people on Earth are closer to the shadows than to the light, since penitentiaries have not been made for the just, but for wrongdoers.

What were we yesterday? What will we be tomorrow? Here are the questions that men ask themselves, but we lack doing our best. What are we today? Today, tells us what we will be in the future. Let us constantly ask ourselves what we are today. Let us study our lives, the aspirations of our spirit, and let us not formulate useless questions, because in us, we carry the solution to the problem of our existence.

In Creation, there is only one pathway: Goodness. Let us follow it, and we will leave this sad planet where the great tyrants of yesterday have chained themselves to forced labor for an entire existence.

Poor little girl, you live in our memory with your little cart, with your dislocated and emaciated limbs, with your rags, your misery and your expiation.

Illuminate us, Lord. We want to progress, we want to live, because we have not lived yet; and may our mistakes never make heaven return us to Earth in the sad state that spirit has returned, that so painfully moved us.

No, no; we want the splendors of the infinite, the abnegation of the redeemers, and the sacrifice of the martyrs. If necessary, we want something great, that we feel and cannot define; but we want light and life, an abundance of science and the divine emanations of charity.

---

[69] A rough equivalency in American money

CHAPTER TWENTY-TWO

WHAT DOES NOT DIE

In the eighteen years, that day by day, we have been studying the phenomena of Spiritism we have been convinced a hundred times a hundred that spirit communications are an undeniable truth; the most absolute reality that does not give rise to the slightest doubt. We can doubt the identity of the spirit that communicates, but not that spirits do speak to us, tell us their impressions of the spirit world and the anxieties they suffer when they contemplate our struggles for existence; a struggle in which a life is given for life. Being that our conviction is so profound, even though all Spiritists of this globe may declare that the communication of the beings from beyond the tomb is a hallucination of the senses, I would say that the communication of the spirits is as true as the light of the Sun that animates us. Therefore, in spite of our own personal persuasion, every time a fact of life beyond the grave is evidenced, we feel a satisfaction so immense that we hasten to impart it to our regular readers to carry it to their mind, in the meager measure of our efforts, the conviction that makes us live consoled in the midst of greatest tribulations.

It has been three days that, speaking to several friends in our sitting room about the disappointments that young women receive at the age of illusions, and how difficult it is that a completely disinterested friendship between two people of different sexes take root, when suddenly appearing in my mind, was a memory of Jose Alvarez (a friend of our early years). We met in the gardens of Alcazar in Seville in the most poetic way you can imagine.

Without knowing why, that memory caught my attention, when in a long period of more than three decades, we had never thought about it.

The next morning, we got up with the notion very willing to work and when we hurriedly finished fixing our room, we began to remember a poem that Alvarez, our friend of adolescence, had given us.

In reciting the composition, we gave the beginning of the second stanza, and with a slight effort we remembered perfectly a poem written thirty-nine years ago of which we did not, of course, retain any copy. The flowers of youth, as all flowers of the Earth, when their withered leaves dry, the wind blows them away and in our fateful existence we have not consecrated the least memory to the past. There are incarnations in which the spirit resembles a sailor lost on the high seas, and in that shipwreck, one only thinks to live for hours; one is not allowed to indulge in memories when the struggle of the present absorbs all our faculties. So, it seemed to me that the reminiscence was very surprising to me, it appeared to me that in those moments an invisible hand lifted a tip of the veil that covered my past, and I saw the garden of the Alcazar of Seville with all its charms, and among the myrtles I saw myself young and laughing, accompanied by my mother and my friends. Is Alvarez dead, and will he want to contact me? We shall see. Or, will it be that my spirit during the sleep of my body, wanted to go tour the places where once were his charms? Not trusting of myself, I took advantage of the opportunity of a medium who had come that helps me in my work, and asked Father German what that extemporaneous memory was due to.

Spirit communication of Father Germain:

"To what is it due? (the spirit asked and then responded), for the simplest and most natural cause, your friend of youth has left the Earth. He extended his flight and after having risen high, he returned to you with the purpose that he himself will tell you; and given that each spirit has its free will, I will not be who will come forward to tell you what he thinks, for it is just, to leave all the merit of his undertaking to him. Accept, then, your communication of a good friend who today is in the spirit world."

Ms. Soler:

Overwhelmed by melancholy memories, I let some hours pass, until taking the pen, I said to my old friend, I await you. [70]

Spirit communication:

"Here I am. You did not expect me ... isn't that true?... So many years have passed for you...! As for me, not even two seconds has elapsed, time is measured in a very different way on Earth than in the spirit world. To earthlings, as a general rule, moments seem like centuries, and, to the disincarnated, epochs that span several centuries are considered as brief moments.

"In the eternal life of the soul, what are thirty-nine years? Less than an atom lost in immensity. However, you are on earth, adjusting my awareness to yours, I will say, it has been much time since we have known each other! Do you remember...? It was one spring afternoon, in the gardens of the Alcazar of Sevilla a multitude of young and beautiful women (because there is no youth without beauty), crossed in all directions by those lovely flower gardens with its covers of orange leaves, with its roundabouts closed with walls of myrtle, with their baskets of roses; beautiful roses that attracted your innocent looks and were the cause of friendship. Do you remember? I still see you in your pink dress, with your white veil, with your blond hair and your white complexion. You never were beautiful, but there was something in you that attracted, it was your soul, that much superior to your body, overshadowed it, that magic of your poetry, of your feelings. Upon seeing you it impressed me in such a manner that anyone would have believed that I had fallen in love with you, but in reality, it was not like that. The course of my life was already marked out, but I had the feeling that you were going to be very unhappy and I would have wanted to save you from the abyss.

"I had a feeling I would love another woman. I would have wanted

---

[70] It is not clarified in the text, whether Ms. Soler received this spirit communication through her own mediumship or by attending a spirit center and writing down the message via another medium.

to give you my name and to tell you, 'Live in my shadow.' However, it could not be, because you did not come to the Earth to rest in a humble place separated from thorns and hardships. You had to struggle with all the miseries, with all the humiliations of poverty and loneliness. I was the one, without me knowing it, destined to awaken in your soul the purest sentiments of friendship. I was the first man to put a rose of a hundred petals, of intoxicating perfume and beautiful color, in your hands. Your mother looked at me smiling sweetly, giving me thanks with her expressive eyes for my gallantry.

"We spoke a lot, you and I, and I remember that you said, with charming naivete, 'What a beautiful afternoon!'

"It's true, you're right,' I responded with the greatest enthusiasm, 'it's an afternoon of the color rose. The sky, your dress and the flower that I have offered you, everything has the same color. The rose, whose fragrance aspires with delight, will lose its intoxicating perfume, but you can keep it if you want.' 'How?' you asked me with innocent astonishment.

"In a very simple manner, dedicating a few verses to that rose whose petals, with as much as you protect them, will become dust, meanwhile your poem will resonate eternally.

"I, thus, ignored that my spirit survived my body, and that thirty-nine years later I would remember the simple phrases of your verses. Copy them now, they are the purest page in the history of your present existence."

TO A ROSE

Flower of ideal beauty,
lovely and dedicated rose,
I proudly contemplate you
in an oriental garden.

There was a being who understood
that I admired your beauty;
Boldly, he plucked you,
in my hand he left you
and I looked at him with tenderness.

Again, we met
and in memory of the rose
we swore eternal affection;
a pure and precious friendship,
a saintly bond we formed.

Today, I contemplate your leaves
without color and bless them;
for they gave me an ignored friend,
who is a flower.

"See how it has fulfilled what I told you in the gardens of the Alcazar of Sevilla? The rose that I plucked for you, you saved for some time, later ... when I joined with another woman, you thought yourself guilty keeping a memory of me, and you delivered it to the mercy of the wind.

"Your verses were stuck in my memory, no copies of them were on Earth, because I destroyed those poems that I possessed, an hour before receiving my nuptial blessings, yet I never forgot them. Whenever I saw you, my heart felt crushed, and I lamented that I had not been free to be united with you, and, it is not because I loved you. No; my wife, the mother of my children was the woman of my earthly dreams. Your poetic and passionate soul, your mysterious something that I sensed in you, made me want your spirit (sad and solitary), I felt I felt I would cross the Earth.

"I wept with your first disappointments without anyone knowing the active part that I partook in your pains, and when your destiny took you faraway from Sevilla, I was glad. I was shaded, by the shadow of your misfortune.

"When I left Earth I went as far as my progress allowed me, and in the midst of the light, in the midst of the immensity, free and entirely blissful, I suddenly remembered you; and continued to read the history of your actual existence, feeling the purest pleasure upon reading on the first page in which there was a rose and a poem.

"Since then, I followed you on your painful pilgrimage, and according to the elevated spirit that you know by the humble name of Father German, I have come to be in relation with you to counsel you; what he has already indicated you for some time: begin to write your memoirs, because you would do a great goodness to poor women who have surrendered, been abandoned and left to their own efforts. [71] Write without reserve, without fear, count one by one all your disappointments, say what you felt when the light was missing in your eyes and in your soul. Tell how you lifted yourself from that prostration, how you searched for the fountain of truth to quench your thirst for infinity. Do you believe it will be an interesting book? Yes, it will be. Your spirit in this existence has taken a giant step. Do you think valuable only the stories of universal slaughter are valuable? (there is nothing else in the general history of the massacre of the towns). No; the story of fallen spirits is of great teaching, and on the pages that you leave written, many women will cry over them. I have wanted to dictate the prologue of your memories. Who has the most legitimate right? None. I was your first friend, the one who introduced you to the flower that symbolizes the life of a woman, brief in its luxuriance and the stem always surrounded by thorns in its existence.

"Rejoice, though you are no longer the girl of white complexion and golden hair, naïve-looking and a cheerful smile. You no longer dress in pink dresses and white veils; the youth of your body has passed…never to return, but what has never left nor will it ever leave, is that tender youth of your soul. You are each day acquiring new perceptions, in each existence you will reach new triumphs, the palaces of science will open up before you and within them you will search with joy.

"In the humanitarian asylums the children await you, and when you are late, they will say to each other, 'Why has not that good lady come?...

"This regeneration of the spirit is not the work of one year nor a hundred, it is necessary for many incarnations of struggles and sufferings to restrain passions, and to do good without expecting recompense, to forgive all grievances and to refrain from inflicting offenses. The work of perfecting the spirit is very slow, my friend, but by its slowness it does not lose one atom of its grand importance.

---

[71] During this time, Spanish laws prohibited married women from working, owning property, voting or traveling without the consent of their husbands. Women could not even attend funerals. There was no welfare or social benefits. Women who suddenly found themselves single (with any relatives to take them in and without money) forced many to enter marriages of convenience, or nunneries or they ended up on the streets.

"See how death cannot break the truest of friendships? Is not it true that you were pleasantly surprised for the remembrance of the poem you had so erased from your imagination? What, then, is elapsed time? In what way has it affected your spirit? You have remembered me (without knowing why) with sweet melancholy, saying with immense satisfaction:

'Our affection was as pure as the perfume of that rose.'

"I, for my part remember, better said, see those youthful days of the body full of illusions and of tender hopes. Those illusions and those endearing hopes, we have an eternity to fulfill them. Why, then, do you lament a few years of anguish, if these will have served to magnify the aspirations of your soul, which is what lives eternally?

"You have always lamented your solitude. You, who say with bitterness that you do not want to deepen any affection, so that mire does not appear on the surface. Then when you least thought of it, you found a friend who turned up that you had on Earth; who today is associated with your work to help you to write your memoirs. Believe me, my friend, it will be a useful work for you, and useful for women, poor and abandoned to their own strength. However, today I leave you. You need rest. Your first friend.

ALVAREZ

Ms. Soler:

All that the spirit has said is very true. His encounter has produced an immense satisfaction and we are disposed to follow his advice. We will take a look at the past thirty-nine years and consecrate to memory our weaknesses and our energies; to our immense pains and to our modest joys. If this work helps us to take a step in the path of progress, we will not hesitate for a second, and the prologue of a woman's memories will follow the chapters of a story of atonement. However, as time has no end, over the centuries we may write interesting stories of heroic events in which our spirit has been the hero for her science and for her immense love of humanity.

Who calls, receives a response; to he who asks, it will be granted. We call and ask for the science to understand the omnipotence of God and the love of loves, to do good for the sake of goodness itself and to transform ourselves into one of the great beings who introduce universal brotherhood on Earth.

CHAPTER TWENTY-THREE

THE SEA OF WHEAT

Ms. Soler:

On December 24, 1887, there occurred a sorrowful event that newspapers recounted on the 25th as the following:

The Double Misfortune of Yesterday

It occurred at half past three o'clock in the afternoon at the pier of Barcelona.

A family from Aragon composed of a widowed mother, a married daughter and a single handsome young man and convalescing from a grave illness. They were seated at the aforementioned hour in a section of one stretch of stairs at the pier of Barcelona. The last one, in front of them on foot, was enjoying the beneficial rays of the sun to get rid of the cold that prevailed, and all significantly ignorant, without a doubt, to the horrible misfortune that threatened them.

In the aforementioned pier, it was proceeding, it seemed accordingly, for the dangerous operation of piling a bulk amount of wheat from one of the anchored ships in our port. Yet, either because one side of the wall or edge may have weakened to contain the heaped upon wheat (it is customary to form sacks filled with the above-mentioned grain around the site for the object it is destined), or the weight of the piled-up wheat ran precipitously towards that direction and it fell like an avalanche outside the pier near the place where the above-mentioned family was, and two individuals, the women, were instantly buried.

The son, seeing the grain spilled, hurriedly and immediately came to their aid, and when he was going to lay his hands on his sister, who he had caught by her leg, a sack that fell from the pier hit him strong in the chest, throwing him to the ground at average distance.

To the cries of those who witnessed the event gave, workers came with shovels to separate the wheat, in whose task many people helped them, but as they worked with earnestness it took a good while to bring up the bodies of those two unfortunate ones; upon being discovered, were already inanimate. They both died of asphyxiation, indicated by the circumstance of them having their mouths open and full of wheat, that gained access to those wanting to breathe.

The youth stayed, as one would suppose, seized with the greatest of despair to see before him those bodies of his loved ones, with whom minutes before he chatted cheerfully, without the slightest thought that such a terrible misfortune could happen.One detail; in separating the wheat away from the site of the accident, a dog was found alive next to the wall to which it was leaning and standing, belonging to the victim's family of the unfortunate event.

A worker who contemplated that horrible catastrophe, pointing to the two bodies, murmured judgmentally, 'What a contrast! ... Meanwhile a great number of day laborers without work die of hunger, these two unhappy ones died drowning in a sea of wheat.'

Ms. Soler:

When we read the preceding story, we were profoundly affected, as was natural, lamenting the death of those two poor women. However, the words of the worker impressed us more. These were for us an admonition, a warning to make use of. So, asking the spirit who guides our work if the words of the worker enclosed the compendium of a history of horrors, our invisible friend told us the following:

Spirit communication [a dissertation regarding a death that occurs suddenly]:

"You have a saying or proverb on that planet, that says 'Voice of the people, voice of heaven.' Never a simple intelligence was better inspired than that of that son of work, contemplating those women drowned in a sea of wheat.

"Understand that violent deaths always obey the fulfillment of an unavoidable law: to give to each one, according to their works.

"Great, and very great, are the faults committed by the spirit when he must die violently; when he cannot prepare his mind for that supreme moment in which he must separate himself from loved ones by breaking those human bonds that, undoubtedly, constitute the whole of his earthly life. Although, the act of death considered philosophically, is nothing more than the detachment of a more or less heavy suit, leaving to the spirit its perispirit [ethereal/astral body] and with this, it has all the sensations of the true life. The position of who abandons the Earth does not lose neither their understanding nor their remembrance nor will, but nevertheless can cease to be sensitive or distressed upon leaving some households where some more or less interesting chapters of the history of the spirit have been written. [72] If it is sad to say goodbye to those places where you have lived and have loved, it is much more violent to see yourself suddenly separated from loved ones, without having been able to give those warnings, those sacred instructions of the last moments, that even the most ignorant beings fulfill and respect as a divine mandate.

"A sudden death, whatever its cause, do not doubt it, is a punishment that the spirit suffers; deservedly a punishment, undoubtedly, but just because a sentence is just, it does not have to be painful in its execution.

"Why do you think that generally the countenance of the old acquires that tinge of sweet serenity, and one even says that the elderly return to becoming childlike? It is because the spirit is personally content of having been on Earth long enough acquiring the knowledge it needed, at the same time paying off the debts it proposed to settle. An old man may say, 'How much the years weigh!... Yet, if that same spirit could speak to you while

---

[72] Subtle and ethereal covering of the Spirit; see full definition of the *perispirit* in Allan Kardec's, *The Spirits' Book.*

148

its body slept, perhaps it would say the opposite, for it thinks in a very different mode when adhered to a sickly body detached from an organism whose multiple and important needs fatigue and overwhelm the spirit.

"An existence is a journey that the soul undertakes for its relative improvement, and you as earthly explorers are happy and even proud when you return from around the world and penetrate unexplored regions, in the same manner the spirit is satisfied of its work. When it gazes from space in the spirit world, on its useless wrapping, it says, 'My poor body! Disintegrate in peace! How good your muscles of steel served me, your red blood, the phosphoric substance of your brain! [73] You were my battle steed, and always saved me from imminent dangers!... Now you are nothing! Your atoms break up, and on each one of them still palpates the sentiments imprinted upon them by my will.

"Every existence for the spirit is an interesting chapter of its history. Woe to him who is obliged to let go of his covering when he is most attached to earthly life, who hates himself when there is sickness of reason, when the spirit does not find in the body all the organs that it needs to manifest itself, if not for the trials you have within yourselves. How many times you say you find life unsupportable, that you want to die, and at the same time, if you feel any threat, you flee instantly and try to save yourself. We have seen more than once a cripple recover his agility when he sees a runaway horse running towards him. This proof you have is in your beggars, that despite lacking all the most indispensable in life (because many of them live years and years sleeping in different places), you will see that it is not for that reason they rail against their miserable existence. Very much the contrary, they grow accustomed to hardships, they are brutalized undoubtedly because misery dehumanizes, but they preserve the instinct of preservation because the love of life is superior to all sorrows.

"The spirit loves its body, no matter how defective or repugnant it is, because it serves for its advancement, and because the law of indefinite progress imposed on that union between the human soul and the organism. They are two entities, the one without the other has no value at all, for if the spirit lives without a body in space, it is also true that in worlds like yours, and in others more advanced (without an organism appropriate to

---

[73] Chemists in the 19th century hypothesized there was a link between phosphorus in the brain tissue and mental ability.

the conditions of the planet in which it wants to inhabit), cannot realize its undertakings, it cannot associate itself with the life of that globe that attracts it, by its magnificence and by the memories that awaken within its mind, of the habitation of loved ones bound to its eternal history.

"Of the many errors spread by the religions, one of them, the most prejudicial without a doubt, is the contempt they have made for the human body; to discipline it with beatings, mangle it with cilices, weakening it with fasting, covering it with filthy dirt. To the extent that wool habits, in contact with the body (has developed parasites with the heat that have mortified it) have made it a disgusting object that has been looked at by educated people with shame and contempt.

"In its infancy, the religions did this and from this error, some philosophies have participated, not precisely of neglecting and forgetting hygienic laws that impose washing, cleanliness, moderate and healthy food. However, yes, saying to those who call themselves Spiritists: 'Oh, when the time arrives to leave the earth! If they let me, I am going to be in space centuries and centuries without this body that so weighs me down, without this matter so demanding! Oh! The life of the spirit is the true life.'

"These innocent exclamations retain the essence of the religious idealism which is the annihilation of the Being. What do you think the spirits can enjoy in space, whose advancement does not allow them to leave the planned trajectory of their work and their relative progress? Do you believe that they enjoy the glory that's painted by the religions?

"The spirits in the spirit world also suffer; they also lament the time lost in useless bewilderment, also they feel the separation of their loved ones and the penalties that these people suffer. The life of the spirit keeps a perfect relationship with its multiple existences; it does not smile with the smile of the righteous who have left the earth without having wept and been blessed. The crisis of a death does not anticipate the events of the eternal history of the spirit. What you do not reach on Earth or the worlds that you inhabit, with your abnegation and sacrifice, you do not obtain by leaving an organism deficient for your necessities. Nothing is gained by assault or fortune; in the regions of truth everything is weighed and measured by the laws of the strictest justice. Those who are more than mediocre in virtues and in intelligence, do not sigh upon leaving Earth because they will not get more glory than their deeds deserve.

"Do not neglect the time that you have at your disposal to progress and perfect yourself, because you have no more wealth nor possess more treasure than the hours that you know how to use in doing good for your fellowmen; which are of great benefit, because he who diffuses the light, it is because he carries the source within him.

"We have put together the considerations, which we have believed necessary. We will tell you something, yet not specific, about the past, of those two beings who left their envelopes in a sea of wheat.

The spirit continues [revealing the past life history of the two women]:

"It is not only you who have asked the spirits what the victims of yesterday's insane catastrophe have done. Other lovers of knowledge, as you, have been given detailed circumstances of how and where they lived yesterday [in past lives], those who died today drowned by that precious seed that serves as food for most of humanity. For our part, we are not in favor of citing places or dates, because your history (which is very badly written) is, according to one of your sages, a conspiracy against the truth, which is so true. You know nothing of the past more than the inventions of excitable fantasies by spirits passionate of your exclusive ideals, and if in your days you observe that the most vulgar facts are disfigured by your historians, calculate whether chroniclers of the past will have lied for your pleasure. So, it is customary to refer to facts omitting date and place, because the action verified neither loses nor gains importance whether knowing that it was executed on the banks of the river, on the edges of the Guadalquivir, under the mists of the Thames, or before the waves of the Seine; the theater is the least, the subject of the drama is what interests and influences the progress and future of the spirit.

"Those two poor women of town were two spirits united by the most intimate bonds of life, and most of all, by the identity of their aspirations.

"They have belonged in various existences to the priestly class which has always been greedy (excluding uncommon and honorable exceptions). Especially, in one existence not too far back, these two spirits contracted the horrible debt that they have paid for a few days ago. They belonged to the privileged class of prominent priests, and they were venerated and feared, by the humble flock that around them lived miserably after paying tithes and offering their first fruits to the saintly mother apostolic Roman Catholic Church.

"Among those who paid tribute, were two elderly workers that were twin brothers. They lived together after having lost wives and children due to so much sickness and death, the total ruin of Juan and Pablo. They having in their old age nothing more than a small old house and some hectares [74] of cultivated land, under writ of sequestration by various creditors. In such a bad situation, they could not pay to the church the amount stipulated by them, and so were presented to the ecclesiastic collectors. These brought it to the attention of their superiors, who in disdain did not visit the humble abode of Juan and Pablo, for they had been smeared by ill will because they were freethinkers; of which there have been those in all epochs and have protested against religious absurdity. [75]

"The conference among the four was threatening on the part of the weak, who complained about a Church that demanded from the poor what she should on the contrary offer them, since they were elderly, poor and with no one to take care of them in their destitution.

"Juan and Pablo told them great truths, and in those times to tell the truth was to sign a death sentence; but faithful souls do not fear martyrdom, although it signified that they were very costly in their boldness. They spoke to the fathers of the Church with that crude frankness that is made use of by free spirits, and the ministers of God sent to put gags on them. They seized the confiscated lands and the poor little house on the pretext that there was buried money, they lied like scoundrels that the men had insulted the church. They were tormented for some months denying them necessary food, making them suffer slowly the most horrible of deaths: one of hunger. They left them without eating until they saw them faint, then after they would feed them to start anew the torment of starvation, until the men died cursing their executioners. The latter, in the meantime, taking advantage of a horrible drought, seized all of the wheat that they could, sold it later at a fabulous price, able to ensure that each grain of wheat was exchanged, in that occasion, into a gold coin for them.

"The hungry crowds asked for mercy, and then pretending a compassion

---

[74] Close to two and half acres.

[75] Those who form opinions about God, the nature of things and spiritual/religious ideas through reason.

that they were very far from feeling, they gave them damaged wheat, that exploited the starving masses which developed by its consumption, a devastating plague that caused countless victims. Meanwhile they, rejoicing in treasure, did not absolve any means for them to trade for foreign wheat, as the fields of their homeland had hardened, refusing absolutely to allow to germinate in their entrails, the golden tassels of the never well appreciated wheat.

"Those two tyrants of humanity, those two villains who were never stirred by the weeping of a babe nor the supplication of an old man, nor the desperate plea of a mother surrounded by her starving children, died tranquilly in their beds. The Church celebrated with pompous funerals, their bodies were deposited in the vaults of the sumptuous temple and famous sculptors made their statues reclining, that still sleep on their marble graves, being visited by many travelers, being that they are true wonders of art.

"It is like everything in this world, usually they who go to the mass grave should be canonized and those true monsters of iniquity are sometimes sanctified. However, what does it matter that in the comedy of human life are represented roles similar to those depicted in your theater? Is it by chance an actor a king, is covered with the cloak of purple and places the imperial crown on his temples? No! His ephemeral reign lasts only short-lived hours; when the function stops, when the coliseum is left empty, the actor returns to what he was before: an actor more or less fortunate. Well, the same thing exactly happens to a spirit when he abandons this world. He could have lived in an alcazar [76], it may have been his slightest whim a shameful law; yet he finds himself in the spirit world as if an actor on leaving a theater, without any more superiority than his many or scarce virtues.

"On the Earth one can continue the farce, one can canonize an executioner of humanity; that will not prevent the executioner from returning to that world to pay an eye for an eye and a tooth for a tooth, like how it has happened to the two ambitious hoarders of wheat that returned to that planet in a very humble position and have begun to pay their debts by dying, drowning in a sea of wheat; like all the food grain that they denied to the starving multitudes. It is just that they drown, one hundred

---

[76] A Spanish palace or fortification of Moorish (Arab) influence.

and hundred times, for there is no debt that is not paid or payment that is not fulfilled. If it were not so, if human injustice and blindness were a copy of [Divine] justice, there would be reason for all thinking men to go mad, because their intelligence would lose itself in chaos.

"So, fortunately, it is not like that; no one is fortunate by privilege, and no one is unfortunate due to abandonment by Providence. Each one has what they legitimately deserve; and if you notice those around you, if you study carefully the chapters that form each family of human history, you will see that leaving aside those who come to settle terrible accounts, the majority on earth suffer no more than the consequences of their mistakes. Many groaned in misery because in the same incarnation they badly spent what they possessed, others acquired debt (and with them, serious concerns) because they do not know how to resign themselves to live in an honest and tranquil way, and more than one serious illness afflicts because of satisfying at times immoderate appetites, and you produce evil with your recklessness. Do not forget that the same relationship applies to all acts of life, because nobody has more happiness than the one who has created it. So sometimes you see beggars who smile almost at the height of bliss, and it is that perfect tranquility of their conscience that surrounds them with light in the midst of the densest shadow.

"Now you know; no one has more repose and well-being than what one creates. Always sympathize with those who die like the wretched women, drowned in the sea of wheat. Woe to those who forsake the earth without preparing their spirit for that solemn act called death!

"Goodbye!"

Ms. Soler:

What great truths, are enclosed within this previous communication. Each man is the son of his own works; we can be convinced that the narratives of history can deceive those on Earth, but not from those who leave this planet.

We must ensure that our acts do not cause us to incur debts in any area, and so, at the conclusion of a theater's function, an actor who plays in the role of king for some moments, manages to take off his mantle of purple and ermine, without leaving the slightest shred on his own suit.

Let us treasure virtues by doing good works, so that when we leave Earth, even if we exhale our last sighs in a humble shelter, the truth of our deeds shines here and there, and although our remains are thrown into a common grave, may our spirit have the immense satisfaction to exclaim, 'I leave the Earth alone with my conscience, and I will incarnate again without fear!'

Happy is he who can contemplate his past without remorse, and smile peacefully before the splendorous dawn of his future.

CHAPTER TWENTY-FOUR

THE LAST WALTZ

Ms. Soler:

Being it was summer in Deva we went one afternoon with several bathers to take a long walk in the country. We arrived at a country house, and we rested in the garden which was very spacious. Fortunately for the young people, there appeared an Italian boy who was carrying an organ with which immediately a dance was improvised. All the girls danced, except one pretty young lady who was with her grandmother.

A gentleman named Alvarez, who had come with his two daughters, asked the elderly lady, "Why doesn't Susana dance?"

"Because as long as I live, she will not dance. Dancing is the ruin of youth."

"Madam, according and depending on; for when young women, in front of their families and decent men are with them, it is an honest and even healthy distraction. Come on, let go of that way of thinking, and let your granddaughter dance with my friend Sandoval. All springs have their flowers, I know it from experience, Madam."

Susana did not speak with her lips, but her eyes spoke eloquently what she desired. She looked at her grandmother, and that one, after a thousand refusals, finally agreed. The pretty girl started to dance with the enthusiasm of her sixteen summers. Alvarez, Susanna's grandmother and us went apart a bit from the dance, and sat together next to a pond. The elderly lady stated, "It was necessary that you asked me to let my granddaughter dance.

She is very alive of wit, and one cannot leave to the girls all their freedom because then there are fatal consequences."

Mr. Alvarez tells his story:

"All extremes are awful, Madam," Alvarez replied gravely, "No one better than I can say, since I have seen it in my family. To serve as evidence for you, I will tell you why I give my daughters all the joys I can. Remember my brother Pepe, the eldest?"

"I think I remember; a beautiful person."

"Yes, he was very good, but very odd. You will remember that he married and shut himself in his house. The year of the marriage, his gave birth to a girl and then died an hour after delivery. My brother remained inconsolable, and for a long time he looked at his poor daughter with offence, because he said that she was the cause of her mother's death. At last, that fatal mania was taken from him. He wanted to love Margarita with delirium, but without studying the character of his daughter, who had an imagination of fire and a daydreaming soul. She had eyes blacker than an abyss; her eyes told a story. She had a voice like an angel. She was a truly enchanting young girl, delirious over music and dancing. However, her father insisted in making her live in a monastic way. In the morning, very early, he took her to mass, made her go to confession weekly and during the day he did not permit Margarita to leave; to go anywhere. At night, with much satisfaction, they would come for a little while to the home I had with my mother. My mother would rebuke my brother, and say, 'You do not want to go anywhere; let Margarita come with me, and she will be well guarded.'"

However, he always responded, "My daughter did not come to this Earth to have fun, she entered it causing a death. If her mother had lived it would be one thing, but in the way that the plan of my life has been changed, for nothing in this world will I change my method."

My mother, in order to avoid his displeasure kept quiet, and counseled my niece that she should be patient. She told me that, she desired that Margarita should be my wife so she could leave that confinement. I liked my niece, but I knew perfectly well that she would not be pleased with me as her husband. She already was a dreamer, and with that life of veritable slavery, her ideas were even more excitable. [77]

The day Margarita reached twenty-eight years old, a sister of mine got married, and for that reason there was a big dance at the house. My brother came with his daughter and did not let her dance one single dance. My mother and I begged him but it was futile, and upon insisting, he said, "Both of you will make us retire." Upon hearing these words, Margarita assured her father she would not dance, but that for God's sake, let her stay until the end of the party.

Her pleading caught my attention. I followed her gaze and soon knew why she insisted so much to remain. A young pianist, a friend of mine, a romantic type, pale, beautiful long hair, with eyes that told a history of tears, had powerfully attracted her attention. Her gaze followed everything. He had not noticed her; so much so he danced with a young girl. They played a waltz composed by him, his satisfaction as a composer was flattered, because his music made your heart beat, or his partner to feel.

The truth is my friend was excited, and Margaret (with her eyes) kept yearning for him saying, 'What a harmonious waltz! Whoever could dance it! You want to believe it?' She told me, looking at me attentively, 'If I was able to dance that waltz, the happiness would kill me.'

"Well then, it's better you not dance," I said smiling, to hide my emotion.

The couples got tired of dancing, and when the piano stopped vibrating, Margarita turned pale, took her hands to her heart and said to me, 'I am cold and hot at the same time, but don't tell anything to my father, he will make me leave.' Further the poor girl started to tremble convulsively and had to abandon the salon, saying in my ear, 'Tomorrow, bring me that waltz, don't forget.'"

The next day, Margarita was confined to bed, but as soon as she saw me said, 'If you brought the waltz, play it. I sat at the piano and began to

---

[77] In the Civil Code of Spain, avunculate marriages (uncles/nieces and aunts/nephews) were generally prohibited, but were not uncommon, and could be allowed with special permission by a judge; as well as for Royalty, as in 1888, Maria Letizia Bonaparte married her uncle Prince Amadeo, Duke of Aosta (formerly King Amadeo I of Spain, House of Savoy) from 1870 to 1873.

play, and she (according to her father) upon listening to the music cried silently. Afterwards, she closed her eyes, and fell asleep.

Margarita continued to still be ill, for twenty-eight to thirty days. She passed the nights with fever, then in the morning she cleared up completely; asking for me, and upon seeing me said, 'Play that waltz; while I hear that waltz, I find myself much better.'

Her father was if crazy, because the doctors had told him that Margarita was dying and there was no remedy; she was being devoured by tuberculosis. They assured him that his method of life had accelerated the death of his daughter because an imagination like hers, with those natural emotions of youth, needed an expansive life; to go out, to shine, to enjoy the delights that the first age of an existence offers. My brother, I repeat was crazy, and wanting to put a remedy, when the damage was already done. He told Margarita that when she was well, they would travel, and he would take her to whatever amusements she wanted.

'Will you let me dance?' asked the sick girl.

'As much as you want to,' said my brother.

'Will we dance that waltz?' Margarita asked, looking at me with an understanding.

I, cherishing hope for her being so young, spoke to my young pianist of the enthusiasm my niece had for his waltz, and, since it produced good effects, he gratefully offered to play it. This is what I was looking for.

I went to the house of my niece, and I told Margarita to listen to me carefully. I told her, that he himself would play the waltz. That poor child looked at me in such a significant manner, that I will never forget that expression on her face. She became so animated and overjoyed that she wanted to get up. Since the doctors had said to let her do whatever she wanted, my brother had that young man come to the maiden. We left the drawing room, and I told Federico to start playing the waltz. Shortly, Margarita entered into the salon, pale as if dead, but her face was illuminated by a divine smile.

Federico looked at her, she to him, and the two of them shared an understanding. My brother was ecstatic. He did not know what to do with Federico, but from that day forward, my friend had free entry into the house of my brother.

My niece got better to the point that her father, in celebration, wanted to give a tea party where the youth could sing and dance. Margarita was stunned to see such a change in her father and had great hopes in thinking that she would dance her adored waltz with Federico; the two made a very good couple."

She herself, with feverish activity, directed the making of her dance dress, that was of white tulle adorned with garlands of daisies. When she was presented into the drawing room, leaning on my arm, all the guests released a cry of admiration; she was absolutely beautiful. I looked at her, and did not know why I felt fear."

First, she sang and was very animated, and Federico very enthusiastic. Later, finally it came the hour of dancing, and they played the favorite waltz of Margarita. She, for the very first time in her life, started to dance."

I did not know why I did not let her leave my sight, and although I was also dancing, all of my attention was fixed on her, and involuntarily, I remembered when she told me, 'If I dance that waltz, that happiness will kill me.'

At first, they played it slowly, but it was such a very special music that unintentionally the pianist played it hurriedly; and those who were dancing continued rapidly in time with the music. My tired companion sat down. I was glad because I would be free to watch Margarita, who danced enthusiastically. Her feet did not touch the earth; she did not appear to be a woman, but a sylph, a fairy, one of those airy figures one sees in dreams. Federico, crazed before that marvelous apparition, continued spinning without knowing where he was. When suddenly, a horrible cry was let out. Upon seeing the head of Margarita (that charming head who breathed youth and life), it searched for support on his shoulder. She emitted a weak groan. He took her as if a small child, and left the drawing room as if insane. I ran after him, and when able to catch up to his steps, I found Margarita in the arms of her father and grandmother, with her eyes shut. Half-opened for a moment, she said with her voice fading, 'Play the waltz, that music gives me life!'

Federico ran as if crazed, and started to play the piano. Margarita sat up, listened for a few seconds with true ecstasy, and smiling as only the angels can do, then fell dead. We placed her in the casket in her dance dress.

I married soon after, fleeing from her memory. I always would see her dancing her first and last waltz. Federico (a true artist) stayed so affected, that he had to go to America to erase the impression that dancing with Margareta caused him. He said to me, 'Believe me, Alvarez, your niece was not a woman, she has left because it was impossible for her to be here on the Earth; a being so spiritual. When I spoke to her, it appeared as if I was already in the other world. I, for my part, who had never been an idealist, and if given to be very logical, I firmly believe that little by little Margarita was murdered by her father.

That creature lived as a martyr and died because it was impossible to resist so much opposition. Her body was weakened by that continuous martyrdom. So, since I have had this experience in my family, when I got married, and when my daughters came to ask for my affection, I was a truly obliging father for them. My wife laughs many times, but I did not change my plan, and much more since Margarita advises me as to how to educate my daughters.

"What are you saying?" responded the elderly woman, "Margarita died. How can she advise you?"

"Very simply, her spirit communicates with me."

"Hail Immaculate Mary, what are you saying?"

"Don't you remember, I am a Spiritist?"

"But Sir, that of Spiritism is a farce."

"You are in error, Madam, pardon me in telling you. I will not say that there are no frauds among the Spiritists, but one speaks of it on how it is [fortune-telling] at a carnival. However, in the way that I got to know Spiritism I have no doubt that it is the truth."

"How did you come to know it?"

"In a most simple manner. My oldest daughter of six years of age, one night when I was writing, I heard that Matilde was yelling for me and I ran to see what she had. I found her sitting on the bed, and she said to me, 'Oh, Papa, here is a lady dressed in white, who wants to hug me.'"

Without knowing why, I thought of my niece. I asked what manner did the lady have, and my daughter described the figure of Margarita. She never knew her or had ever seen a picture of her, because her father, among his many oddities, never let anyone take a picture of her. What most struck my attention was that she told me, she carried in her hand on her chest, a bouquet of white daisies that was stained with blood, the same as the dress. And with reason, for Margarita, at death, had expelled a mouthful of blood that stained her entire chest.

That particularity vividly caught my attention, and made me think even more that my daughter had become accustomed to seeing that apparition and told me very often, 'Here is the lady dressed in the white dress, she says, she loves me very much and loves you, too.' I consulted with a friend (by the way, a healer) and he told me, 'I do not have the least doubt that your daughter sees the spirit of Margarita, the dead live. Buy the books of Kardec, read them, study them.' I did experiments to see if she was a medium, and had the immense happiness that Margarita would communicate with me; she was a good spirit who suffered much on the Earth.

She has helped me in educating my girls; she always tells me to sweeten the hours of their lives as much as I can, for how bitter they often are on Earth. That's why today when I've seen what you did with your granddaughter, not letting her dance and take pleasure in such an innocent enjoyment, I remembered Margarita, who was a victim of parental tyranny.

The danced finished, Suzanna hugged her grandmother, and we all returned to the inn satisfied with our walk, in particular the girls and young people.

We, who have a basic knowledge of Spiritism, that very night asked Alvarez if it would be inconvenient to evoke the spirit of his niece, to see her write. He told us no it would not, and after dinner, with his wife and daughters, they came to our room and with great concentration we evoked Margarita. First came another spirit, and then her, who gave a large communication as it refers to the education of youth. We believed it opportune to copy some paragraphs. Alvarez was kind enough to give us a copy, that started like this:

Spirit of Margarita communicates:

"How beautiful youth is! How ungrateful you are on Earth! Many of you do not grant at that age their innocent enjoyments and purest joys! In all ages of man ambitions dominate, but in youth, all is pureness, all is abnegation, everything is poetry!

"Fathers of families! Concede to your children those pleasant things, to those sweet innocents those expansions that so much flatter the spirit, that both encourage and serve them, and to sweeten their sentiments.

"Youth is content with so little! I, when on Earth, I would have rather been so blissful walking through the countryside with a friend who I could tell my dreams to. However, I lived so alone and frustrated that my daydreaming imagination came to the exaltation of delirium. I loved music with a madness; I gave certain dances such charm. Deprived as I was of all juvenile distractions, the compressed force of my emotions, destroyed my organism, when my weak body stirred to the tempo of those sweet notes that caused me such a profound impression.

"Fathers of families! Don't add to the sufferings of existence with your methods of education. Concede to your children a moderate freedom that harmonizes work with recreation; make them work according to the measure what you give to time there, a week if necessary, and the day consecrated to the feast let them have the whole day. Let them, if it is possible, to go out to the country, that they breathe freely. The conditions of earthly life are monotonous, there are some existences that become painful expiations because of the ignorance that dominates you. I lived dying, the trial that I chose was superior to my strength. Those who inhabit your world must make a special study so that those who depend on you may live pleasantly; observe their tendencies, their inclinations, and if it cannot harm them, do everything that is possible for them because their dreams are made by those young souls thirsting for love and of light.

"The spirit is very enslaved by your laws, your paternal authority, your old-fashioned customs. Everything conspires against the poor young woman who has to live deservedly from her parents. If these do not seek to diminish the sufferings inherent in human life, the spirit in its first epoch lives stationary or it leaves its covering as I did because suffering comes to wear down the organism; or to live without making any progress. What parents should want is the progress of their children, since they are spirits who have come to ask for support and protection.

"When a friend asks for a favor, if you care about them, you try to accommodate them. Well then, your children are friends from beyond the tomb that have associated with you, not for you to enslave them or mortify them or to make them live frustrated, but for you to advise and help them, and to smooth down the obstacles that are always found in the rough pathway of life. Children look at their parents for allies, companions that offer them a means to progress, because with love, the spirit progresses; parents and children united by a superior affection to all the loves of the Earth, both progress because they love and mutually help each other.

"A child without the care of its parents, cannot live; and an elder, without the attention of their children and the caresses of their grandchildren, is like a dead tree with its dry leaves, nothing is left behind.

"It greatly suits those on Earth to study Spiritism, so that parents can convince themselves that the parents are not the arbiters of the fate of their children, that their obligation is to love them, instruct them, doing with them what maybe those same beings did with us when they served us as parents in previous existences. The duty of the spirit is to love all that surrounds it, and by natural law it must care with more desire those beings bound to it by material ties, without ever asserting its authority as a father, to mortify the tender being that Providence placed its care. Do not become responsible for new mistakes, since the mere fact of incarnating together on the Earth is proof that you have to settle long accounts.

"Fathers of families! Love your children, love and sympathize with those poor young people; those weak lilies that wither and die if they lack the warmth of your caresses. I was one of those pale lilies; my soul could not exhale the perfume of his love. I loved art in all its manifestations, I had a world of feelings in my heart, and the exuberance of my extreme sensitivity broke all the fibers of my being, giving a superhuman value to a few certain notes. All the illusions that my soul dreamed of, all the desires that I wished I had nourished, all the love that burned in my soul, I found expressed in that waltz that made me feel all the emotions of the heavens and all the tortures of the Earth.

"Your language is not the most purposeful to tell you what I felt with that waltz; there is a history between that music and I. Upon ultimately hearing it on Earth, I could not understand why it caused such a profound impression on me. Today, all has been explained to me; everything is linked in life, there is not a smile that does not have its yesterday, there is no lament that is not comprised of multiple memories. The love of the spirits is responsible for closing all the wounds of the heart within oneself. [78]

"Love one another; give to the beings that you have in your care an expansive and pleasant life. Smile; make sure that the young smile, learn about Nature, for each season has its flowers and fruits; likewise, in the same manner the ages of man have their distinct aspirations.

"Let the child play and get excited; let the youth dream and smile, since later on at the age of maturity and in old age offer to the spirit serious meditations, deep disappointments and bitter boredom. Do not poison the water of life that is already clouded with your tears.

"It is sad to contemplate a centennial tree that tilts its treetop, overwhelmed by the weight of the centuries, but it is even sadder to see a bush cut down by a hurricane.

"For spirits, when they incarnate, it is appropriate for them to prolong their stay in the world they have elected, because that is how they utilize their time, to work and strengthen themselves. However, being surrounded by a suffocating atmosphere that is not theirs, lacking the necessary vital conditions to their organism, they will succumb as I did, drowned by emotions. There were so many, that I still do not find the sufficient serenity to tell you the mysterious link that exists between my life and that last waltz; that made me glimpse the heavens and made me suffer that supreme crisis you call death. Love! Love a lot; for love is the breath of God!"

Ms. Soler:

We find the reflections by this spirit very logical; we believe that youth should be granted hours of rest and solace, without intimately distracting from linking the useful and the pleasant. If the character of each individual were carefully studied, life would be much more productive and the incarnations of spirits more advantageous; from a frustrated being nothing good can be expected, neither for his own good nor for the good of others.

---

[78] Previously, the spirit of Margarita felt she chose a trial superior to her strength, but that may not be the case as she states "all has been explained" to her by loving spirits, "everything is linked in life" (present and past lives), especially her connection to that particular waltz.

Pain is very selfish; it does not take care of more than itself. Happiness is more generous, it is like the Sun that spreads its rays for all, the same way souls spread pleasure around them. Yet, beings who live as poor Margarita lived are not living an authentic life, for their feverish imagination makes them delirious, and even die, listening to the sweet harmony of a waltz. The spirit, to progress, has to live dominated by the logic of reason upon the firm ground of truth.

CHAPTER TWENTY-FIVE

JUSTICE!

A Judicial Error:
Thirty-Five Years in a Prison

"A few days ago, he came to Reggio de Calabria [Italy]. Francisco Crea was an old man of seventy-two years old, tall, withered and sickly. His face revealed long suffering and by his way of speaking it was deduced that he had spent many years in prison, thirty-five according to the certifications that he carried.

"The news that an innocent prisoner was returning to his homeland, a small village of Palizzi located in Calabria, had circulated in the press, and two reporters went out to meet the freed man in Reggio. They got him to tell some interesting news of his adventures and of his captivity.

"I ran on February 13, 1865, the last day of carnival (he began saying), when my brother Antonio had a dispute with Pedro Calba in Palizzi. He had mistreated him and sought refuge in a cottage of mine in order not to be detained, and to avoid further issues with the victim.

"However, a son of his named Francisco, having news that my brother had struck his father, armed himself near the refuge, to surprise Antonio. Since my brother did not go outside, the hateful Francisco tried to set the house on fire.

"In the sinister light of the barn, turned into a bonfire, he saw [Pedro] Calba go out of his house to Antonio D'Amico to kill him, and believing that he was my brother, he pointed the gun at him, leaving him dead of a bullet wound. I knew that [Antonio] D'Amico had been murdered near my dwelling, but I feared nothing.

"When some person said that they had accused me of homicide, I protested.

"There were some unimportant controversies with the murderer, to affirm that to this one, my son, had caused damage to his garden. Yet, those questions were of little importance, considering that I could not be accused of a serious crime. Nevertheless, I was imprisoned, and through craftily combined statements, I was tried and brought before the jury in Reggio de Calabria.

"There they condemned me to death, in spite of the efforts of my defender, the respectable Baron Guiseppe Nanni.

"I filed an appeal before the court of cassation [79] and my attorney Casella, obtained an annulment of the sentence. The case was sent to the court of Monteleon Calabro. I was defended by lawyer Fernandino of France. His report was so eloquent that even hearts of stone had been moved.

"I was condemned to death by majority due to a sole juror, and my sentence was commuted to life imprisonment.

"Always, I bitterly mourned my misfortune. I was always inconsolable: first, me being innocent and for them having condemned me, and in addition, because I left an angelic woman in my house (my wife Bruna Luciano) and three children: Vincente, Saverio and Eurico.

"The condemned were conducted to the prison of Civitavechia and I stayed twenty-years there classified with the number 21-28. I was then transferred to Portolongone, and finally confined to Portoferraro, where I lost all hope of freedom.

"Thirty-five years had elapsed when Francisco Calba, gravely ill, and given that he had committed the crime, declared himself the person responsible for D'Amico's death before the notary Ajello and a protector of Crea the Baron Vicenzo de Basio, which caught the attention of the minister of justice regarding this dreadful judicial error.

"The director of the prison, continued Crea, (speaking of the last days of his incarceration), had announced to me that I would become free in two or three days. Yet, I doubted so much luck, for when the guard

---

[79] A judicial decision by a higher court.

ordered present before him, number 21-28, which was me, I trembled, and embraced and kissed all of my partners in the prison block. A man arrived, an anvil left in the ground and a cold chisel, broke the chain that I had carried for thirty-five years which had made indelible signs on my body. I was sent, continuing to be released of the prison, to the cell of Pasanante, where a tailor took steps to make me these clothes. The next day I was free, but without having anything to eat. Some young Englishmen who worked in the mines of Portoferraro gave me food and drink, and handed me about six liras, gathered in a collection.

"A security delegate gave me afterwards a lira and twenty contesimi. I traveled with a pass until Naples, and finally have come to this city."

Later, he announced that he would travel to Palizzi, where lived three of his children, all married, and one with the daughter of Francisco Calba. He lamented the misfortune of the poor D'Amico. Then, before saying goodbye to the reporters, he showed them his arms, tattooed as those of all old convicts, in one of which were drawn scenes of Calvary, as if he had proposed to constantly remember that he [Jesus] also was sentenced but innocent, and that he also had recovered in the end freedom, but not the youth and strength that justice is unable to return.

Ms. Soler:

Is it not true that the preceding story is horrific? Undoubtedly. The toughest of fortitude, the strongest of spirit, the soul with the greatest courage, trembles terrified before the idea of being a victim of a judicial error. Many judicial errors are registered in the histories of trials, many unlucky persons have risen up the steps of the scaffold without having committed the least crime, and more than one skeptic has said with bitter irony, 'And, they say that there is a…God!' Where is eternal justice? Who sustains the balance of the divine scales that slant towards so many blunders, and slander weighs more than innocence?'

Well considered; there are motives more than sufficient to express the way that the skeptics do. Only the reasoned study of Spiritism [what the spirits teach us] is the one that raises the tip of the veil that covers a past life; this undeniable life without which they would be right to renounce to have been born and to serve as a plaything of the ignorance of so-called bad judges who so blindly condemn, and so impassable they remain after having committed the most horrible of blunders. Even studying Spiritism, before the judicial errors so horrible as the ones committed by the judges with Francisco Crea, we are left perplexed without knowing what to think, and in such a state I always resort to my spiritual counselor to enlighten my understanding and to save myself from thinking without clarity. As my questions never intend to meet puerile curiosities, maybe that is why (so far) I found a good welcome from my friends in the spirit world. Inspire me, oh you, who suffered so much on Earth, and so well did you know how to read within the human heart.

Yes, Father Germain, speaks with me one more time to calm my spirit, that before certain judicial errors it seems that I lose the reflection necessary to search for eternal justice. Acceding to my desire, here below is what the guide of my works said.

Spirit communication:

"Indeed, you find yourself disoriented because you understand that martyrdom as horrible as that wretched one suffered must have submitted to very powerful causes, and that before the imperative necessity of punishment, a large part of the guilt of the judges disappears, and their error is, as if to say fortuitous because instruments of torture are needed to torment the condemned. However, I must tell you that you are in grave error. The judges are criminals; and their crime does not receive the slightest reduction. Also, the role of executioner is not necessary to represent the guilty on Earth for punishment and suffering. When a man deserves to suffer the torments of hell, he doesn't need anyone to throw him into the abyss, he throws himself in.

"Remember that not many months ago you read in the newspapers and trembled with fright, that a learned explorer had fallen from a high altitude down a precipice, dragging behind him his guide. The snow covered them up, the guide died and the explorer was subject to being held in a hole formed by rocks. There he remained two days, writing his last thoughts in his writing tablet, until the snow covered his grave. The next day, concerned friends looked for the explorer, and they found him in his improvised tomb with the writings pressed to his chest; an invaluable treasure for the wise and to science, since in its sheets were written the agony of a martyr, one with the most precise data to know how he died, for those who insist on reading in the book of Nature.

"You see, that man did not need that he be placed in a chapel and a priest speak to him about eternal life to comfort him of the loss he was going to suffer. He, himself, sought in his fall, the appropriate place to meditate during his last hours. He, without the necessity of being required to be compelled to do so, confessed his sins before the closeness of an inevitable death, and cried, contemplating his guide whom he involuntarily dragged with him, in his fall. The sentence of eternal justice is bound to the fault. That is how judges, make so many stupidities due to their little study and scant interest taken of the unhappy ones who appear as criminals, that in due time will receive their deserved punishment. And, if there are disturbed spirits in the spirit world, most of them are our robed ones, those who emotionlessly signed death sentences without knowing in the slightest the guilt of the accused. You can never believe or say if a person deserves to go to a place of execution, it is necessary who provides for such an act, that it be verified; each is the executioner of himself. Study a little of humanity, and you will be convinced that I am right.

"Look, for example, a person who is unexpectedly rich, and if he does not deserve to enjoy the pleasures that wealth gives him, you will see that he lives poorly, that he does not enjoy much or little of the well-being that has entered through the doors. He does not need thieves to leave him poor, he himself maintains the habits of poverty.

"Why? Because he does not deserve to be rich, because the enjoyment of the satisfactions offered by abundance has not been justly earned. The strictest justice reigns in Creation; you do not understand it, as you do not understand many, many other things. Do you see with the naked eye the millions of worlds that rotate in space? No, you don't see them, but they exist; well, in the same manner so does eternal justice. [80] That is why the lives of souls are eternal, because they need to study in the grand book of which the title is very short, solely seven letters compose it: Justice!... [81]

"Regarding that unhappy one who has experienced the prisons for

---

[80] This took place before science proved the existence of planets (exoplanets) outside our solar system.

[81] In the original Spanish it's eight letters – *"Justicia"*

thirty-five years, in this existence, yes, he had been an inoffensive being. However, he has not always had such good qualities. Since centuries ago, he was one of many Cains who had killed his brother; that unhappy man in that epoch was a nobleman named Count Selvio who had many parchments, but his coffers were empty because his brother, the eldest son was the absolute owner of the great assets of that wealthy family whose members all lived in the shadow of pleasure in humiliating dependence. Selvio did not settle with such a guardianship. He claimed a large part of the property of his brother, who did not agree to his request. Hence, Selvio had him kidnapped, made him disappear without anyone able to find him, took out his eyes, and as a courtesy did not kill him, but had him buried for forty years; living underground dragging heavy chains. For greater security, he handed him over to a petty king, saying, 'This prisoner is the guarantee of your reign, the day he dies I take possession of your estates.' This one, for the account that he had, gave the prisoner good food and would even remove the chains so he could freely walk around underground. Selvio, would visit his brother several times a year, always demanding that he make a donation to him of what he possessed, and telling him that he should consecrate himself in writing to God [join a monastery]. The prisoner always refused the requests of his brother. Selvio had his only son secretly murdered, and his wife died insane.

"Selvio seized all the inheritance, but did not dare to kill his brother because of a vague fear; he believed if his brother died, he would die, too. He was not fooled in his calculations because upon the death of the prisoner, almost instantaneously, Selvio felt the contact of his iron hands strangling him. It was the spirit of his brother who avenged his long captivity. [82]

"Yet, as a second of pain is not enough to settle an account of thirty-five winters, that is why he had been thirty-years and five winters in prison

---

[82] Direct violent physical encounters (slaps, scratches, being pushed, marks on the skin, etc.) by spirits on humans have been reported and documented; much by the Catholic Church, especially during exorcisms. Spiritists do not accept the existence of demons or the Devil. See Allan Kardec's, *The Mediums' Book* and Jon Aizpurua's *Fundamentals of Spiritism* for information on physical effects by spirits, spirit influences and spirit obsession. I believe it would be presumptuous for any human being to absolutely know all the nuances, of what is permitted or not, in accordance with the Divine Laws (material or spiritual) or of the Divine Will of the Creator.

dragging a chain, although happier than his victim, for he had not lost his sight and had a reduction of five years. If he had not found thoughtless judges, he would have become accused of an imaginary crime, because when a spirit proposes to settle an account, and elects the epoch that appears best for him, nothing or nobody stops him in the fulfillment of his plans, since each spirit knows when it is convenient for him to lighten a little of his heavy burden.

"Goodbye."

Ms. Soler:

What can I say, after what the guide of my works has said? What the wise man said, "I only know, that I know nothing."

CHAPTER TWENTY-SIX

THE RELIGIONS AND SPIRITISM

The Spring and The Sea

By the Sea, from a rock burst forth
a humble Spring that distilled,
drop by drop, its clean stream;
And the frothy Sea said to it:
　　"Who commands you to throw, tearfully,
within my bosom, thy poor torrent?"
　　"Vast Sea," responded the Spring,
without boasting and with gentle current,
"Of my pearls, I do a favor for you,
because lacking within your ferocious waves,
what remains in my tears is a drop
that quenches a thirst."

Luis Romero Espinosa
19th Century Poet from Spain

Ms. Soler:

The foregoing apologue that precedes these lines, I was so profoundly affected by their reading, that I can only write some considerations on their interesting subject; comparing the waves of the sea with the religions, and the drops of the spring with the spirit communications that calm the souls' eagerly desirous thirst for comfort. I know it from experience.

Before knowing of Spiritism, I would enter the churches, look at the images of the suffering virgins, of the dying Christs, of the miraculous saints. I would look at the relics of the martyrs and it seemed to me that I was inspecting a collection of antiquities more or less authentic, leaving my soul completely unmoved, without my temples nor my heart quickening a beat or feeling the least excitement. Also, it is not that I looked on with prevention as they surrounded me (quite the contrary), because I wanted to believe, and to be able to have hope. I envied the good women who prayed fervently at the foot of the altars. I said with sadness, what should I do to believe in the mysterious religions? Am I so bad that God has thrown me from his church? And, thrown me out it is true, because these images did not inspire in me the least respect, for they were not artistic marvels. As they were of mediocre or less than medium work, I would destroy them like the iconoclasts of the 8th century that did not want the cult of images, and worse still, is that I laughed at the sculptures and gross figures I saw painted on great thick [pieces of] cotton. Although they say that faith saves, I do not admit in any way that to worship God, they make puppets of clay and paint strange caricatures. [83]

And, I would leave the church upset, because I wanted to believe in something! Yet, I could not believe in anything!

But I did not relent in my endeavor, I returned to advance with new determination visiting cathedrals and temples of great luxury, and listened to different sacred speakers and at the end of the religious function, I murmured with discouragement remembering the famous phrase by Saint Augustine, "Vanity of vanities; and all is vanity." [84] In those ferocious waves there was not one drop of water that quenched the thirst of my soul.

Many years I struggled, looking within the religions for something that spoke to me of God. I remember being in Madrid on Holy Thursday in the afternoon. I left the lavish church of Saint Sebastian (where all the rich people meet of Atocha street) and I directed myself to the humble street of Calatrava, where an evangelical chapel was located. It was a large, dilapidated salon, with whitewashed walls which were covered with some Bible verses. The faithful sat on benches lined-up well and the pastor

---

[83] Spiritists respect all religions and beliefs that encourages mankind towards peace, love and charity; e ach to their own practices. However, objects which inspired others at churches, did not inspire or console Ms. Soler.

[84] An early Church Father, in his book - *City of God*, Ch. 3 – discussed the Book of Ecclesiastes from the Bible.

dominated the multitude on a podium or platform; behind was a great Bible resting on a table covered with a red tablecloth.

I extraordinarily liked that simple décor and I said to myself, 'yes, I have found here what I desired!' However, as soon as I believed, my illusion was as brief as the freshness of the roses, for the one who believed in Jesus was saved, but what of the millions of individuals who didn't believe in Jesus? What about them? In short, I was convinced that all religions were the same, none brings consolation to wicked souls. Those who have the pernicious habit of thinking, cannot believe in the stories of the religions; it is impossible on all points.

When I got to be knowledgeable of Spiritism, I then put myself very much on notice. I turned all eyes to see and ears to hear, because for all, absolutely all, one could arrive to become wise and good, if one insisted on becoming so. It was highly consoling that the believer and the atheist, the fanatic and the sceptic, that all could progress eternally, filled me with joy. They had collapsed the foundations of heaven and hell. There were only countless worlds where humankind acquired scientific knowledge and purified their sentiments by means of loving sacrifices. This could be touched, looked at, there was no place for doubt, because the dead spoke: the tender mother, the loving father, the spoiled son, the enraged lover snatched by premature death. All rise up from their tombs and call out to their relatives by making noise: translocation of furniture, the throwing of stones, to others flowers, to those sleeping innocent girls who spoke and said marvelous things. These were not the hallucinations of a few, but it was a general revolution on the Old and New Continents. [85] It was not just simple people who had seen these strange phenomena, it was also the wise, kings, princes, and theologians. At a given hour, the tongues of fire had spoken in all countries fulfilling biblical prophecies, and these communications were not those ferocious waves; they were the drops of

---

[85] Referring to the beginnings of Modern Spiritualism considered to be started in 1848 with the Fox sisters in Hydesville, New York in the U.S. (widespread interest began with physical spirit phenomena, then writing and trance mediumship and spirit communications) then spread to England and Europe and further. Spiritists formed societies and centers, Spiritualists generally established the religion of Spiritualism and formed churches, and the scientists formed scientific research organizations such as the *Society for Psychical Research* (est. 1882) in the U.K. and the *American Society for Psychical Research* (est. 1884) in New York City.

the fountain that quenched the thirst of troubled and anxious souls. [86] Oh, the communications of the spirits!... There is nothing more consoling nor more persuasive. They, the speaking and writing mediums have done much better than all the martyrs who have died defending their religious creed. Blessed are the communications of the spirits!...

Spirit communication:

"Oh, yes, how blessed they are! (a spirit tells me) You do not know how immense the consolation they provide, because you have not seen one of those horrible difficult situations in which human justice seizes a criminal and condemns him to death.

"I, yes, in my last existence have seen myself at the foot of the gallows. I killed a man out of madness; the fiercest hatred lifted my arm and I wounded him thoroughly, a single stab was enough to kill my rival. Further, I did not avoid punishment. I gave myself up to justice, saying, 'I killed him because he wanted to snatch away the woman of my dreams, and if one hundred times he was resuscitated, one hundred times I would kill him. I was satisfied with myself; it did not matter if I died. The mother of my victim, was a woman of great social influence who worked unspeakably to have me taken to the scaffold. However, the family of my adored was also rich and powerful, and they used all their advantages to save my life. Since they struggled with equal force, the process took a long time, until finally they condemned me to death.

"I was in the chapel for three days; a large number of priests were lurking around trying to obtain a confession, but I refused to confess and continued to keep silent. The second night in the chapel I laid down, telling them to leave me alone. I succeeded in part because my guards went as far as possible from my bed. Shortly thereafter, I saw before me the spirit of my victim, not threatening and vengeful, but sweet and smiling. I remained astonished and my amazement grew, when it told me very softly, 'They're going to kill you because they believe I am dead, but

---

[86] Bible, New Testament in Acts 2-21; spiritual acts of the Apostles and others receiving spiritual gifts (ex. prophecy, healing, distinguishing spirits, revelations, or, Spiritists would say different types of mediumship)

I am alive; my hatred is dead. I am no longer your rival; I have been for many centuries, the two of us have always only wanted the same woman. After my death, I have visited many pages of my history, and have arrived at the moment of our reconciliation. I have come to tell you that you will not die on the scaffold. I have worked it so they will pardon you from the death penalty. Tomorrow confess; show repentance, it suits you to do so. We will see each other again, do not reveal to anyone that you have seen me,' and the spirit vanished.

"What did I feel then? I don't know, but it did not surprise me that it occurred. I confessed the next day, and I knew that the greatest influences to achieve my pardon had been put into play. I was surrounded by many priests, and next to me I say anew the spirit of my victim, that indicated with his lips and demeanor that I remain quiet. I stayed quiet and the next day, tranquil and serene, I climbed the steps of the scaffold. The executioner and his assistants worked slowly and awkwardly; the spirit took care that their movements were slow. They had already sentenced me and the spirit was next to me. Suddenly cries were heard, 'A pardon! A pardon!' and, effectively, the bishop of the diocese, surrounded by a group of gentlemen, arrived at the foot of the scaffold waving a paper and extending his arms, and the spirit of my victim pushed me towards these...

"Since with gold all can be obtained, sometime later I was able to evade prison. I arrived in New York and there the woman of dreams awaited me. There I united with her with an indissoluble link, and there the spirit of my victim took leave of us, saying, 'Love your first child very much.'

"Much time passed, a lot; and the awaited child did not arrive. Ultimately, he did come and my wife and I received him with palms and olive oil, supported him with his first steps, listened to his first words, helped him with his first games. He was of an impetuous character. He was seven years old, and he admirably handled firearms. One day, he was playing with a pistol that I believed was not loaded. A shot went out, and went through my heart. My wife believed she would go crazy, but my murderer was a child, an innocent child, and that child, was our son!... They still continue to visit my grave. My wife has consecrated herself to her son, and he has kept an affectionate remembrance of me. My death completely changed his character; from impetuousness he became calm, from excessive pride to humility. Now, I watch over both of them. My son was my rival of yesterday, my death became the final point in a period of our history. Study; study Spiritism and bless the supreme hour that it irradiated its light over the Earth.

"Goodbye."

Ms. Soler:

Yes, I will study it, my good spirit. I have no other sentiment, but that my body decays and I cannot do all that I would want to, in the dissemination of Spiritism, a fountain of consolation whose drops calm the thirst of troubled souls. [87]

Religions! They are wild waves that do not have one drop of water to calm the thirst of thinking beings. Spirit communications! You are the humble source that spills its clean stream into the dungeons of the prisons, the hospital beds, the beggar's shack, in the prostitute's dresser, in the palace of the kings, in the workshop of the worker, in all places. Like the Sun, which illuminates the whole surface of the Earth with its rays, so the voice of the spirits resonates in all the areas of this world.

Blessed are the communications of the spirits, because they are the drops of water that calm the thirst of sick souls!

---

[87] **Spiritism**, a spiritual science and moral philosophy, based on observation and study of spirits and spirit communications. Through these spirit teachings we know why we suffer, the purpose of life, that there is no death, and that our eternal spirits continue progressing from lifetime to lifetime very slowly progressing, morally and intellectually so we can suffer no longer and finally reach a state of happiness and nearness to the Creator.

CHAPTER TWENTY-SEVEN

YESTERDAY AND TODAY!

Ms. Soler:

Continuing my studies in the grand bible of humanity, I have found, at times, certain beings that awaken within me an active interest. I observe them, contemplate upon them, try to get close to them until they tell me a part of their history. Then I say to myself, I have not been fooled, for this being is a very precious volume, and one can learn listening to their narratives. In effect, there is no better book than that of man, and who says man also says woman; because, like who said I don't know who, reality surpasses all stories of fantasy. The best novelist will never arouse the interest that a real-life episode awakens.

It was some time ago, that a distinguished middle-aged woman was presented to me; elegant in her mannerisms, thin, pale, with sad and expressive eyes and within those eyes could be read an entire past full of tears. Cecilia a widow, has a married daughter, and an adopted twelve-year-old son who she loves overwhelmingly (with the child reciprocating). He has abundant motives to love her because at fifteen days old, he was left without a mother or father. Cecilia (who lived a little less than in misery) did not hesitate for a second having him stay with her.

In spite of her family telling her, "Are you crazy? You don't have enough for you or your daughter, how are you going to raise that poor unfortunate boy?"

"God is great, she replied, "my daughter loves him, and I love her. I already have enough."

"Yes, yes, Mama," said Amparo, kissing the little orphan. "He will be my brother. He will be called Enrique. I don't want to be separated from him."

And, Cecilia, Amparo and Enrique formed the loveliest trinity, and the boy grew up among caresses, without knowing orphanhood.

The years passed and when they dressed her in long dresses, Amparo got married. [88] Enrique was crazy with happiness when Amparo became a mother of a precious child. His joy knew no limits; all his caresses and praise went towards the newborn. He dreamt that when a man, he would earn a lot of money and buy little Lusita velvet dresses and pearl necklaces. The child returned his affection in such a way that when she stammered her first words, in place of what other children say, mama and papa, she only would say "Quique" short for Enrique which she created. The figure of the boy was so engraved in her mind that when he was separated from her (because her parents went far away), Lusita would say to her mother when she saw any boy, "Mama, there is Quique." In turn, Enrique, when he saw a blond white girl, he would yell, overjoyed, "Mama, look at Lusita."

Ms. Soler:

When Cecilia relayed these details, I felt shaken within my whole being. I said to myself, what is it between these two beings? On this Earth it is not customary to love so much. Children spend more time hitting each other and arguing over a toy then in caressing and remembering each other.

Generally, a little girl calls to her mother first, but Lusita called to Quique. Did she know him before? Did she love him with all her soul? Who knows!

Not for curiosity's sake but for study, I asked the guide of my works if indeed Luisa and Enrique had known each other before, and the spirit told me:

---

[88] Woman considered grown up enough to be dressed in long dresses.

Spirit communication:

"You are not deceived in your suppositions. Cecilia, her daughter Amparo, her granddaughter Lusita and Enrique have been united by the strongest of blood ties known on Earth. Cecilia and Enrique have been mother and son in various existences, the two have had troubled lives.

In their third to the last incarnation, Cecilia committed a crime to conceal the dishonor of her daughter, who in that epoch was a charming and passionate young woman belonging to a great family of many parchments, shields of nobility and stately castles, but today is none other than who is called Enrique.

"Cecilia, who today you see so modest, so suffering and resigned with the multiple adversities of her expiation, was then a haughty Castilian who did not believe that commoners were children of God. [89] Between her and the village, in her manner of thinking, was such an immense distance that nothing or no one could shorten it.

"So, her astonishment and grief were frightful when she heard from her daughter's lips the most horrible confession, she was dishonored! Her dishonor could not be hidden because stirring within her was the fruit of a shameful love. She loved a man of the village, a troubadour without fortune, who sang to her the beauties of Nature that he transferred to canvas with an artist's magical brush. However, he was a vagabond artist roaming from castle to castle offering his verses and landscapes. He did not know his parents, and he had no surname! They called him solely Ivan. What a disgrace! And, that lost and abandoned one with a handsome body, wearing very threadbare clothing, without even one bad shield in his pockets, had dared to seduce the heiress of a hundred dukes hoping to join her, until the mother discovered her dishonor. Alas, the artist could read the great book of Nature, but not the heart of a prideful woman; for then, Cecilia then, could not believe that love is the great equalizer of the Universe. She preferred a thousand times more, to see her daughter dead than to be joined to a man without any title of nobility, and stealthily, (without giving any understanding to the poor daughter of her wicked intentions), had Ivan seized accusing him as an agitator of the town. He was embarked and deported far from his home, while his beloved gave birth

---

[89] A person from Castilla (Castile), Spain

to a child her who was seized by its grandmother, disappearing forever. The child dead and the father deported, the honor of her granddaughter of a hundred dukes remained without blemish. No one suspected what occurred. However, the young mother could not endure the separation of the love of her heart and the tender being she had carried within her. She did not murmur one complaint; she understood her mother acted dominated by her pride of race. She forgave her because she loved her so much; but slowly her splendid beauty withered, and dying in the arms of her mother, she said, 'I forgive you...!'

"Then Cecilia was horrified by her work, but at the same time she breathed with much more freedom because the victim of her pride of race had disappeared, the dead do not speak. The dishonored youth was clothed in a white dress and they placed between her hands a palm frond of her virginity (which was the palm of her martyrdom), and on your white forehead delicate roses withered. She did not lack any attribute of purity to her virginity. Yet, all the demonstrations seemed insufficient to her mother to conceal the dishonor, for although every one ignored what happened, she knew; and she always saw the figure of her granddaughter and heard, trembling, a voice that said, 'I forgive you!'

"No news was ever heard of Ivan again; he died in exile cursing his unfortunate luck. Cecilia was tormented by remorse and at the same time satisfied with her work, for having saved the honor of her opulent family, and she did not live much longer than her poor daughter. She left the Earth in the midst of the greatest disturbances, without being able to realize if she had committed a horrible crime or if she had carried out a heroic act, sacrificing what she loved most to avoid a major scandal.

"Now good, on Earth today Cecilia is completely transformed; her pride of race has disappeared. Today, she is humble, patient, resigned. Today, she knows how to love; love is her religion. An active spirit, when she realized the error in which she had lived, with the same decision-making she had used to do evil, she consecrated herself to practicing goodness. Since she was no criminal but halfway, the spirits [in that past life, the dishonored daughter, the deported Ivan, and the killed newborn] who were victims of her pride of race, have not separated from her, having forgiven her and they have accompanied her on her incarnations of expiation.

"Her daughter Amparo is the spirit of the child that she caused to die at birth, and her granddaughter Lusita is the spirit of Ivan (who follows Enrique still loving him). That is why, in this actual existence when she started talking, she called to him because it is Enrique who is the love of her soul. They have been together many centuries (together is not the most appropriate phrase) because there were many times that they had been impatient; they committed a crime to unite much faster. Since then, they meet, love, struggle to live together, and always a hidden hand separates them. That hidden hand is their expiation, since happiness cannot have foundations of blood and tears. [90]

"Study well this true story because it is of great instruction. Cecelia was guilty; out of her pride, for her ignorance, for her hardness of heart. She became the owner of the happiness of three beings causing the death of her daughter, of her grandson and of Ivan. The three spirits have pardoned her. Her grandson could not be more generous by choosing to return goodness for her wrongfulness. Her granddaughter Lusita, (who died in exile [who was the deported Ivan] cursing the hour when "he" was born), today claims her sweetest caresses, and Enrique adores his adoptive mother without remembering the past. Her victims not only have forgiven her, but love her delightfully.

"So then, her victim's hatred having disappeared, has Cecilia the right to be happy? No, she does not, and that is why she is not. That is why she struggles with misery, with humiliation, that is why she gives a life for a life. That is why she cannot be with her daughter and her grandchildren, and only has at her side an adopted son, costing her immense sacrifice the power to enjoy his company. It is logical that this occurs because yesterday she broke into a thousand pieces a nest of love: her daughter died a martyr, Ivan a desperate person and her grandson could not sleep in his crib of flowers. That is why today she yearns for her daughter, for her grandchildren and sacrifices for Enrique (giving him all her love) because one day of insanity she denied it to him. Cecilia is a redeemable soul. She has seen the light; she wants to live in the light. The love she feels for her family is immense, she would gladly give up her life with pleasure for them. A thirst for love has awakened in her that she never sees satisfied. It always

---

[90] Further clarification: **Cecilia** – was the Castilian woman of nobility; **Amparo** – was killed as a newborn; **Lusita** - was the deported Ivan; and, the adopted son **Enrique** was the dishonored daughter who died of a broken heart.

appears to her that she does not love enough, she always is unhappy with herself. Blessed are the souls that think solely to love! Cecilia is one of them.

"Goodbye."

Ms. Soler:

Indeed, Cecilia's story is of great teaching, because it is seen that no one can be happy if one has caused the misfortune of one's relatives or servants. Happiness exists, there is no doubt; it is a very delicate plant that needs the water of abnegation and sacrifice to flourish. Blessed are those who know how to love!... Only those who love, know how to struggle and to overcome the rough battle of life.

CHAPTER TWENTY-EIGHT

ONE MORE HISTORY

Ms. Soler:

Reading articles in the newspapers, I noticed a very special report that is transcribed below, and that gives motive for so many considerations!

THE MARTYDOM OF A CHILD

Paris 18th – At 6:40 in the morgue there was a most horrible "confrontation" or meeting of criminals, although in that place the most horrible is common.

Three people have been placed in front of the corpse of a child who was found lying in the street, who died a victim of the torments that his own father unsparingly laid upon him.

The man is called Gregiore, who shamelessly confessed (which explains his mental alienation) that he effectively tormented his son and abandoned him alive on the street of Vaneau.

The judge noticed that in the child's clothes he did not see a single hole, when the body was riddled with punctures. Gregoire calmly explained that when stabbing his son with the knife he looked for his flesh, so as not to spoil the clothes.

A woman, dear to Gregoire, has declared that it was impossible for her to prevent the martyrdom of the child, because she had assurances that she would have also been abused by him.

She explained that she tried to save the child from being thrown into the Seine, and that it was she who advised his abandonment in the middle of the street, believing in this way to save the life of the child.

THE BURIAL OF A MARTYR

Paris witnessed yesterday one of those spectacles that are never erased from the memory of a people. Little Pierre, a child of three years old martyred by his parents, was carried from the morgue to the cemetery followed by an accompaniment of 300,000 people. There is no ruler on earth that has had another the same. His small casket disappeared among the piles of flowers, offered by working class fathers and mothers in the name of their children. When the cadaver was deposited in the grave, all those people who passed by and before it, deposited a handful of dirt over this victim of barbarity by his unnatural parents. The city of Paris wanted, with that great demonstration, to prove to the world that inhumanity is a rare exception among its members.

Ms. Soler:

The horrible story of the martyrdom of that child and the burial of that martyr, profoundly affected me. Firstly, it reveals an appalling perversity. Secondly, it reveals the advancement of humanity that, undoubtedly, is raising awareness, becoming more caring, affectionate, slowly losing its ferocity.

Spirit communication:

"Do not judge so lightly (a spirit tells me), humanity works according to the circumstances, and believe me, it has been many centuries that earthly humanity knows how to sympathize with the helpless and knows to persecute an offender.

"To that spirit the city of Paris has paid thoughtful homage, that same city, that great mass that is always the same in all epochs (impressionable and just), but that city to that same spirit in the first days of the eighteenth

187

century, persecuted it through the streets of Paris with the sole eagerness to haul it away and quarter it.

"Do you know why? For the spirit of little Pierre, was at the dawn of the last century a noble of the house of France, plentiful with everything of parchments and coats of arms, but he was lacking of feeling and of humanity. He was of such a violent character, (beyond all comprehension hot-tempered) he frightened numerous in his servitude, in particular a few children he had as pages. One of them, the handsome Isa, was a child that everyone in Paris knew for his gallant figure for how well he handled his horse. The mothers of the town, when they saw him pass by would be envious of the mother of such a good-looking child. One morning, Isa went out with his master, both on horseback; that of Isa's stumbled and fell. The rider was unscathed, but not his horse which resulted in grave injuries, and the noble Lord forced Isa to lie down and lashed him until he left him dead. The people were incited to rebellion, the women roared like wild animals and chased the nobleman so closely, that he had to shelter in the royal residence, and, even there the people en masse were asking for his death by the hand of the executioner, since they could not destroy him at their pleasure. The people saw him as so despicable that to avoid greater evils, the noble had to be condemned to death; and he ascended to the scaffold listening to the curses of a generous people.

"The noble of yesterday was little Pierre, that recognizing his inferiority thanks to the spirit of Isa (that is, one can say his guardian angel [91]), he elected one of his many enemies to create a family on Earth. Pierre came ready to begin a test of reconciliation, but his father, who in another life was a victim of his cruelty and died on the scaffold due to him, has not been able to see anything more in his son than a being that he hates with all his heart. So, he has been pleased to torment the child with unprecedented ferocity; which is a disgrace, for every spirit as a child always inspires by his helplessness, being the only means of reconciliation that can be used on Earth. One need be a monster of wickedness in order not to feel moved before a child who, whether ugly or as repulsive as he may be, is powerless and cannot defend himself and has need of all. If an irrational creature inspires compassion when it lacks food, should not it occur with a very small child that cannot defend itself? That is why the father of Pierre is

---

[91] A morally superior spirit

truly a criminal who has placed new links on his long chain [92] and he will have to go after the spirit of his victim now requesting mercy. Although the spirit of Pierre is willing to progress, his forgiveness does not remove an atom of the enormity of the cruel revenge of his old and defeated enemy. Pierre did not come this time to suffer such martyrdom, it was a trial of reconciliation that he intended to do, willing as he was to work for his progress. The punishment of his guilt does not require anyone to impose it, he will be judge and cause at the same time, as are all spirits. It is not a necessary fate that any being become the executioner of another because one has to settle many accounts, each one is their own executioner.

"When one has to die in a violent manner or in major misery, suffering cruel pain, the odious role of tormenting is done by a spirit dominated by its bad instincts, not because he came to the Earth with orders from superiors to torture the guilty from yesterday [a past life]. The law is fulfilled without need of any executive agent; you have only to glance around you, and you will become convinced. Have you not seen or read many times powerful men, with good fortunes, a gifted life, with an affectionate family, put an end to their days in a most horrible way? Do you not remember that old man who, in Paris, enjoying a good income and excellent health, left a portfolio of great value, placed himself completely naked in front of the chimney, smeared his whole body with oil and hid his head between the burning logs? What does his way of dying prove to you? That he had hopelessly charbroiled his body to suffer the painful passages that others had undergone at the stake.[93]

"When the press reports horrible crimes, feel sorry for the executioners [the criminals] because they have condemned themselves to forced labor for many centuries. The pleasure of revenge is truly a hellish pleasure. Woe to those who enjoy watching a helpless being suffer! Woe to those who become deaf to the moans of children!

"Goodbye."

---

[92] Debts that he will owe in future existences.

[93] In a past life, he had burned others at the stake.

Ms. Soler:

I am in agreement with that communication received. I have always believed that the role of executioner was not necessary for humanity; man's own history is enough to climb to the heavens or to descend into the abyss. [94]

---

[94] Each person through freewill decides his/her own destiny. As a Spiritist, Ms. Soler did not accept the existence of a Heaven or Hell, only the conditions (good or bad) we find ourselves in life by the consequences of our own actions; whether in the material world or spirit world (the afterlife).

CHAPTER TWENTY-NINE

HOW MANY SHADOWS!

Ms. Soler:

Among the many persons who visit me, the image of Teodora Ortiz stayed very vivid with me; a very pleasant woman, very well educated and very much a Spiritist. She promised to write me when she arrived in Madrid, and she has kept her word, writing to me in the following letter:

"You will remember that the day of our meeting I explained, along with my husband, the persecution of which I was the object of on the part of our grandmother (my husband's grandmother), of which it has been thirteen or fourteen years since she had disincarnated. Which, after three years in the spirit world, I have been feeling the effects of her hatred towards me; continuing since then her persecution with such tenacity bordering on the incredible, as much physical and moral, as material. So much so, that if we were not lucky enough to have known Spiritism, and to enter into relations with good Spiritists, with assurance that given the mortal blows that we have received from that spirit, I would have succumbed without taking this test to a happy conclusion.

"We are thankful that we have good invisible friends that give and have given their valuable help, that we all need. I have forgotten to tell you that when it is very troublesome, my daughter Ines, of which it has been three years since she disincarnated (when she was going to turn two years old), comes to give me life. We know that she is a very elevated spirit inasmuch as that in her presence, that rebellious spirit that persecutes me retires, and

191

she gives me the strength that replenishes me and that drives me to pardon and even to love my tormentor.

"Having already told you the story in broad strokes of what is happening to me, I dare to ask you a favor that I would be forever thankful for; that when you have the occasion to consult the guide of your works to see if it can tell you what is between that spirit and me, between our grandmother and us. What causes there is in the past that bestows so sad and so distressing the effects in the present? I think it is useless to say that we are not moved by childish curiosity, much less, but by the desire we have to progress and make peace with this poor spirit, because if I succeed, I will consider myself completely happy. I suffer so much! ..."

Ms. Soler continues:

Teodora's letter profoundly affected me, because she reminded me of her previous story, which was very convincing because she has the misfortune of being a clairvoyant and sees his [her husband's] grandmother continually with hands touching her neck, wanting to strangle her.

How many mysteries! How many shadows of the past, the night keeps!... Given the suffering of this family, I have not hesitated to ask my invisible friends because Teodora has to suffer so much, and they have answered me the following:

Spirit communication:

"To properly respond to your question, we will have to give you a series of communications regarding the history of Teodora, but for today, we will concretely tell you that when the Tribunal of the Holy Office [of the Inquisition] dictated its horrible laws, the best of the Spanish nobility residing at Court confessed to one of the most powerful judges. In that epoch, Teodora was a beautiful young woman who was to be united in matrimony with a man worthy of her, and before she was to receive the nuptial blessing, she went to confess her innocent sins to the fearsome inquisitor, who when he heard them, completely lost his reason and swore to make that young girl his. When Teodora got up, her fiancée prostrated himself before the confessional, with whom the confessor used his evil cunning to cover Teodora's immaculate honor with disrepute. However, he was unable to achieve his villainous intent because her future husband was convinced, that his beloved was an angel disguised as a woman. After they exchanged their impressions, the two lovers tried to make their bond quickly, but before carrying it out, Teodora was accused a heretic and violently removed from her paternal home. However, her fiancé was a very influential man; he put into effect all his power, utilizing large sums in buying off bailiffs and jailors. Theodora was able to leave prison by fleeing to foreign lands, where her marriage was brought about. This maddened and made furious her pursuer; that he could not overcome Teodora's resistance. She was very happy with her husband, but she could not return to Spain until after the furious inquisitor died.

"In the spirit world, he did not recognize he was dead, and continued to believe for a long time that he lived, while hating, yet desiring the possession of Teodora. The inquisitor and Teodora returned to Earth. The two lived under one roof when Teodora married, and her grandmother [the spirit of the inquisitor] felt incomprehensible aversion towards her.

"The spirit left the Earth in the most major agitation, was late in realizing its disencarnation; and upon recognizing the state of its spirit, its hate redoubled towards Teodora. Fully materialized, it has and does all the wrongfulness it can. Thanks to the husband who Teodora had in her previous existence, and who in this incarnation was her daughter Ines (a spirit of great power), she helps her mother a lot and strengthens her to resist the horrible persecution of a spirit completely materialized, and dominated by such violent passions. [95]

"Teodora and the spirit of her daughter Ines need to work without rest to make the inquisitor of yesterday comprehend his true state, counseling him, urging him and forgiving him of all his offenses. He is an insane one that they need to cure and pity.

---

[95] This spirit's strong influence is such that it can produce strong moral and physical effects, almost as if he IS alive (what she means by "materialized"). Since Ms. Soler's friend is a medium, she feels him and sees him as if alive. Moral superiority of other spirits can provide spiritual protection. Spirit obsession can be a trial and/or a test (of patience, resignation, etc.), yet as always there is a *just cause* for all suffering. See Kardec's, *The Mediums' Book*.

"Later in another communication, I will tell you more regarding Teodora's history. A strong, valiant, honorable spirit that, yes, sinned in the night of Time. Yet, has come later to heroism and to sacrifice, in defending her honor. She knows how to suffer, now it is necessary for her to be able to forgive, and later...later on, to love her enemies.

"Everything good will come to be achieved because she has the will and desire to improve herself."

"Goodbye."

Ms. Soler final comments:

What shadows! How much shadows the past! Blessed are the Spiritists who can tear away the veils of yesterday and contemplate the shinning sun of the future.

Blessed a thousand and a thousand times the communications from beyond the tomb! Mankind no longer walks blindly! The star of truth already shines in the east!

CHAPTER THIRTY

SADNESS

Ms. Soler:

Sometimes, how heavy life weighs! What coldness is experienced evoking the shadows of the past! When one stops to spell out the alphabet of a long existence, one weeps without spilling a tear, one cries inside. It seems that melted lead or ice water runs through our veins, and the despondency is so profound that one does not want to die, fearing to find beyond the grave the continuation of the history begun here. When a desire is not nourished nor hope is possessed, how heavy life weighs!...

Living without hope!... It is not living! To live without desiring, is to die without agony. Living, dominated by indifference is to anticipate the crisis of death, it is to open oneself the pit to bury our body in it; it is to become a gravedigger. Oh, the ones who say with this poet:

"No pain reaches to my pain,
I have no memories, nor hopes."

Spirit communication:

"He who has no hope (a spirit tells me) closes the eyes of his understanding. It is like someone who dies of hunger because he is obstinate in not eating; and burns with thirst because he does not want to drink; and feels the cold because he tears his clothes off; and who hurts his feet because he throws his sandals away; and feels the horror of asphyxia because he is enclosed in a cave rejecting the air that is the beginning of organic life.

"He who says he does not want to live, is he who dies without hope. That is to say, he believes he dies, but he lives (more than his disbelief and his desperation) in the eternal reality of life. When in his daze and in his tribulations, he closes the eyes of the body (believing where there is no sensation, there is no agony and that all concludes in the last pale that falls on the coffin), then, it finds that it hears, sees, feels and contemplates its body as it disintegrates inside the mortuary box. It is tormented by sensations it never felt and sees other beings that surround it, and it sees that life extends beyond the grave. Then hope comes to meet it, and says, 'Do not reject me, it is useless. I'm the spirit of your body, I am united to you by indissoluble ties, the knot that binds us there is no sword that can break it. Hope is the essence of life, the spirit lives eternally, and hope, which is its inseparable companion, like it, is immortal.'

"The sadness that those on Earth experience is one of your vices, it is one of the manifestations of the ingratitude of man. Sadness!...

"No one should let discouragement enter in, since one lives, and one who lives does not die. I was one of the many ungrateful who swarmed upon the Earth. Since young I dreamt of - not being. I lost my parents when I was still unable to call for them, and although I did not feel the horrors of hunger, I found myself so alone... so forsaken of affection!... The master of my actions since such an early age!... So unattached from the great human family! I became sullen, distrustful, suspicious. I did not know the sweetness of love because I did not love anyone. I formed an emptiness around myself, and finding the weight of life unbearable, I put an end to my days [suicide] believing that my whole being would be lost in the sea of the unknown. Vain chimera!... My astonishment had no limits, it is impossible to explain the surprise I experienced when I saw my body shattered at the bottom of a deep abyss, and I, next to my remains, remembering perfectly all the details of my past existence, listening to a voice that told me:

Spirit communication by the mother:

"My poor son! You are ingratitude personified! You surrendered into the arms of sadness, and you had no right to be sad because you had a healthy and robust body, a well-balanced intelligence! You never knew what a day without bread was or a night without a bed. You were not tormented by the coldness of hunger or the fever of thirst, because I always gave you what is necessary to attend to all the imperious attentions of your life. Why were you so ungrateful? My poor son!... They tell me you needed to torment yourself because you did not deserve the tranquility or the well-being of a quiet existence; that you had sinned a lot and you had to be your own executioner; that all those who surrender into the arms of sadness are unrepentant sinners who drown in the sea of their own miseries. My poor son! I left you with so much sorrow!... I have followed you with so much anguish on your painful pilgrimage! I approached you with so much eagerness to give you breath! All useless! You closed your eyes so you could not see! You closed your ears so you could not hear! You obstinately remained reclining in your bed so as not to walk! My poor son!... Poor crazy one without a straitjacket! I misspoke…there is no straitjacket more than your invincible sadness! It left you without movement, without initiative, without will. It turned off your juvenile enthusiasms, it made you insensitive to the sweet compliments of love, it pulled you away from the arms of love, it brought you out of the arms of friendship, it made you an ungrateful being, and ingratitude is the most horrifying prison where your spirit lives chained. You condemned yourself to forced labor, you forged the iron chain that oppresses your throat, injured your hands and bloodied your feet. My poor boy! Open the eyes of your understanding and contemplate hope, that benevolent fairy you have despised so much. Yet, hope is the driving force of humanity, so good to her children, that never abandons them, and if these are ungrateful, her love is much greater than universal ingratitude."

Spirit communication by the son continues:

"What good my mother's words did for me! The bandage fell from my eyes, and I saw the reality of life. My sadness vanished as the mist vanishes when receiving the rays of the Sun and I began to live in the arms of hope."

Spirit of the mother responds:

"I heard your complaints and you inspired in me compassion. You are also your own executioner, also you do not know the divine justice. Look; you can see! Listen; you can hear! Come; you can walk! The ungrateful are those who are sad. Reject sadness, which is the ivy that binds to man and oppresses him, until it reaches in the strangulation of your body.

"Goodbye."

Ms. Soler:

The spirit states it very well; sadness is a symbol of ingratitude because it is a demonstration of the ignorance that man has of the divine justice.

Hope; eternal mother of humanity! Receive me in your arms, give me the nectar of consolation that only you possess, because I want to trust in my work and wait on my limitless progress.

CHAPTER THIRTY-ONE

KARDEC'S MISSION

As the Sun gives life
to what is born on Earth,
So Kardec with his works
the teachings spread,
of supreme truths,
as sublime as they are great.

Sun of intelligence,
it is just to be called a
source of love and consolation.
How much they teach!
How many his books [have] attracted,
that in gold letters
they should always be preserved.

Spiritists! We must
honor him with our deeds,
imitating his virtues
and working eagerly,
making sure that his works,
his teachings spread.

Praise to Kardec! Your mission
was so great!... So great!...
That there is no wise man in our time
that is equal to his greatness. [96]

---

[96] Ms. Soler was very grateful to find in Kardec's books, the **spirit teachings** that made sense of life on Earth, of her own sufferings and which provided her great consolation. As millions of others around the world, she greatly admired Kardec and his compilation of information due to observation of phenomena and what was taught by morally superior spirits through spirit communications.

CHAPTER THIRTY-TWO

ETERNAL LOVE!

Ms. Soler:

How much sorrow we suffer in this world!... What a somber mansion the Earth is!... How many unfortunates oblige me to share in their troubles!

Here are fragments of a letter that I just received:

"It has been approximately some nine years that a granddaughter of mine has been secluded in the insane asylum of this capital. Then, as she is at this time thirteen years old, her state is one of the saddest that the human mind can conceive. She is already a true automaton; disabled of both extremities, deaf and mute, without knowledge or reasoning of any kind. She remains in that state because my resources for the moment do not allow me to have her by my side, which are my keen desires. I feel an affection and fondness so immense for her, that frankly, I cannot explain. This fact makes me suffer horribly and when I visit her, she is completely indifferent to my presence, which causes my spirit to suffer in a dreadful way.

"For all the above, I beg you fervently to ask the guide of your work for some information about the past history of this unhappy creature, and what previous relationship exists between her and I. Do not disregard my plea, I believe in Spiritism, in the reality of successive incarnations, and I need to calm my spirit with a new revelation."

Ms. Soler continues:

The demands of a suffering being have always been sacred to me, therefore I have procured to ask a spirit about these two unfortunate beings; one who has answered, has responded with the following:

Spirit communication:

"The anxiety and perplexity from that brother is just, who has addressed you in need of help; and, since one who asks, it is given, listen carefully to my communication. The deaf-mute, idiot [97]and paralytic girl of today (seemingly, but she is not in reality; more so, for her for greater torment) was in her last incarnation a man celebrated for his misdeeds.

"He was born in Spain and was the amazement of the people for his skill, for his audacity, his boldness, for his temerity, carrying off the greatest dangers to rob travelers, and to attack stately homes to seize the most hidden of treasures. He was a terrible outlaw; the proudest rulers secretly admired, but surrendered to him. He was an arrogant man with the beauty of the angel of darkness. Since he was of noble lineage, his manners when it suited him, were the most distinguished that the most demanding lady could wish for. So, it is not strange that he went crazy for a young woman from a very good family, who he carried off from her home, and he took her far away to avoid complaints and serious disgust from her parents. The seduced young woman understood too late the misstep that she had taken. She wanted him so much and was in love with him, that she set out to convert him from a fierce outlaw into a good man. However, all her efforts were useless. She was very Christian; she believed in the effectiveness of fasting and penance and wore cilices [98]martyring her beautiful body to redeem the man she loved so much. However, he got tired of her sermons

---

[97] The actual professional psychological and medical term used at that time, which is now considered inappropriate, to describe anyone who did not have the capacity (or very limited capacity) to communicate in any way due to mental, emotional and/or physical limitations.

[98] Originally, a cilice could be a sackcloth or any rough undergarment (called a hair shirt) and/or a spiked garter causing its wearer discomfort and/or mortification of the flesh and done to show penance.

and lamentations. After committing a robbery with a gang and killing several of those who they had robbed, he said to one of his companions, 'The woman who continues to follow me from so long ago hinders us, is becoming more and more fussy, and more devout. Make her disappear for the good of us all, and we will gain time.'

"The bandit complied with the orders of his captain. In a deserted place, where the earth was furrowed by mushroomed ravines, into one of them he cast the young girl in love; good and a believer, who had converted into a redeemer, which is why, naturally they crucified her.

"Later on, during an armed encounter, part of the bandits died and among them the captain; he upon arriving in the spirit world was received by his redeemer, willing to remain his guardian angel. [99] She loved him so much!... They have been in the spirit world for quite a while, and she is who was preparing him to begin the balancing of his accounts. So much effort was put into his conversion, and so much light was given by other spirits, that the bandit of yesterday is the paralyzed girl today. So much running around to commit horrific crimes, that today he cannot move and cannot speak; the one who yesterday spoke to issue death sentences.

"The anguished grandfather, who visits his granddaughter (who does not recognize his victim of yesterday), is the one who wanted to be his redeemer; a spirit of love, a spirit of light that will always follow him, until he is converted into a superior being. [100]

"Much more I will tell you about the love of this spirit that is an envoy

---

[99] The so-called guardian angel of the religions according to the spirits themselves is a spirit of a higher morality that has elected to watch over another of a lower level. The spirits teach there are separate created beings as angels, demons or devils. All spirits were created ignorant and then after many reincarnations they develop, learn and progress themselves from spirits of low ignorant moral/intellectual levels to higher and higher levels. Very morally superior spirits have been perceived as angels, and spirits of evil intent have been perceived as demons or devils in many beliefs and religions throughout history. No matter how perverse a spirit may be, it will eventually elevate itself and come to realize that only by being good and progressing, will it lessen its suffering and find happiness. Yet, progress is very slow, each spirit progressing at their own pace; that is why we see so many people at different levels of development. We are all on our own individual spiritual journey!

[100] The current grandfather was the spirit of the girl that the bandit had murdered.

of God in order to improve a guilty one, since the sickest are the ones who most need the celestial doctors."

"Goodbye."

Ms. Soler:

How beautiful is the mission of the spirits that love! If it were not for them, what would become of those on earth, since most of us have such a horrible history? Blessed are the spirits that love and blessed also those who are loved!

CHAPTER THIRTY-THREE

THE ALARM CLOCK

Ms. Soler:

Victor Hugo has said that "eyes do not see God, but through tears," and it is a great truth. In the midst of happiness, thought is not elevated, neither little nor much, the soul is content with what it has before itself; either a horizon without limits or a piece of sky within the reach of our eyes. They say nobody remembers Saint Barbara until it thunders; and that is sad, but it's true. [101] This gives a very poor idea of who we are as terrestrials, but before the facts you have to bow your head, and declare yourself defeated.

Reading *The Latin World* (El Mundo Latino), I noticed an item that I copied, and continued:

An Italian correspondent reports a terrible tragedy in Castellamare in the following manner:

Pascuale and Carolina Sarrubbo, distinguished young persons of wealthy position married yesterday.

Last night, when the happily married newlyweds had gathered in the bridal chamber (on the second floor of the old palace of Mosca), the floor of the room sunk, and among the rubble, the newlyweds fell to the room on the ground floor, where a lady and two children slept. This resulted in

---

[101] Patron Saint of artillery and mining; legend has it her father was killed by lightning and therefore her name is invoked against it.

them being seriously injured, and Carolina was left dead in the arms of her unharmed husband.

Ms. Soler:

What a painful wedding night!... What had these unfortunate people done yesterday? A terrible history, which must have such a moving episode; for, a spirit tells me:

Spirit communication:

"Yes, they have one; and for useful teaching, copy down the narrative that I will give you in broad strokes. Carolina and Pascual in their previous existence were father and son; Pascual was the father and Carolina the son. They belonged to the highest nobility, were knights safeguarded by the king, and spent more time in the palace of the monarch than in their stately home. Pascual was the most prideful noble of his epoch and he placed all his hopes in his only son, his heir, in his beloved Carlos, the most smiling and flattering of hopes, having the firm conviction that he would be married to some infanta [102] related to the reigning monarch of his nation. However, as proud as Pascual was with his shields of nobility and his family tree, his castles, privileges and all the greatness of his illustrious lineage, his son Carlos was of simple, humble and carefree ways given that he hated palatial parties and enjoyed only dealing with his numerous servants. In particular, a young girl who grew up by his side, daughter of a ranger, with whom since childhood, they climbed trees to get nests and eat ripe fruits. They took long walks in the woods and they were always seen together, the same in the mornings of spring as in the nights of winter.

"Pascual had not noticed these two adolescents, yet knowing his son needed a lot of air and a lot of sun to develop his weak body.

"Carlos turned twenty years old, and his very happy father called to him and told him, 'My son, God has listened to my prayers, you are going to form part of the royal family, a niece of the king has deigned to

---

[102] Title given the daughters of the rulers of Spain.

fix her eyes on you, and when the monarch arranges it, a marriage will be celebrated with the infanta Elena.'

"Very contrarily, Carlos said, 'But Sir, you already know my desires, I prefer the life in the country. I choke in the palaces, there is no air for me to breathe. Also, I do not like the infanta Elena; for me to get married, I want to love my wife and I would never love Elena. She is very prideful, very domineering and I do not want to be a toy for a woman, even if this one was born on the steps of a throne.'

"Pascual was amazed at the response of his son and took note right away that Carlos wanted another woman, but hid his suspicions. He put spies onto his son, who told him a few days later that Carlos loved the humble and simple Anita, the ranger's daughter who had been raised with him since very young.

"Pascual upon learning that his son loved a commoner, became angry, he called Carlos and told him, 'I know everything, Anita's life depends on you. If you accede to my demands, I will give her a good dowry and I will marry her to someone in her class. If you persist with your crazy passions, I will confine her in a convent and I will send you far away from here until you recover your reason. I'd rather see you dead than see you married to a woman unworthy of you.'

"Carlos, whose health was very delicate, felt mortally wounded by the mandate of his father, but wanting first of all to free Anita from confinement in a convent. He gave up, and told his father, 'Give Anita a dowry with generosity and I will do your will.'

"The father fulfilled what was promised and gave Anita a great dowry. Yet, Carlos, hurt in the depths of his heart (meanwhile his father prepared a sumptuous palace), felt faint, and as he desired to die, a few days before his wedding he delivered his soul to God, in his final moments calling for his idolized Anita (the companion of his childhood). And she, when Carlos died, entered a convent dying before professing. Pascual arranged a luxurious funeral for his son, and between seeing him dead or married to Anita (the humble daughter of the town), preferred the death of his heir before dishonoring their heraldic coat of arms with a marriage so unequal.

"Feelings were asleep in Pascual; his son, seeing him in the spirit world, made an agreement with his unforgettable Anita. He proposed to return to Earth electing that the father of yesterday be his wife of today. Since

Pascual did not know how to mourn his son, he would undergo the test of awakening his feelings at the moment of being his. Pascual was not bad, he was only vain and proud, and it was necessary to awaken his feelings, for this purpose there is no more powerful alarm than the pain we feel for our dearest affections.

"Pascual, as he shook his wife's corpse in his arms, felt what he had never felt in his previous existences, his feelings have been violently disheartened, and he has wept with the most immense grief (the man who rejoiced at the death of his son before seeing him united to a commoner). Today, he weeps with tears of blood, the loss of a beloved woman [his newlywed wife]. He has heard the alarm clock of all time, he has heard the voice of infinity that calls him to judgment, and from now on he will not prefer parchments to virtues. In this sad episode, the sentiments of a soul that slept in the midst of its earthly riches has been awakened, and children who were wounded [in the accident] had been the spies of the love of Carlos and Anita.

"For all, there is what's deserved, since there is no debt that is not paid or deadline that is not met.

"The awakening of a soul is a great event, because from a sensitive one, good works can be expected; while of a spirit puffed up with its riches, one cannot get from it more than the coldness of its selfishness and its petulance.

"So, the alarm clock of the centuries' ring, even if souls weep when they wake up, for the man who does not cry does not see God. We have to cry a lot to see the rainbow that is formed by our tears, and in that rainbow is where God is seen.

"Blessed are those who cry, because they will be comforted.

"Goodbye."

Ms. Soler:

The spirit is right; pain is the great alarm clock of humanity. The spirits that sleep, are like dry trees, and for them to reanimate they must be watered by their crying, due to pain.

Translator's Note: Summary of a history of nobility

One may question as to why there appears to be so many nobles or nobility mentioned in the stories of this book. However, the history of the region (the Iberian Peninsula) reveals there were so many small individual kingdoms (including all with their own nobility) living throughout the land before Spain even became one country. The Visigoths (5th to 8th century) had numerous feudal kingdoms ruled by medieval monarchs; the Muslims (Moors) conquered the Peninsula by 720 and ruled for about 800 years and had separate kingdoms, emirates, and taifs (Muslim principalities) that had their own emirs, caliphs, dukes, nobles and knights, and, ancient royal bloodlines existed (with ties to the royal houses of Europe).

In addition, there were also lower-level nobles around the 12th century called the Hidalgos (translation, "son of something" in Castilian Spanish). Some were wealthy and owned land, but some were poor. A person could be granted this type of nobility due to a special accomplishment, having a profession or having performed a special task.

Even when King Ferdinand II of Aragon and Queen Isabella I of Castilla (known as the Catholic Monarchs) married in 1469, they continued to rule their separate kingdoms for many years, working together to rid the Iberian Peninsula of the Moors with support of feudal lords in other kingdoms. In 1492, they took over the last Moorish city of Granada. Yet, it could be said that the very first monarch was King Charles I in 1516 to rule in totality what is considered now Spain.

CHAPTER THIRTY-FOUR

JOHN TOMORROW

(Juan Mañana)

Spirit Communication:

"When a thought or an impression inclines you to correct a defect or the fury of a passion, be it in word, work or purely mental work, never wait for tomorrow to correct yourself, but do it at that moment, immediately, because by waiting you could find yourself on the day of your transformation [103] and then you will have to suffer the consequences of your laziness to act.

"Many, think and say, 'When I see my hour is close and notice signs that the end of my existence is approaching, I will make a resolution. This is a wrong way to think! Each day you receive warnings through impressions that the spirits cause you to feel, and also physical pains that indicate that your organism is losing its energies and that you are approaching the time to render accounts.

"If you take advantage of these warnings and are swift in acting well, instead of maintaining your flaws, you will have paid for at that moment, a portion of your debts and your responsibilities, they will be extinguished, with what you worthily prepared yourself for, that solemn hour when death presents itself.

"If many would work in the way I have indicated, they would not find themselves in compromised situations when the deadline comes. However,

---

[103] Your physical death and your spirit's return to the spirit world

the majority of you think and say, 'Yet, there is still time, and although physical pains cruelly torment me, I will endure it with courage.' Bravery that would be better used, and be of greater benefit in your resistance; for you try to distract yourself and say...tomorrow ... tomorrow can be the beginning of my improvements, today is too early.' Then you continue with the same impure desires, dreaming about enjoyments that afterwards bring untold misfortunes."

Ms. Soler comments:

This is what a spirit told a fellow-believer, and in truth, what this spirit says from beyond the tomb is reasonable. We always leave for tomorrow the fulfillment of good works. On the other hand, we rush to think badly of our neighbor, for that, we are so diligent!... Yes, we are so occupied with our murmuring and what others are thinking (our tongues are silenced by admonition, and advice from the spirits). We work tirelessly censoring the actions of others, and how many times do we call indolent and lazy those that surround us; and we are the first to leave for tomorrow, what we should be doing today!...

Spirit communication continues:

"Don't get tired of writing about this topic (a spirit tells me), everything that is said in reference to this matter is small in comparison to the serious damage that this vice produces (that seems even insignificant) of leaving for tomorrow the work that should be done today. What are a few hours on the watch of Time, if you let unproductive hours and days pass by, you say, yawning indifferently? There are so many days in front!... Yes, there are many days, but each day has its work marked out, and when that work is not executed, an imbalance of life begins for who do not realize it.

"Unfortunately, I know it from experience. I have been my own victim; for tomorrow, has been my condemnation (I will not say eternally) because never is the punishment superior to the fault. Yet, it is enough to suffer lamentable stagnation, not only in one existence, but in various incarnations. I have always arrived everywhere an hour later then when I should have arrived, and in that hour, at times, there have developed so many dramas! Dramas? Even worse. Tragedies!

"In my last existence, laziness was my most primary defect. An only son, my parents loved me so much they did not know how to fight my indolence; afraid to lose me they let grow up without correcting my wrongful condition. As they had enough to live on, they did not distress about thinking of my future, which they believed was completely assured; that is why I reached twenty-one years old knowing only the first rudimentary of an elementary education. A brother of my father, captain of a merchant vessel, a practical man and very knowledgeable about life, spoke very plainly to my parents, painting for them with the blackest of colors of my future. My mother, who adored me, never ceased to comprehend that I was completely lazy, useless for all study and all manual work. She tried to make amends for her mistake, although too late, by giving me to the brother of my father, so that he could make of me a man of profit.

"I undertook the first trip and changed quite a lot of my ways of being, seeing around me excellent men who worked all day, obedient and happy. My teacher [my uncle] was obliged with the work of teaching me to read and write correctly, not ceasing in his effort, despite my inherent laziness; which always impelled me to leave for tomorrow, what I could do today with time left over.

"It had been one year I was traveling. When I was in Marseille, I received a letter from my mother telling me to immediately put myself on the road because my father was gravely ill. His brother could not leave his vessel at the moment, and I strode alone to walking to the family home; but halfway down the road, I wanted to rest for the night, leaving for tomorrow the continuation of my journey. The next day, a wheel broke from the post-chaise [104] that was to drive me to my parents' house. So, I lost another day because it did not occur to me to look for another vehicle. When I arrived at my father's home, I found present the body of my father, and my mother completely desperate telling me bitterly, 'Now collect the fruits of my criminal disdain for you, surely you have not come directly, for you have entertained yourself along the way.'

"I confessed my faults, and my mother recriminated me so harshly that for the first time, I was ashamed of myself. I stopped traveling to

---

[104] Horse-drawn carriage for mail and passengers

accompany my mother, and to manage the fortune that my father had left. However, my indolence and my inactivity were so much (leaving for tomorrow the most urgent matters) that my fortune began to diminish in such a way that my mother was seriously alarmed. To see if my activity would awaken, she arranged for a marriage with a very good young woman who fell madly in love with me, and I with her. However, my love was not sufficient in uprooting my major defect; I was still as lazy as before.

"I had to take a long trip because my father's brother called me to his side to give me all his savings, since he sensed he was dying. My fiancée, during my absence, entered a convent, swearing that it would be either God or me. My journey should have lasted a year, but due to my laziness I left various matters for tomorrow. After having fulfilled to my old teacher of closing his eyes and leaving him in his grave, I let the departure of a ship pass by and lost six months without being able to board because there was no ship to sail to my country; when I was willing to deal with and finish all my matters, I fell slightly ill and did not try to combat that evil, so I lost the opportunity to embark again. As always, I told myself, 'I will write tomorrow.'

"My mother and my betrothed cried over my death, and when I finally arrived at my home without having advised them of my arrival, I found out from the servants that my mother was at the church of the convent crying, where my betrothed had taken her vows that day. That unhappy woman, upon hearing of my return, threw herself into the street from the highest top of the bell tower. She did not want to live without me, and my mother was so affected by my arrival (and with the death of the poor nun), that in a few days she [died] and entered the cemetery. I remained in such a state (without losing all of my reason) that I was not useful even to myself. My possessions completely disappeared, handed over to stranger's hands. I was left to beg for my living, and mocking me, many told me, 'Come back tomorrow.' I went hungry and thirsty. I found myself with nowhere to shelter; and so, I lived for many years in the greatest destitute, listening to the mockery of the boys that would tell me, 'You did not eat today? You will eat tomorrow.'

"Nobody ever worried about me. I did not deserve it!...

"I lost my name and surname, and they put on me the nickname of Juan Mañana.

"When the street children saw me pass by, they yelled, 'Where are you going, Juan Mañana?' I would recover for a few lucid moments my ideas, and I suffered much remembering my youth; in which I was so loved, so respected, so attended to. And, all of it was my work! I had loving parents, a teacher of good faith who wanted to make of me a man of profit. I had a woman who loved me so much that she preferred death than to live separate from me. I had a sufficient fortune to live moderately to enjoy all the joys of earthly life.

"I did not have any physical defects, and although in my childhood I did not enjoy robustness, in my youth I acquired the necessary development to be what you call a good tall, slender, vigorous young man. I was a sympathetic being, therefore, met all the combined conditions to be relatively happy, and instead, I was profoundly miserable.

"And, all of it was my work...! Even to die, I was too lazy to go to the hospital, and I said, 'I will go tomorrow.' In the doorway of a dilapidated house, where several beggars would meet every night, there I exhaled my last breath, [my spirit] stayed with my remains until the gravediggers came. When they arrived at the cemetery, they brutally threw me, (saying one to the other), 'We'll bury it tomorrow, that would give him pleasure, since that poor one left everything to do for tomorrow.'

"How hurtful, that cruel mockery was for me!... Thanks, that no one lacks of those who love them; for my parents were responsible in removing me [my spirit] away from the cemetery. There my body was left unburied upon which abundant rain fell, as if compassionate clouds cried in the face of so much misfortune. When I realized my true state, I made a firm proposal to make amends. My current job being to follow those lazy ones [in the material world] and inspire in them the greatest activity, associating myself gladly to all those who want to work for the good of Humanity.

"I have lost so many centuries!... I've squandered so many material and intellectual assets!... I have been the owner of so many treasures! ... And, all for what? In my last existence, to be the laughingstock of the people and to carry the nickname of Juan Mañana! The one who in another century, wrote his name with letters of gold in the great book of history! How one falls, when one becomes a toy of one's vices!... It is true that I have lost nothing of what I have gained; that tomorrow when I return to the Earth, I will be a tireless worker. I will make the night the day, and I will take advantage of my acquired knowledge to be both artist and philosopher, historian and great politician; all manifestations of human knowledge will seem too few to use in my existence, and I will be a model of activity and generous initiatives.

"How pleased I am to dream of my tomorrow! I will be great among the greats! Wise among the wise! Good among the good!

"Goodbye!"

Ms. Soler:

Enclosed within the communication that I just received is a great teaching. If I was not stingy of time, if I did not believe that we should not leave for tomorrow what we can do today, the story of this spirit, or better said, one of the chapters of the story of this spirit, would have served for me to put into practice one of the virtues of the Christian doctrine: hard work - the opposite of laziness.

If each day has its own concern, each day we must leave finished, the work that concern demands, leaving free all hours of the following day, because already they will come new concerns to take possession of.

There is an old adage that says, 'keep from eating and don't know what to do', and it is true, because increasing of work generates fatigue and the tired worker does not do good work. In order to work with relative perfection, one has to have accumulated strength, lucidity of ideas and physical agility, and that is only achieved by orderly arranging work, giving with eagerness every day to all the activities that we can dispose of, to be able to say when reaching nightfall (and giving ourselves rest), 'Lord, if time is gold, today I have taken from that mine all the veins that I have been able to, to enrich myself in talent and in virtues.'

CHAPTER THIRTY-FIVE

ON A BED OF FLOWERS

Everyone in this world has their consuming passion, and mine undoubtedly is with flowers, all of them appearing beautiful and enchanting to me. When the fruit trees' branches bend due to the weight of their fruit, it causes me the greatest of impressions. My favorite trees are of almond which are the first to bloom; and they have always captivated my attention in such a way that I will never forget a hundred of these trees that I saw in Tarrasa, their branches covered with white little flowers. The next year, I returned to the same place and upon seeing that all the almond trees had disappeared, I felt such an acute pain in my heart; as if at that point I was thinking of finding a loved one and he had made a trip to eternity. I had to make a great effort to not cry bitterly. All year I had dreamt of that oasis, only to find a desert in place of a flowery forest. What a tremendous sorrow I experienced! Next to my house is a garden that has many fruit trees, and when these are covered with little flowers, I spend delightful moments contemplating those rows of flowers because looking at the flowering trees from a certain height, it seems completely a network of flowers held in the air by invisible threads.

One afternoon, I stared at that paradise in miniature. I saw over the branches covered with flowers, that a slight mist spread. This condensed and formed into the ideal slender figure of a vaporous white woman, covered with a wide transparent tunic that one could see a luminous body. She was a beautiful woman, her splendid hair as soon as it appeared seemed formed by golden threads, or it was a charming cloak that floated; and when floating, those abundant curls seemed that they gave off a brilliant rain from those luminous strands.

That lovely apparition did not dissipate quickly, I saw her with sufficient time so that beautiful figure stayed photographed in my mind, and I would see her both day and night. I have seen her in my dreams, the same as awake. How precious she is!... Her face is so sweet; so pleasing! I could not comprehend of what material her organism was composed of, because all her being was transparent; she carried within her a soft light. Under her skin was a clarity that changed colors so quickly that the delicate shades of pink scattered their color as the dawn, and reflections of a pale blue increased the beauty of that enchanting apparition.

One night, I saw her in my sleep and I observed that she carried in her righthand ribbons of different colors; the ribbons, as if they were taken by invisible hands, that interlaced and formed some letters that read Rosablanca. I woke up, and a sweet voice murmured, 'Rosablanca'. From then on, I knew that the spirit wanted to communicate with me, and I waited to be in a condition of repose as possible, so as to transmit the least imprecise of her inspirations. She presented herself, and the spirit of Rosablanca had waited without showing impatience, since the angels cannot be impatient.[105] How much I feel, I cannot convey to paper what Rosablanca inspires in me! She is all light, and in me there is so much shadow! However, it will be partly supplemented by my goodwill. Rosablanca smiles compassionately, she looks at me fixedly and speaks, but her voice is so sweet and so muffled, it's such a distant murmur, that it barely resonates vaguely in my ears, that a special languor (pleasant state of calmness) takes ahold of me and I let the pen run over paper. Run? It is not the word. Slide? Neither of those is the word, since I wrote very slowly.

Spirit communication:

"Amalia, chronicler of the poor, humble troubadour of the unfortunate, all to be relayed must not be bitter; a flower also has to sprout among so many thorns. I am that flower; I, who solely live to love. Do you like my name? In my last existence they called me Rosablanca, and my body was as

---

[105] A morally superior spirit

delicate as those beautiful flowers in your gardens; the fruit of some lovers that could not legitimize me due to absurd laws, my mother for being of royal stock and my father a poor gardener. The latter, obedient to the orders of my mother, placed me in a beautiful wicker basket, covered me with flowers and left me in the palace gardens of a wealthy businessman whose wife was sterile in body and soul. Poor Eloía! To awaken her dormant sentiments, I descended to Earth.

"The hues of dawn illuminated the horizon, when the woman who was to be my adoptive mother, after a night of insomnia, rose up feverishly seeking tranquility from her fatigue, and crossed the gardens that surrounded her dwelling; an enchanting forest where the most delicate flowers covered the earth that linked to the trunks of the flowering trees, forming a truly lovely vault, surrounded by a small lake whose margins shaded trees of greenery. There, Eloía sought refuge fleeing from herself.

"Allowing herself to fall on a shell of mother-of-pearl, her eyes noticed my little cradle, she screamed and I let out a groan. Then, that woman, hitherto disinherited from the purest joys of motherhood (she hated children fiercely, for her being a fruitless tree) she leaned over my cradle, impatiently removed the flowers that covered me. When she saw my little body, which looked like a bubble, a cup of white foam, she felt what she had never felt before. On looking upon me, I extended my arms, and my crying and moaning seemed to say, 'Love me!' She, dominated by an unknown emotion, I squeezed against her breast, and without knowing what she was doing, she screamed with amazement, with joy, with immense joy. She called for her servants and soon I was surrounded by pages and maidens. No one missed examining my crib, and in it they found a small parchment on which my mother had written, "Rosablanca." They put Rosablanca on my baptismal font, and Eloía lived only for me; her husband looked at me with indifference, but he never opposed the demonstrations of tenderness of my adoptive mother (that woman who had hated children, she, who had never noticed the looks on beggars). However, to please me, for seeing me smile and enjoying my tender caresses, founded an asylum for orphans and a hospital for the elderly which still exists, and is supported by the income of an allowance that Eloía left for such a noble purpose.

"Eloía, in other incarnations, had been my rival; had made me suffer horrible persecutions and we had been what were called implacable enemies by having different political and religious ideals, and belonging to families who hated each other with that hatred of different races that have caused so many victims on the planet. I, more fortunate than Eloía, worked with ardor on my progress, because the call to love inflamed my being, and in loving much, one progresses a lot. So, when I saw my old enemy within the wrapping of a sterile woman, who at this time was a disgrace and more than enough reason to be thrown out of the bridal chamber. On seeing her so miserable, so selfish, so inclined towards wrongfulness, I said, my God!... I want to go to Earth to start a good project to disperse the feeling in a being that has known nothing but hate; and my efforts were crowned with the happiest success.

"Eloía would hold me in her arms, fill me with caresses. She looked at me enraptured, and when she saw me so beautiful, she considered me as a supernatural being. Much more so when during the night, I would hold her around the neck and say, I want you to be very good, and when I leave the Earth, I want to present myself before God and say, 'I have redeemed a soul, receive me in your glory.' I would say this while asleep. I arrived at the age of fifteen, my beauty was an amazement to those around me, each day that passed, the affections of Eloía increased towards me. The love of the Earth offered me its tributes, everyone told me that I was very beautiful, lovely, but no man attracted my attention, because I loved a spirit to whom I owed my progress to, and with it, I conversed in the little flower grove where they left my crib.

"That was my favorite place, there I saw the beloved of my heart, with him I spoke, with him I smiled, with him formed I venturous plans for the future. One afternoon, I left as usual to my flower bed, while Eloía visited the arrival of patients by my direction. I became dominated by the beginning sleep of my beloved spirit, and enveloping me with his mantle of light, he told me, 'Your banishment is finished because you have redeemed a soul that needs to lose you to purify itself through pain. Come, my love! Leave your bed of flowers, that in my arms another bed you will find better; leave from the place where you appeared with your beautiful envelope. Eloía will cry over it, and her crying will be the divine baptism that will sanctify her. Come, Rosablanca, leave your petals on Earth and with your essence you will perfume the infinite.' [106]

"Upon hearing such sweet words, I felt immense pleasure, but one mixed with pain, because the suffering that my separation would cause Eloía disturbed my celestial bliss. More so, my work was finished, not a second more could I remain on this planet, and without agony, without fatigue, without any suffering, I separated from my envelope [physical body], which I left in a flower bed. My body did not have the slightest alteration, on my face the sweetest smile, my open eyes waited for Eloía's kisses to close with the pressure of her lips. This one came joyfully to tell me how well she had employed her time; she quickly believed that sleep had subdued me when I did not come out to meet her, she wanted to wake me up with her caresses, as usual, and when convinced that my sleep was eternal, her pain had no limits. She would have searched consolation to her immense grief in death, if my spirit had not given her instructions and advice, so her sad existence would be less painful. [107]

"A monumental tomb guarded my remains, and for many years, on the green moss that surrounded my grave gushed flowers forming letters to passersby - Here are the remains of a White Rose! ... Eloía, without making religious vows, became a sister of charity, curing lepers and those with the plague, and when her strength was missing, she would come to my grave and there she heard a voice saying, 'You will find Rosablanca in a flower bed, those flowers do not want Rosablanca to wither, water them with your weeping, and when you return to the Earth, Rosablanca will choose you as a mother and your arms will be a bed of flowers.'

"I will fulfill the promise, Eloía will be my mother when we can unite ourselves with those sweet bonds with which the spirits unite in this world, and we will form a blessed home that in reality will be a flower bed.

"Do not be saddened by your helplessness, Amalia. You have goodwill, and with it you will throw down productive seed which in turn will offer you a bed of flowers."

---

[106] Rosablanca, a spirit of goodness, knew her mission on earth and was in constant conversation with her spirit guide that now came for her at the time of her departure from the Earth.

[107] She spoke to Eloía's spirit in the spirit world, so she would not commit suicide, when her physical body was asleep.

Ms. Soler:

The communication by Rosablanca to me is of great value. Good spirit, you are right, among the thorns, a flower has sprouted. Blessed be Rosablanca; blessed be your inspiration! [108]

---

[108] This chapter makes clear Ms. Soler was a medium; apparently, she could see, hear and receive spirit communications directly, but based on her autobiography it seems she was primarily an inspirational medium.

CHAPTER THIRTY-SIX

AMPARO

Ms. Soler:

Speaking some time ago with the spirit that most guides me in my work, referring to funeral prayers, obituary notices, he told me among other things the following: [109]

Spirit communication:

"Do not give away virtues they did not have, to those who leave. Speak only of the good qualities they possessed without increasing their number or diminishing the sum of them. Speak on solid ground, with knowledge of cause, about one single virtue if he did not possess the aforementioned, but do not take out for public auction weaknesses and defects. For what? Is it necessary perhaps for you to bring out bitterness of their crimes or errors? No; unfortunately, earthlings are condemned (with rare exceptions) to forced labor. You carry the shackles of imperfection, and the chains of crime link each one to the other like the convicts in your prisons, the only difference is that they can see their heavy iron chains and your chains cannot be seen; but perhaps (and perhaps not) they are much stronger and more difficult to break.

"The plan of a crime is not made without immediately finding out who supports it, who seconds it, who sponsors it, who will employ all his

---

[109] Also, regarding eulogies.

cunning to overcome difficulties and leave expedited, the path assassins or swindlers will have to follow. On the other hand, to do a good work, to facilitate the dissemination of an invention which has countless benefits to a town or a nation, how unfortunate the inventor!... How many difficulties! How many obstacles! How many barriers he finds on his rugged road!... Everyone laughs at him! Everyone thinks he is crazy!... Even his most intimate friends, own families, are those who throw firewood at the bonfire of the ridiculous, in which they want to sink a man, superior to the general majority. The wise man or philanthropist, who loves his fellowman with a love that is higher than the abilities and sensitivities of the common masses, is morally crucified if the barbarism of his contemporaries does not get his body destroyed, for recreation and the satisfaction of human ingratitude.

"There are still plenty of murderers, the envious, the hypocrites, the hoarders of wealth, the moneylenders without hearts, those who only think of themselves. Why increase the catalog of human vices and put them in relation with those who left the Earth with the vices they had? If, those who shared the hazards of life one day with you, had in their frivolities a delicate thought, if they were moved by the nakedness of a child or an old man, if they trembled before the desperate woman who sold her body to receive bread or a burial for one of their beloved relatives, they would grab ahold as the shipwrecked man grabs ahold of a small board. So, grab to yourselves to that virtue in the corolla (the petals of a flower) and make its petals open so that its intoxicating perfume exhales to the ambience and that delicate essence serves as a teaching for the ones on Earth. At the same time, as comfort for the spirit, that in the midst of its many vices it had one virtue, because it will see that the only feeling that ennobles it is a star whose pale light gently illuminates the dark path of its eternal life.

"Do not tire of circulating to the four winds the happy new virtue that perhaps for many went completely unnoticed. Therefore, in your obituary never use hypocritical praise for which one was not worthy to be praised for, but open the book of its existence, examine all of its leaves, as you will undoubtedly find a leaf bordered with flowers, make your comments on that, and do not read on any other page. For what? You will have plenty of volumes that only tell terrifying stories. Spiritists never convert into historians of crimes; from this painful and disgusting work a great number of sages have already been occupied with. You must do another kind of work, giving God what is God's, and Cesar what is Cesar's. Give silence and oblivion to the mistakes of your brothers in captivity [living on Earth] and fear not that they will be punished for the evil they did. Woe to him who lights the fire to throw one's brother in! If nobody lights it to throw it at him, he will look for the flames, he will produce the fire and he will perish incinerated.

"Yes, if the being to whom you consecrate your memories had only a single virtue, talk about it simply; goodness is endorsed by itself. Be the historians of good works, since you have plenty of historians for cruel tyrants and brutally oppressed peoples."

Ms. Soler:

Following the beautiful counsels of the spirit of Father Germain, I am going to dedicate some lines to a woman that I have admired in silence for many years. I spent four months in her pleasant company, and I have never been able to forget this sister of our beliefs, because Amparo loved and admired everyone.

She belonged to the middle class, and married for love. When she started wearing long dresses, she left her dolls; then to be wrapped with the symbolic orange-blossom crown around her forehead, and herself wrapped in a virginal veil. Amparo was practically still a girl, when her first son embraced her neck, and told her, "My mother!"

I knew her at twenty years old after her wedding, and never have I seen in any woman with the perfect balance Amparo kept of her maternal tenderness and her conjugal love.

As a general rule, in the heart of a married woman, the immense love she gives to her children and the passionate love she lavishes on her husband do not occupy the same place. Women who want to be frank often say from their heart in the most intimate of confidence, "My children before anything!" says one. "My husband is my life!" says another, "without him, I do not care if I die" ... "But, your children?" they ask. "They have already have been raised, God will not [let them] miss anything." Only in Amparo, have I seen the two loves balanced, the conjugal and the maternal.

Her Pepe, as she would say, was always outside the house, he was a commission agent and traveled most of the year. You had to watch her the days she waited for her husband's letter; rain or windy, she waited for the postman on the balcony, like a girl in love waiting for the first love letter.

What anguish! What anxieties!... What worry if the postman was late or did not come! What horrible forebodings assaulted the feverish mind of Amparo! Already in her afflicted imagination she saw her Pepe rolling down the cliffs, not leaving a healthy body or a limb, or wrapped in whirlwinds of snow or killed in the middle of the mountains, and she cried silently with the greatest grief of the imaginary death of her husband. In the middle of that anguish, their children arrived from school, asking, 'What does Papa say?' Amparo responded, feigning the best of tranquility, 'The postman has not yet come, it is because I erred about the date; not until tomorrow or more there will be no letter.' Therefore, this drove away fear from the minds of her children, all fear and suspicion; and the same when she was happy as when she trembled before her terrible visions. Whenever they went to school, she would go to the balcony and they would say goodbye to her with their loving looks, until the children turned around a far corner. No more tenderness could be asked for by her children, no more tender care, more solicitous efforts, nor more love for her husband; you could not ask for more from a woman on Earth. Speaking with her I learned much more; in no one have I seen so admirably balanced in economy and spending. Amparo saved on superfluous expenses to accustom her children to be generous, and to look at the poor as their younger brothers. There were several beggars who collected alms at their home, and in particular children. Amparo would say to the children, "Do not be content with giving them half your lunch and some broken toy, invite them to play with you. Poor little ones! Do you not see that face so happy when you treat them with love?"

I remember one afternoon while walking, we found a little boy who went daily to Amparo's house. The boy, accustomed to playing with the youngest child, approached his familiar playmate and tapped him on the shoulder; the other, who was wearing his new suit, looked at him disdainfully. Amparo noticed it and did not say anything then, but when she returned home, when she undressed her son, she told him simply, "Pepe, you will not wear this suit anymore."

"Why?" he asked in an angry voice

"Because it makes you wrongful; I have already seen that you have looked at the poor boy with whom you play every day with contempt when you are at home. Then, you're not the wrongful one, it is the suit that makes you proud, and I do not want my children to reject the poor."

In this way, she educated her children without annoying sermons, without violent quarrels, on the contrary, she was the inseparable companion of her children. She went out daily with them so that they could enjoy a break, she made life pleasant for all those around her. There are very good people who are only good for their family, but Amparo was good for everyone. She had a special grace to comfort the unfortunate and she was so modest and was such any enemy of drawing attention in any way, that she did good, for good itself.

When I separated from her, I felt a pain without a name. I felt cold in my soul, very cold, my spirit felt that I would never find another woman on Earth like Amparo; in fact, my feelings were well-founded ... How could they not be? This world is not a place of perfect beings, and I could not, a poor prisoner of this planet, be in relationship with beings like Amparo. I knew it as a special grace, maybe because at that time I needed my spirit to be very close to the light ... So much of a shadow enveloped me!... So many sorrows tormented me!... I found myself so alone on Earth! Amparo did everything she could to keep me at her side, she had for me, the sweetness of a mother, the benevolence of a sister, the sweet compassion of a true friend, but I walked away from her convinced that my spirit was not worthy to live along side of Amparo.

Ms. Soler final comments:

Many years had passed; I had always tried to make sure [I knew] what Amparo was doing, and some time ago, I found out with deep sorrow that she was immensely miserable!

Her Pepe, that man she had loved so much (after twenty years of marriage of waiting for his letters with the ecstasy of a woman in love) the companion of her dreams, of her fantasies, to whom she surrendered in her mind true adoration, that man so beloved, spurned his wife's immense love, turned to superficial love and morally killed the mother of his children.

. She, who had made her children see in their father the most perfect man in the land. morally killed the mother of his children.

Poor Amparo, how much she has suffered!... How immense must have been her despair!... What such a terrible debt she must have had to pay in this existence! Perhaps her spirit has great virtues to resist heroically such a terrible test, because in the way that Amparo loved her husband, to be convinced of his infidelity, she would have needed an unknown moral force in this world to not kill that unfaithful one or die violently; because death was undoubtedly preferable to the abandonment of that beloved man... What energies she must have needed to put forth, to not die of heartache!... In the end, she died in the arms of her children. Yes, Amparo asked in this existence for the settlement of a terrible account. [110] How happy she will be, of herself! How well she has fulfilled all her obligations! She is the woman in whom I have seen more virtues gathered. If there was only one existence, one would have to go crazy seeing so much injustice in the rewards and punishments of this world; but no, the same inequality observed in human events shows that an existence is a page detached from the book of life, in which there is neither prologue nor epilogue of the history of a spirit. It is nothing else than a chapter, where a few, more or less interesting actions, are worked out.

Amparo! Not out of curiosity, not for a trivial desire to know something about your history, I ask you to inspire me or my spirit guide so that this one can tell me the debt you have had to pay in your last existence. We desire to know and study those great pains, those pending accounts since the night of the centuries.

You deserve to be loved by all for your virtues; because they were very good, good within your home struggling with a thousand hardships, and good for your friends and generosity for the unfortunate. You read in the soul of those who suffered and gave the medicine of your affection with your touch, with care, with a truly maternal care, and you... have had to suffer the pain that would hurt you the most!... So many wounds you have healed with your tenderness, and you had to receive the stinging dart of contempt, of the abandonment of the one who was your God! Your religion!

Oh Amparo! Speak! Yes, speak, it would be as useful as when you were

---

[110] No response was received to our knowledge, yet, Amparo fulfilled her life's obligations and paid "the settlement of a terrible account" as Ms. Soler stated due to the many virtues that Ms. Soler saw in her and felt the need to write about them.

here on Earth. It is necessary to understand why one cries when one least expects it, and when one seems less deserving of misfortune.

Many years have passed and I have not forgotten you, show me that my memory has not been erased from your mind either.

Let us resume our friendship of yesterday, I'm far from being as good as you, but my spirit, eager for progress, is more courageous today than yesterday and asks for your assistance by your work.

Yes, Amparo; get close to me, I need you. If on Earth you cared for me, you should care even more for me from the spirit world. That is how I believe, and I trust that when you awaken [in the afterlife], you will tell me, "Amalia, listen; I present an attentive ear, and a new story I will make known of the women who suffer and cry in this world."

Amparo, I wait for you. Wake up! Wake up, and speak! It has been so long since I have spoken with you!...

CHAPTER THIRTY-SEVEN

EVERYTHING HAS ITS CAUSE!

Ms. Soler:

One of the catastrophes that most affected us are fires. Twice in our lives we have been threatened by fire, and once by water in one of the many floods that Sevilla has suffered. We were horrified more by the fire than water; and with this last one, that was rising without rest and turning the patio of our house into a wide pool where the furniture of the low rooms swam, that blackish water produced such a distressing affect in our mood, that if it had been blood, it would not have caused us as much fright. Yet, in the middle of everything, our suffering was tranquil, leaving us completely clear-thinking. Our being languished and without bewilderment we thought our death near. It seemed that we were preparing ourselves to an imposed sacrifice; we saw the fatal fulfillment of a law, and we said, like the Moslems, "It is written!" When we were free of that danger, we looked without horror at the place where we had been exposed to die ... However, when in Madrid being delivered unto sleep one night, we heard thundering voices shouting, "Fire!" The emotions we experienced... we could not find phrases to describe them. We believed that if we could have climbed up to the gallows, we would not have to suffer anymore.

When we looked over the balcony and saw the broad street full of cars that conveyed the fire engine, soldiers, firemen, an immense crowd that all shouted at the same time, we were overwhelmed in such a way that in spite of the fire not being in our abode, and a street separated us from the house caught in the flames, these seemed to envelope our very being. We saw that they were far away, and nevertheless, its terrible heat burned our insides. For this reason, for a long time, even when someone lit a match, we felt a painful emotion that we tried to hide because they would have described it as childish, but our impressionability was stronger than all our reasoning, and now we understood perfectly that perhaps we paid some debt, because without wanting to, we suffered extraordinarily.

Given these slight explanations, our readers would not miss that whenever we read the story of a fire, all our being was moved, and we felt profound compassion both for those who died by burning and for the families of the victims who will keep a terrible memory of those violent deaths, that torment and crush the body, impressing upon the spirit so deeply. For we have been assured by some spirits from beyond the grave, those that leave their envelope while in the midst of the flames, for a long time their perispirit remains in a very sensitive state (despite the fact that their ashes have disappeared from Earth), for them there still exists the devouring flame that has consumed its material envelope; so acute is the pain experienced by those who die burned. However, they have also told us, and this comforts us and we find it very logical, that often the spirit in use of its free will, even if it has a terrible debt to pay, does not settle its account until a number of affections have been created, enough for them to give it consolation in the midst of its agony so that when it dies, it is not alone fighting with its terrible pains. Friendly spirits try to move it away from the place of its torment, and as this consolation is legitimately earned, since it is the consequence the result of its good deeds, of its sacrifices, of its abnegation, this lessens its pain. [111]

It is natural, to strictly pay what is owed, but to not increase one's suffering because of what happens on Earth like two that have ruined themselves. One, for example, loses his fortune and tries through work, not to recover his riches, but to yes, not live in misery; and stifling foolish pride and vanity, is not ashamed to perform humble jobs or go to serve a master (having himself had numerous servants). Although he does not live well off, at least he suffers neither hunger nor cold nor thirst, and after some years he comes to live in a melancholy tranquility. He lives tolerably,

---

[111] We reap what we sow (based on the law of cause and effect and the law of attraction) in the material and spiritual worlds, as well as during the transition process we call "death." Each spirit's physical death experience is unique.

but not in desperation. On the other hand, he who has ruined himself and is desperate, and playing everything for the whole, mixing in illegal businesses, surrendering to fraud and all sorts of mistakes; at the end there comes a time that he lacks position to sustain himself, and holding a gun to his temple, dies cursing an existence that has not provided him nothing more than just suffering.

Well, the exact same thing happens to two spirits that have committed a crime. If the one recognizes himself guilty and he tries to make amends by asking for incarnations in order to exercise goodness, when it is time for him to suffer the pain that he made another feel, his torment will only be momentary, because the spirits that owe him a benefit will come to encourage him and comfort him. However, the rebellious spirit that after his crime increases debts to his account committing new excesses, when the time comes to pay eye-for-eye and tooth-for-tooth, finds himself alone in the midst of the shipwreck, without having even a board to grab onto, because what is not earned, is not obtained. Also, if he has to suffer martyrdom of fire, he will believe in his despair that the hell of the established religions is a reality, since he feels the tortures that the religious traditions assure that it exists in Avernus.[112]

So that is why, when some or many unfortunates die in a fire, as happens when a theater full of spectators is burned, our thought is not solely fixed at the terrible moment that flames, confusion and impatience determine the dimensions of the death to the hundreds of individuals. What horrifies us most is the tomorrow of those unfortunate ones, because we do not know what moral level they were, and we cannot calculate the relief they can find in the spirits beyond the grave.

Recently, the newspapers brought the description of a fire that occurred in Granada. The *Gazette of Catalonia*, of February 9th, said this:

"On Thursday, it had been a busy day at the home of Mr. Juan Granizo, an honest merchant of groceries on San Matías street. At ten o'clock they finished salting the pork meat, and the married couple and their eight children, four women and four men, rested on a stretcher with the love of

---

[112] A lake in an extinct volcano near Naples, Italy that in ancient times was thought to be the entrance to Hades (Hell).

the fire. At twelve o'clock, at the request of the father, the children went to bed.

"We are going to fall into bed like a stone in a well,' said the fourteen-year-old, who was very tired.

"It was two or three o'clock in the morning when a serene glow was noticed inside the store, he called, and they did not answer him. Everyone in the house was sound asleep.

"Shortly afterwards, the smoke betrayed the increase in the fire. Much later, a terrible explosion was heard and great flames appeared through the cracks of the door, so it had to be thrown down.

"Upon Granizo awakening, one could no longer leave through the door. He called for his woman, the two of them carried one child to their chest and went up to the roof where they also reunited with the two eldest boys, all being saved by the roof of the adjoining house, in nightshirts and terrified. The mother, especially, arrived in a grave state produced by the terror, and bleeding heavily, cried loudly for their children.

"The father could not speak; none could realize all that was frightening and horrible about that reality.

"Word spread in the street that there were still five children in the house, when the soldiers and the artillerymen fought the fire that threatened the adjoining houses. A few of those had climbed to save the children, but a horrible explosion forced them to throw themselves on the balconies, resulting in bruises or the wounding of three or four firemen, a soldier and a clerk at the Simaneas inn.

"The confusion somewhat passed, two men arrived after breaking a partition to the room next to the bedroom, and found the burnt corpse of Angustias, the young girl of fourteen, who fleeing death, had climbed on a shelf.

"Then it was dawn! The fire spread to the Simaneas inn from which they evicted all the guests as they could, the burning flames reaching the door of the house in front.

"In this, the main and second floors of the house had sunk and the hope of saving the other four children (whose destroyed and charred corpses were found later) was lost. The one, Encarnación of seventeen years old, had in her arms her little brother of seven. Carmen's body, an eleven-year-old girl, lacked a hand and head. All of them, except for the first one, had their legs separated from the trunk.

"The losses of the house were great because nothing could be saved. Also, the inn was all burned, except the furniture. In this, the fire devoured the library (which was very numerous) of the son of the owner and the editions of three important works of geography of the professor of the university, as well as the originals of Mr. Artero's *History of the Orient and Rome*, the fruit of great efforts, and a thousand other documents.

"Also, in Mr. Godoy's house were lost the drafts of a work of medicine that carried five years on it, many bushels of wheat, a lot of oil and a thousand other things; without counting other works and documents, the losses are calculated at 60,000 duros [dollars].

"This unfortunate disaster resulted in the five children dead, eight wounded and bruised, as well as two combat engineers, and a sick father and mother (and what is worse of their reason). When they were informed of the atrocious misfortune, they did not even understand what was being said to them. The boyfriend of one of the young ones who died, fell ill to know of the terrible news.

"They believe that the cause of the fire must have been the burning of some boxes of matches that the store owner did not keep in his tin box."

Ms. Soler:

This account painfully struck us, thinking of the parents of the victims, who undoubtedly believe that they are a joke of a terrible nightmare. Losing five children in a few seconds! Among them, three beautiful flowers in the most promising time of life. Encarnación, seventeen years old!... When perhaps she already was preparing her wedding ball! Angustias, of fourteen summers; a girl that already dreamt of losing her angel wings to become a woman! Carmen, of eleven winters, that maybe upon sleeping thought about her dolls! What a horrible awakening! And, when the more immersed we were in our reflections, the spirit that guides us in our literary works told us this:

Spirit communication:

"Do not occupy yourself solely with the facts, it is necessary that you write something about such a sad event. You know why? Because the parents of the victims need consolation, and it is indispensable to awaken their attention regarding the afterlife communications so that they can interact with the beings that they believe lost forever.

"The spirits that left their envelopes in the flames are in very good condition because they had already made great progress. They have waited to settle their terrible account for some centuries, within which they have worked tirelessly, and have formed great spiritual sympathies that have now served them to immense relief, given that they have not suffered more than those essential pains that they had to experience because, in former times, these spirits were pleased to see their fellowmen burn. Yet, do not have the slightest doubt that those terrible sinister acts that affected you so much, those gruesome fires in which the immigration of hundreds and even thousands of spirits are tested, are nothing other than (have it well understood) expiations; balances of overdue accounts, promissory notes of which you have no choice but to pay them. You can be very good, you can be a true champion of progress, but if before possessing so many virtues you have been pleased in the harming of others and have made others suffer, you have to feel their personal anguish because just as we are compensated for good desires in favor for another, the just law of compensation in the same way returns to us, moan for moan, torture for torture, pain for pain.

"When the Inquisition raised its terrible tribunal in Sevilla, the spirits who left their bodies in the fires of Granada were then in Sevilla. I know the whole story very well, because intimate ties bind them to me. In that epoch, there were women of the highest nobility of Andalucía who clapped their hands when they saw the first beams of wood burning, whose flames were to devour the infidels; with their clothes and their armor, they went ahead to the bonfire, they waved handkerchiefs, cheered the executioners and provided many victims to the Holy Office, *even from their own families!* Carried by their religious zeal, and also wanting, to erase with death, traces of their own mistakes, they persisted with the erroneous adage that a dead man does not speak.

"How many crimes mankind would have saved, if it had comprehended that death does not end after the grave, and those violent deaths do not give any other result than acquiring enormous responsibilities to those who cause them, attracting implacable hatreds that are a little less than imperishable.

"The spirits to which I refer, I have the intimate satisfaction of having worked hard in their advancement, the victory being easier, by them not being of such great perversity.

"There are spirits who when they commit crimes often do so dominated by circumstances or are subjugated by the religions that have so prevailed in humanity, to which have led them to such deep abysses.

"These spirits that today are so mournful for their relatives and friends, in actuality deserve all the feelings for them that have been awakened, because they possess great virtues and dearly love their family that they have left on Earth, so what they want is to communicate with them to calm their pain. For this, utilizing you, I tell those parents which are without consolation, 'Poor wounded souls! Listen to me! It's not so sad, it is not so horrible their current situation. Of those beautiful young women, of those lush flowers that enchanted your life, their intoxicating perfume has not been lost.' Their bodies have been charred, crushed, but their position and their perispirit (a wrapping much less gross than their material body) exists enveloping the spirit. Or better yet, assimilating beauty without having lost any of its charms; rather they have been increased because the body, however beautiful, never has the heavenly beauty of the spirit, because the material body has the first highest density. You cannot understand spiritual beauty no matter how we present it; giving your saints gleaming aureoles. Well then, that light that you imagine is a weak reflection of the luminous atmosphere that surrounds the spirits that have enhanced themselves by their immense love, not wasting opportunities to be useful to humanity.[113]

"Poor wounded souls! Your reason falters, and it is not strange, because

---

[113] Allan Kardec called the semi-material covering of the soul/spirit the *perispirit*, whether living in the material world or in the spirit world. The perispirit has been called other names such as: astral body, ethereal body, and the like. The physical body, the denser of the three, is only what dies at what we call - death. See Allan Kardec's, *The Spirits' Book* and *The Mediums' Book* for further clarifications and explanations.

seemingly you have suffered an irreparable loss. However, believe me, your pain can find a great balm if you study the Spiritist works and try to get in touch with your daughters who want to communicate with you; to comfort, encourage and fortify you. Few families are found on Earth in the special conditions that you are, because not all who leave are willing to communicate, nor all those who leave are as dear as you are. On this occasion, many circumstances are met, all favorable to take away some of your grief because if you want you can communicate with your daughters, who today, lament your grief, caress you, and murmur in your ear, Awaken! Do you not see us? Do you not feel us?

"Awaken! Do you not see us? Do you not feel us? Poor suffering souls! As much as it seems impossible, the dead live! The dead are with you! The flames consume everything less the spirit and the perispirit that serves the soul to manifest itself in the spirit world, as it serves the body to manifest itself on Earth.

"You are submerged in the darkness of pain, but the dawn of tomorrow will illuminate your horizons. Open your eyes and look! Pay attention and listen! I promise you that if you are dead in desperation, you will be resuscitated in hope.

"Nothing is impossible! What you think is outside of natural laws, really is not. The only thing that happens is that you ignore the plan and the method of those laws, which are many in Nature that escape your penetration, but that is not why they are fixed and immutable.

"Amalia, we work for the good of those sick spirits who today cry in the city of Granada, land of flowers, whose soil has been fertilized with blood and tears.

"What horrible expiations there are on that planet! But do not doubt it, they are all deserved. You are resistant to believe it is that way, but this does not stop this all from having its cause.

"I remember the last time I was on Earth I wrote great volumes that encompassed my thoughts, which constituted a treasure for me. When I was the most satisfied with the fruit of my diligent tasks, without knowing the cause the library caught fire, and in less than sixty seconds the work and vigilance of my life was all reduced to ashes. I felt very much that mishap, but I felt even more what I might have caused another to suffer, for I had a clear intuition that I had lived yesterday. Consequently, as I left the Earth and realized that I existed, when reason dominated my new state, I saw my past existences, and I immediately found the cause of the destruction of my work - since 'he who kills by the sword, dies by the sword,' I had thrown into the fire thousands and thousands of books, the fruit of long vigils bravely supported by hundreds of sages. I, in the destruction of the first library that was founded in Alexandria by Ptolemy Soter, took a very active part, and in other incarnations, I also continued to destroy the seasoned fruits of human understanding. In many existences, when I have been more reasonable, I have consecrated myself to writing, but never did my works came to see the light, always fire was responsible in destroying them - 'who does such, pays such.' He that enjoys the destruction of the greatest that there is on the Earth, which is a good library, does not deserve to have his thoughts perpetuated, these must be lost, just as a man's footprints are lost in the sand.

"Work, Amalia; do not rest for a second in spreading Spiritism, because that philosophy will be the redemption of humanity. [114] Do you know why? Because you will avoid great abuses, punishable acts of which today you suffer the consequences, because humans live very badly on Earth. Fraud seduces you. Hypocrisy flatters you. Your customs leave much to be desired and it is time you began to regenerate. Does it not fatigue you to live in the shadows? Does it not sadden to see your geniuses, who on one part arrive to the heavens of wisdom, and on the other descend until lost in an abyss of debauchery?

"The true life is more harmonious, more peaceful. Your days without calm and your nights without sleep are the result of your previous mistakes. Do not doubt it! Life was given to us for high purposes.

"Looking at the loveliness of Nature, the beauty and perfection of all its species, does it not distress you to look at the man who always has in disagreement the declarations of his intelligence with the demonstrations of his feelings?

"Study! Inquire! Question! Don't lose hours in vain pastimes, employ

---

[114] They refer to Spirit Teachings: that we are eternal souls, there is an afterlife, mediumship allows communication with loved ones on the spiritual plane, reincarnation provides us the ability to make amends, correct mistakes, make better choices and having infinite time to redeem ourselves and constantly progress (which allows us to suffer less and live happier no matter in the material or spiritual worlds).

them in useful work and you will avoid innumerable sufferings. If you were to see what different a manner you live when you walk among thistles, than when you see nothing but flowers!...

"All of the sorrowful, dream of the pardon that comes to reduce their pain. Don't you dream of a better life?"

Ms. Soler:

Yes, we dream, good spirit, and we are grateful to Providence because it allows us to communicate with you and other spirits, giving us the facility to receive your thoughts with which we link our ideas, just as the humble ivy is linked to the giant tree.

How consoling is the communication from beyond the grave! We are happy that when misfortune hurts us, we can say with intimate conviction, everything has its cause! Let's try to be good, and we will be happy!

God-willing, these lines that today we write through advice and inspiration by a spirit attracts the attention of the unfortunate family that lives at the foot of the Alhambra, doubting God and of his eternal justice!

They have been wounded in the heart for their most beloved beings. Only Spiritism can calm their grief, only the communication of those spirits that left this world suffering the pain of all the pains can make them smile. Bless the greatness of God, saying with immense jubilation, 'Death does not exist! Life radiates into infinity! How beautiful is the future of humanity! Praised be to God!'

CHAPTER THIRTY-EIGHT

SAVING

In the newspaper of Granada, we read an article entitled "What Savings Can Do," and in which the distinguished and anonymous writer, after making very good considerations about the convenience that is savings, he refers to an incident that provides a great teaching, and this leads us to transcribe the below:

"About seventeen years ago, a manufacturer in Barcelona had a very skilled worker, therefore, the highest wage earner, but very fond of wine; so much so that he used to get drunk without any means to correct himself. The manufacturer dismissed him many times, but he soon took him back again in the interest of his factory. However, the wine came to dominate the unfortunate worker in such a way that it was deemed almost impossible to keep him in the workshops, no matter how great his skill was.

"The man, in a lucid moment, understanding the reason of the owner of the factory, went to beg, but the owner only consented to receive him by a very reduced salary.

"In this way, he told him, you will not have money to go to the tavern, since what I set as salary was barely enough for you to eat.

"The worker, who except for that fatal vice was good, consented, persuaded of how much it suited him to cure himself of such an abominable habit.

"For a few months, there was nothing to reproach him for; he fulfilled his promise. But a time after that, he returned to the tavern. Although at first, he apologized for drinking, in the end he succumbed again to the vice, and returned to being drunk.

"The manufacturer called him, and presenting him with a notepad from the Savings Bank in which he had recorded the amount of ninety duros, he said, 'Jose, on my behalf this notebook represents what I have stopped paying you in order to correct yourself from the vice of the wine. [115] I see that you are once again giving yourself in to that vice, failing on your promises and proposals. I do not want you in my house, one who manifests such a weak will in fulfilling what he promises. However, this money is yours, I will endorse this to your name and you can do with your money what you want.'

"The worker was amazed and confused to learn that he owned a sum of ninety duros. The unforeseen position of such capital had a wholesome, astonishing effect for him.

"'No, no,' he exclaimed, 'you save it, keep those ninety duros as mine and bless you! There's nothing! Keep them and save them for me, and keep saving until I settle down and need them. Now I can think about getting married one day, and having my little house and children.' The worker fulfilled and kept his word. Today, he owns a factory in Catalonia whose products are sought in the market and receive awards in all exhibitions.

"Capital formed slowly by work, has been for him the basis of his independence, his health and his happiness. What would it have been worth spending it in the tavern?"

Ms. Soler:

It would have served to sink into the mud of the most complete degradation, because drunkenness is one of the vices that most brutalize and demean man.

We have always believed that saving is as necessary to us as the air we breathe, although some say that money should not be loved because those who love it become greedy. We believe that it is one thing to have greed, and another thing is to have foresight. Many mothers have the good habit of buying their children, when they are little ones, a bank, and she throws

---

[115] 1 duro equaled 5 pesetas; 60 pesetas equaled 1 US dollar

money into savings for the child so that one day it will be used to buy a beautiful toy or a nice dress.

We remember that being in Toledo we went to spend a day at a country house whose owners are an honorable matrimony with seven children. Most of the year they stayed in their beautiful country house, and according to what they said, wanted to take advantage of their children's childhood because when these get older, they would have to spend most of the year in Madrid for the children's studies.

It is a truly patriarchal family. Juan and Eloisa love each other so deeply that, despite being married for many years, they cannot live one without the other. They have been lucky, that is, they have deserved that happiness; that all their children are advanced Spiritists, obedient, affectionate, expressive so that to spend a day among them is to spend a day in Gloria [116] and we always remember the day we spent in their company in their country house in Toledo.

In the afternoon, while the children played in the garden, Juan and Eloisa thoroughly showed me the whole house, calling my attention to the children's bedroom, which was a large room where there were seven iron beds wrapped in white muslin draperies, rolled up with large bows of blue moiré ribbon.

On a chest of drawers, there were seven red money boxes of earthenware, each one with its owner's name written with white pencil, and under it a sign that said: box for the poor.

Those primitive savings banks made us happily laugh because they reminded us of our first ages. What child (if he has had a loving and farsighted mother) has not fixed his anxious gaze on one of those closed earthen vessels with a single opening as the future; which he has looked with eagerness on trying to attract with the magnetism of his gaze the treasures contained in that childhood safe? What child has not believed himself richer than Croesus [117] by dreaming of his bank? Blessed hours, moments of repose that does not happen again in an entire incarnation.

---

[116] A biblical reference; the feeling as if one were in the presence of God and/or Jesus.
[117] An ancient king of Lydia (595 B.C. – c. 546 B.C.) renowned for his wealth.

Juan relays his story:

Among the savings boxes, our attention was vividly called to see a broken bank under a glass globe on a blue velvet cushion.

"What is that?" we asked.

"My first savings bank," Juan said seriously, "The rest carry a history."

"Can we know?"

"Yes, I will relay it to you with much pleasure."

The three of us sat down and Juan started his story, saying it with an emotional voice, "I had the joy of having as a mother such a good woman, so caring, so loving of her children, that she lived consecrated to my sister and I. My father died while I was very small, and she dedicated herself to continue with the modest store of threads and silk which had been the only inheritance of my paternal grandparents. To my sister and to I, to each one was bought a very large bank, and all the money we collected from our relatives from the Christmas Passover and the Days of the Saints, we saved it in that bank. She telling us, 'Look, my children, you are well fed, you do not lack for clothes to wrap up in, you have toys to distract yourselves and books from which to instruct yourselves. Anything you could buy would be superfluous; so, keep that money for a true necessity,' and she herself put the coins in our hands and made us throw them in the bank.'

"We continued living tranquilly without any more disagreeable incidents, but for a terrible illness that my sister got on completing fourteen years old. Her convalescence was very painful, and the doctors arranged for her to travel, for a change of air and water to recover her strength. Then my mother left me in the store with her uncle, and she left with my sister; the savings serving to cover the expenses of the trip. She recovered her health and found her happiness, for she met a good young man; one that after three years became her husband.

"I, while my mother was away, being one day in the store (I would have been then seventeen years old) saw a blind man enter dressed with decency and guided by a girl of ten or eleven Aprils. This one gave me a letter from a brother of my mother, a resident in Madrid, who recommending us very specially about the poor blind man who had lost his sight working in diamonds. He wanted to go to Paris, where there was a German oculist who worked miracles (because a priest confided that he would do it for free); for that, he needed to raise money for the trip for him and his daughter. This was such a good man, that we would do for him a true charity.

"I did not know what I felt upon reading that letter. I looked at the blind man and his daughter, had them sit, and I asked them for more explanations.

"The poor sick one relayed what happened to him and the eagerness he had to recover his sight to be useful to his daughter, who was an angel of kindness. Meanwhile, the girl cried silently, knowing that it was very painful for him to be asking for charity.

"Without knowing why, seeing that moving scene, I recalled the words of my mother when she made me keep my Christmas bonuses in the store, telling me tenderly, 'Reserve that money for a true necessity.'

"Here is a true need, I said to myself, and I went up to my room for my bank, and giving it to the blind man with the greatest of joy, saying, 'Here, you have all my savings. My mother has always told me to save the money for a true necessity. What greater need than yours? Sight is life ...! God-Willing, you can live!'

"The dignified sick man in no way wanted to accept my donation without my mother's permission, but my uncle assured him that my mother would be very happy of my actions. After many entreaties, he agreed to my wishes, and he himself struck a blow to the bank, one that broke it into two pieces. We counted what it contained, and our joy was immense since there was more than 4,000 reales. [118] He took a title of loan, saying that he was convinced that he could pay it back soon (the amount that I gave him so generously).

"If I have to be frank, it was more than his misfortune that moved me; the tears of his daughter (that girl who was still mourning her mother) absorbed much of my attention, for I would not have separated from her. I made them stay to eat, and that same night they marched in the direction of Paris. The poor blind man called me son, upon squeezing me against his heart, saying to his daughter, 'Eloisa, hug your brother, your savior, for he has a father.'

---

[118] 8 reales roughly equaled one dollar. During these stories we are dealing with possibly different monetary equivalencies, currency fluctuations and an unknown time period. Nowadays, Spain uses the Euro.

"We became aware that while our friend was talking, his wife cried in silence. Immediately, we comprehended that it was she, the girl who would accompany the blind man, and then we shook hands with warmth. Juan smiled, and he continued saying, 'You have understood that this is the girl; I am happy you guessed it.'

"Well, they left, and I did not notice then, that Eloisa had kept in her handkerchief the broken bank. When my mother returned and I relayed to her what I had done, she did not say anything to me, but gave me a hug, that to me, it seems, I can still feel her sweet impression. Eloisa carried out as a woman, by writing to us all about the procedures for the healing of her father. Six months later, I saw him enter the store with his eyes full of life; that moment has been the happiest of all my existence. My mother took a very active part in my joy; as she was so good!

"As soon as I saw Eloisa, I hit it off with her, understood what that girl was worth and also recognized that I loved her. They rested at home for eight days, and on returning to Madrid, I obtained permission from my mother to accompany them.

"What a happy trip! Eloisa was never a girl, she looked like a woman, so her looks made me know that my love was reciprocated. When I returned to Toledo, the world seemed too small to contain my happiness.

"The money that my wife's father earned, in the first week that he returned to work, a third part was used in the lottery, and one morning I saw him enter with Eloisa, both radiant with joy.

"'Listen Juan,' he told me, 'When you gave me your savings, I told you that I accepted it as a loan. Today, I come to return it, here you have it with interest.' He presented me bank notes worth ten thousand five-peseta coins, for he had fallen into luck in the lottery.

"Since then, we formed a single family; that generous man did not consist in handling that money, he left it in my mother's charge as a dowry for Eloisa. He continued working, but living in our company. Being crazy about me, he was the one who kept the remains of my bank as a sacred memory. He was such a grateful spirit, that he paid me with profit for the good I did for him. When I married my Eloisa, we believed he would go crazy with joy.

"As our happiness has been due in large part to my savings bank, we have not neglected to endow our children with the same treasure, and we do our best to use their savings as my mother said, in cases of real need."

"You have a very good thought."

"Not everything is our work," said Eloisa smiling, "My father always advised me to get my children accustomed to saving."

"Well, did not your father die?"

"Yes, two years after we got married, but he comes to see me often."

"How does he see you? What are you saying?"

"Don't you know I am a Spiritist, and also a seeing and writing medium?"

"I know you were a follower of Spiritism, but I did not know that you were a medium."

""And, very good," Juan replied, "We have a book of communications obtained by her, some of which are of great value."

"Do not listen to my husband, for him everything I do is remarkable. I get purely familial communications. My father continues to advise me from beyond the grave in the same way he did on Earth; nothing more, nothing less. He is a very loving spirit of the family, linked to Juan and to me for having been our father in many existences, he goes out of his way for us."

"Ah! So that explains the action Juan took regarding him, one needs to feel much to do an act like that."

"The only thing that I will tell you is, that on seeing him, I felt what I had never felt; although in honor of the truth, the tears of Eloisa were what moved me the most. Apart from that, I loved him so much that when he died, I confess, I had more feeling than when I lost my mother; and, that same sorrow made me look for Spiritism. For me, outside of my wife and my children, I have no more pleasure than reading my father's communications because I always find something to learn in them."

"Read me some."

I did not have to tell him twice, because Juan immediately brought a luxuriously bound book, and he read us the following communication:

The Father's spirit communication:

"Savings! How well this modest store of wealth produces! How useful man can be to humanity when he reserves for it the fruit of his savings! To live thinking about the needs of others, is to live within the law of God.

"He who saves for the pleasure of saving is worthy of compassion, but he who deprives himself of the superfluous to give another a necessity, has walked half the path of glory. That has happened to you, I have collected the seed that in another time, I planted in your heart.

"I inculcated in your mind the love of saving. Who said that my work, later supported by another spirit of goodwill, would provide me with the greatest joy that I could have on Earth: the recovery of the sight of the body and to find a sensitive soul that are scarce on that planet?

"Accumulated work is a deposit of virtues; it is a savings bank that the spirit finds when it needs it most. I had to suffer the horrible test of blindness for a long time, but I had loved you very much in successive existences. I had instilled in your mind the most generous of sentiments, I had educated you with the most unveiled tenderness. I had deposited in you all the vitality of my love; that is why I found in you such a noble generosity, because it was an integral part of my being and because I had loved in your previous incarnations. For this reason, my son, I will never tire of repeating that you love your children very much, that you make your savings box like I did, because in the midst of my just expiation I found your affection and support that were part of my salvation.

"Remember the advice of your good mother, do not accustom your children to live in misery, because the spirits become greedy if they watch with stinginess.

"But neither let themselves rejoice in opulence, because they be will be made indifferent to the misfortunes of others, since they do not know suffering.

"Virtue consists in a just equilibrium; make them love life providing them honest and moderate satisfactions. Tell them continuously of the unfortunate and let them grow their savings bank so that they get accustomed to prudent savings; and, in this way you will be able to take your children by the pathway of virtue and you will live happily between docile and humble spirits; the only happiness that is given to man to enjoy on Earth."

Ms. Soler:

"Your husband is very right, Eloisa, that communication is very good. Certainly, savings is the first basis of the wellbeing of the family, because it is not enough that two beings love each other with delirium, they need to have the talent to live providing the means of subsistence to enjoy lasting peace."

Ms. Soler's final comments:

Whenever we read something about savings, we remember Juan and Eloisa, of those two virtuous beings who educated their children with the soundest moral principles.

Blessed are they whose advancement have permitted them to enjoy a tranquil existence, surrounded by their tender children!

Happy families are the seasoned fruit of the tree of progress.

Blessed are the spirits who know how to progress!

CHAPTER THIRTY-NINE

THE GREED OF ONE
HUNDRED CENTURIES

No matter how accustomed we are to see men whose oddness and eccentricities are called powerfully to our attention, it is always surprising to see an unfortunate victim, undoubtably due to his own self; for as the spirits say very well, the role of executioner does not have to do anything to anyone to punish the faults of another. Each one is an executioner of himself, because in the eternal justice of God each one collects the harvest of his sowing.

Reading the newspaper, I found an item, and on reading it I murmured, what cause would have given this effect? "The greed of a hundred centuries! …" said a voice.

The item stated:

A MISER

On Paloma Street, number 22, a dying homebody was found days later dying of hunger.

Taken to the hospital, he died.

That man lived in the worst misery, sleeping in a bed of rags in a corner of the room.

Yesterday, the judge appeared in the room where the miser lived; he found under the bed 31,000 pesetas in bank securities.

Spirit communication:

"Yes, (repeated the voice of a spirit), the greed of a hundred centuries is what has given this unhappy one the torment that he has suffered in this existence; which has had all the tortures that hunger produces. Being the owner of a medium size fortune that covered him for all material necessities, he had enough to live neither envied nor envious. He had no choice but to begin to balance his accounts, of which this poor spirit was willing. For at last, he had been convinced that the riches of the Earth, with all its courts of greatness and splendor, did not represent in the eternal life of the spirit more than shadow, isolation and the most complete solitude.

"The man that today died of hunger has been for a hundred centuries the king of gold. He has had enough talent to always undertake lucrative businesses; in his hands the sands of the deserts have become dust containing gold, pebbles without any value into precious gems and the stones of the East into incalculable value. He has been the spoiled son of fortune, as they say on Earth; in all the companies that he took part, luck smiled. Yet he never satiated his thirst for riches; the more gold he treasured, the more gold he wanted to accumulate. However, the gold in his hands became unfertile sand, because his treasures never served to console the inconsolable. He never dressed an orphan, never heard the cries of a helpless old man or a troubled widow. Yes, he enjoyed his riches. He lived with the magnificence of the sovereigns of the Orient. He satisfied his minor caprices, but the leftovers of his table were not taken advantage of by any poor person; his dogs, well fed, did not consume them, but his servants could not give out even a piece of leftover bread. Woe unto the servant who dared to be compassionate! They would soon be dismissed for disobedience.

And as such, he lived a hundred centuries, until at last he heard the voice of his spirit guide who said, 'Unhappy one!... Are you not tired of living in the shadows? You have not stained your hands with the blood of your fellowmen, but...you have given the worst example that a man can give while not being a murderer. You have had abundant water in the fountains of your properties and you have denied water to starved pilgrims. The fruits have rotted in the trees of your gardens, before you would give to the little ones who asked you with their anxious looks. You have not

249

shed a drop of blood for your fellowmen, but to increase your fabulous wealth you have monopolized foodstuffs, and due to inaction hundreds of children and elderly have died of hunger. What has this behavior given you? Gold on Earth, and shadows in the spirit world. And, if you have seen any ray of light, it has been the fires produced by the crowd's desperation of hunger. Also, if you have heard any voice, that voice has said, you are cursed! A greedy hangman! You are cursed!'

"Convert yourself, unhappy one, convert yourself. Accumulate virtues, and not coins. Then the unhappy miser listened to the voice of his spirit guide, and he asked to suffer the anguish of poverty. That is why in his last existence he could not resist his old vice of hoarding, but his treasure did not give him any pleasure. He has been strong to resist the temptations of earthly joys and he has taken a great step respecting his purpose of amendment. When he returns, he will begin to be generous; giving water to the thirsty and bread to the hungry.

So, when you see those scenes of misery, suffering and contemplate over a mountain of gold hidden among dirty rags, do not say, 'What an imbecile! How much greed and stupidity!' No, bow with respect before a spirit that with a start of energetic will has said, 'I want to see the light! I want to regenerate myself! I want to take the first step on the path of sacrifice! No more selfishness, no more exclusivity, no more spiritual misery!'

"Respect these poor spirits, who take the first step to elevate themselves and keep moving forward until they become a model of self-denial and generosity.

"Goodbye."

Ms. Soler:

I am very satisfied with the communication that I have obtained, because it is a good lesson for not criticizing or making erroneous conclusions about the actions and the ways of others.

Each being is a chapter in the history of life, and each one develops their feelings, their aspirations and their purposes to the extent of their knowledge acquired in their past incarnations. We should not judge anyone's behavior by saying if it seems idiotic or wise, because as we do not know their previous existences. We cannot make an exact judgment of their way of being. I am very grateful to the spirits for the teachings they give me because by them I learn not to judge by appearances, which are the masks that men put on in the great masked ball that is celebrated during the carnival of our lives.

Translator's Note: As the communicating spirit said, it was this poor man's "first step" to elevate himself. In this life, he needed to have that wealth around without using it for himself. Maybe soon in future lifetimes, he will finally find the effort to part with any wealth acquired to do charity for others. For many, progress is very slow.

CHAPTER FORTY

SALVATION!

Ms. Soler speaks with a friend Clotilde, who relays a story of spiritual awakening.

I was thinking of my friend Clotilde, when she entered my room pale and sad, wrapped in black crepe.

"For who do you mourn?" I asked anxiously.

"For my political father."

"Well, you must have felt a lot, because I find you pale and worn, the traces of pain can be seen on your face."

"Indeed. I've had one month of trials. Imagine, I was in San Sebastian with my husband, very tranquil and very happy, because I had realized one of my dreams which was to be in San Sebastian enjoying the charms that town has in the summer, when we received a telegram from my brother-in-law saying that we immediately travel to Madrid because my father was dying. We got on the train without delay (with nothing and delaying our luggage) arriving to receive the last breath of the venerable old man who, surrounded by all his children and grandchildren, died smiling as only the just should."

"Was he very old?"

"He was ninety-nine years old."

"Well, dear, such a death was to be expected and there is no reason to become so extremely disturbed...more so, since your father-in-law had a good reputation."

"Yes, right, but my grief is not caused by his death, because as you say

252

very well, dying of old age is a law. Although, one always feels the absence of a loved one, before the just one has to bow one's head, and say God's will be done. However, the situation is such that, I met a girl next to my father's funeral bed of about sixteen who had all the virtues of a saint, all the charms of a woman and all the grace and mischief of a little girl. Guillermina was the only daughter of a wealthy couple who saw heaven in their daughter's eyes, and these are so expressive, so attractive, so loving, so kind, and so grateful, that it made everyone love everything in the world. My father loved her as if she were his, and Guillermina cherished him and spoiled him as if in reality he was her grandfather. I can tell you that seeing and loving her was all one thing, and she matched my love with her cares, with her attentions, with her efforts. Guillermina was like the sun; the light of her kindness radiated around her, giving warmth and life to all those about her. As I was affected a lot with the death of my father, she did everything in her hands to comfort me. She reasoned so well! She seemed as an old woman very tired of life. I found myself so small at her side, and at the same time very happy. As a child searches for her mother's lap, I looked for her and reclined my head on her chest to calm down and bless the will of God. I won't tell you anymore, but I made the intention of staying in Madrid, and that my husband ask for his transfer to the Court, so as not to separate myself from Guillermina... For when one night the beautiful girl grew pale and told me, 'Come, I have to entrust you with a secret.'"

"I do not know why she scared me. We retired to her room, and she said, 'I have to ask you for a big favor.'"

"What?"

"That you console my parents, because they are going to receive a very painful blow."

"Very painful?"

"Yes, very painful; they are going to lose me."

"What are you saying?"

"Tomorrow, I will die. I have seen myself in dreams, shrouded, covered with flowers, and my dreams are warnings from heaven."

"You are delirious."

"No, I am not delirious, I am going because I need to go. My parents adore me, but their love is all for me, and it is necessary that they love humanity. I have come together with them to awaken their feelings. They have been happy with my love, with my caresses, but their happiness has made them greedy, and in hoarding a great dowry for me, they have denied a piece of bread to the poor. I have often spoken in dreams with an old man who looks like a saint, who tells me, 'Awaken the feelings of your parents, tell them to take advantage of their time, that they be grateful to Providence that has given them an angel to have by their side, that they do good works in your name, because if they do not do it willingly, later they will be forced to.' I said all this to my parents. Yet, my mother told me, 'Stop being silly, don't you remember what Calderon said? That dreams, are dreams!' [119] Last night, I saw the old man again, who told me, 'The one who is given light and does not want to see it, is left immersed in darkness.' I am the sun for my parents, and tomorrow I will reach my sunset. Poor things! How alone they will be! ...."

"Then, Guillermina threw herself into my arms, and cried with the greatest of despair. Then, I do not know what happened to me, but I also let out tears, and I must have shouted, because her parents came over very alarmed, and seeing their daughter crying bitterly, they believed that the world was sinking about them. What a night, Amalia! What a night!... Pale and disheveled, Guillermina got up and spoke in a prophetic tone advising her parents to wake up, to open their eyes to reality, and that she was leaving them for their own good. She was leaving for them the inheritance of an alarm clock, and that alarm clock was the immense pain of her departure. I do not know how the words came out of her mouth, she appeared as if an oracle. In the end ... she became mute, extended her arms, and her parents and I embraced her... I do not know how long we were embraced with her. I was the first to recognize that Guillermina was dead, because her arms fell motionless; everything was over. Everything but our despair, because her parents and I accused God of injustice, of cruelty, and I do not even know how many blasphemies we uttered..."

"We three, attended to her burial; we did very crazy things. My husband took action on the matter, and whether I wanted to or not, he made me leave Madrid and here you have me, more dead than alive."

"And, Guillermina's parents?"

---

[119] "...all of life is a dream, and dreams, are dreams." Written by Pedro Calderón de la Barca (dramatist, writer poet of Madrid, Spain) in his book *La Vida es un sueño* [*Life is a dream*].

"I think they are crazy, utterly without hope, because the father locks himself up in his room, writes long and hard, and then comes out very happy. He says, 'Listen to what Guillermina tells me,' He reads some beautiful communications, while the mother cries. Later, the two go to visit the poor sick, and spend hours and hours in the hospital keeping company with the most abandoned of sick persons, and there they are.

"Since their craziness is contagious, I also wanted to communicate with Guillermina. I wrote, 'You do not need an alarm clock.' My husband, upon reading that let out a cry to the heavens; and since Barcelona is lacking people, here you have me, doubting and believing at the same time that the dead live."

"Yes, Clotilde, they live, and many of them serve as alarm clocks for humanity."

"Then, Guillermina was not dreaming?"

"No, she was not dreaming. A spirit was speaking to her and preparing her for her disencarnation."

"Then, her death has been profitable?"

Amalia replied, "I do believe so; with her absence, her parents have awakened and have entered the path of their regeneration. They were given flowers to see if they knew how to breathe in their delicate aroma, and seeing that they did not appreciate the treasure they had, they were given thorns. The pain was an alarm clock for those lethargic spirits in their selfishness and in their smallness. Does God, in the joys of Nature, give more to some than to others? No. The sun shines for everyone. Well, that is the way the love of spirits has to be; and when you do not know how to love, the alarm clock serves as a teacher, and through pain you cry, and later…you love."

CHAPTER FORTY-ONE

THERE ARE NO PHENOMENA

A Spiritist from Rosario of Santa Fe (Argentina), wrote to me, sending me the following short item: "A rare phenomenon." *The Daily Mail*, an English newspaper of great circulation, not only in England, but throughout the world, reports the following interesting facts:

"On February of 1905, a servant John Lee was convicted of having murdered in London a woman whose house he served many years before.

"But John Lee, meanwhile enduring the trial proceedings, protested vigorously of his innocence.

"The day that he had to be hanged, an extraordinary phenomenon manifested: the scale of the gallows did not function, which had to go down and leave the body dead. Three times the executioner renewed his attempts, but in vain. The scale worked perfectly when the condemned was not on the gallows, but when John Lee was put on, it did not move.

"The judges and the solicitor who were present at the act of execution were perplexed at this strange phenomenon.

"After long deliberations, they revoked the execution of John Lee.

"Well then, the condemned never ceased declaring his innocence; the prosecutor ordered a second trial proceedings and a review of the process, and last month the Court released John to liberty.

"This extraordinary fact has made an impression on many of the judges and much of the public."

Ms. Soler continues:

"Truly, it is a very rare case, for which many Spiritists of Santa Fe have asked me to ask about the cause of this extraordinary effect. So, I, wanting to indulge my brothers and sisters in my belief, and have asked the guide of my works. I have obtained the following communication:

Spirit communication:

"There are no phenomena; the event that seems strange and so amazing to you, is nothing more than the result of yesterday's acts, the natural consequence of our good or bad deeds. If it were not so, the eternal laws of Nature would lose their perfect equilibrium and the laws are never altered; everything continues its rhythmic march, everything develops and unfolds in due time. The events that make time in the life of a man do not advance a second or delay a minute. Time is the clock of the centuries, its maker is God Himself, and that Great Mechanic makes his machines function so perfectly, that, I repeat it, the events that decide the future of a man are neither delayed nor advanced. [120]

"That spirit that has ultimately suffered all the agony, all the pains of his next execution and that the scale of the gallows did not work, it is because its movement was paralyzed by spirit friends of the condemned. In this existence, that man who in reality has not committed any crime, and that human justice has fulfilled its duty by declaring him innocent, has not always been as good as now. He has a page in his history so full of stains, that he proposed to leave it completely clean in his present existence, and he has succeeded; because the three times that the executioner tried to fulfill his mission by hanging him, he suffered at that those moments a thousand deaths per second. Thanks that he is a strong spirit and has very good friends in the spirit world; especially one, to whom he made him suffer something similar to what he has just suffered now.

"The spirit of John Lee, in one of his past life existences belonged to the nobility. He inherited from his parents many parchments and medium-size

---

[120] The superior spirits teach that the Creator - the Supreme Intelligence and First Cause of all things, is Eternal, Unique, Supremely Just, All Love and All Powerful and created Natural Laws, for both the spiritual and material aspects of the Cosmos. The spirits teach the Creator is not anthropomorphic or pantheistic.

riches that he proposed to increase, thinking that gold opens all doors, both on Earth and in Heaven.

"Among his many servants, he had one that served him as squire, as a secretary, help in the bedchamber, being in reality his faithful dog who blindly obeyed him in his wicked plans, because John Lee was very adept at making false wills and other kinds of documents with which he appropriated goods that were not his, leaving many of his relatives and their neighbors in the greatest misery.

"His faithful servant, his squire Daniel, was aware of everything his lord did, and John Lee began to fear him. His soul was seized with panic, and he said to himself, 'This man could make me disappear. The thirst for gold that I have would be able to overtake his soul. He is very clever, he understands perfectly that if he spoke, he would get paid very well for his denunciations by my many enemies. A dead man does not talk, or hands to work.' For the time being, I will accuse him of being a great thief, saying that he has stolen a fabulous amount from me; if the accuser is rich, a conviction is obtained quickly; and, said, and done. John Lee accused Daniel of having stolen 'so much and how much.' Daniel was reduced to imprisonment, and not only appeared before justice as a thief, but was accused of murder, attributing to him the death of a public officer who in a time previously had been found under a bridge with the head separated from the trunk and a dagger stuck in the chest.

"John Lee spread out money to full hands, and a judgment was completed in a few days.

"Daniel always said the same thing, that he was innocent and he knew nothing about what they were taking about. However, his declarations were not paid attention to, because there was a powerful man who wanted to see him dead.

"On the eve of the execution, John Lee suddenly felt an agonizing pain in his heart. He looked within himself, and muttered in horror, I am a miserable person! Daniel is innocent, I know full well. I do not have the least complaint, he has served me selflessly; when I wanted to reward his services, he told me, 'I have the best reward, with being by your side.' Solely due to an unfounded fear, I will have murdered that unfortunate one. Oh, I choke! Remorse will cause me to die ... fire, not blood, runs through my veins ... but it is not yet time. Dominated by the most horrible anxiety, he ran to the place of execution at the moment when Daniel said to the executioner, 'I forgive you the crime you are going to commit, because I am innocent.' John Lee yelled, 'Yes, he is innocent! Under a secret of confession, they have returned to me the amount that they had stolen, and I have been told that the murderer of the official who was under the bridge has confessed his crime knowing that an innocent was going to die for his motives.'

"The bewilderment of the judges was indescribable. Daniel was overcome by so many emotions, and he was sick for a long time taken care of by his lord, who took him to his house again, treating him with the greatest of affection.

"Daniel, while he was on Earth, ignored the behavior of his owner, and died blessing him, but in the spirit world he learned everything and sympathized with his lord for having fallen so deep. However, he cared about him so much that he was his good angel [or spirit protector], and when they were both reunited in the spirit world, he counseled John Lee to make haste in suffering what he had caused him to suffer. Yet, John Lee needed a lot of time, to decide to pay such a terrible debt. Finally, in this existence, he has bravely suffered the greatest of his pains.

"Daniel and other spirits prevented the scale from working. The one who had repented of his crime should not die; the sincerity of his repentance has received the well-deserved reward, since for the repentant is the kingdom of them heaven.

"Goodbye."

Ms. Soler:

The spirit is right; there are no phenomena, there is only compliance with the eternal laws. [121]

How much must be studied in Creation!...

A wise man from Greece rightly said, "I only know, that I know nothing!" [122]

---

[121] The influence of spirits on the material world whether the effect is of a physical or mental nature are in accordance with the Divine Laws and it is one of the forces of Nature (yet not taken seriously or much studied by the scientific establishment).
[122] Commonly attributed to Socrates

CHAPTER FORTY-TWO

THERE IS NO FAULT, WITHOUT PENALTY

Adages, sayings and proverbs are poems written through experience and form a volume that people have not been careful to bind. Therefore, their loose pages fly from the huts to the palaces, already in tropical regions, already at the north pole, corrected and supplemented, but always preserving in some its satirical element and others its profound reasoning.

There is a refrain that says, "Justice, but not for my house," vulgar and simple words, but they are the compendium of all the feelings of humanity.

Who can deny that we rejoice when the law punishes an offender? Even the death penalty which is anti-religious, anti-social and anti-human, finds acceptance with the majority of society, telling itself, upon seeing a victim pass by, "It's well deserved to have it." He who does such, shall pay; nothing, nothing, but the penalty of the law of talion, an eye for an eye, and a tooth for a tooth...

Of course, these staunch supporters of harsh justice, when the time comes for them to be asked to make an accounting of their acts, they let a cry out to heaven and make use of all the subterfuge imaginable to escape punishment, because they see the speck in the eye of another, but the beam in theirs does not bother them. [123]

---

[123] In Matthew 7:3 of the Bible, Jesus says, "Why do you look at the speck in your brother's eye, but do not notice the log that is in your own eye?" Basically, we will notice small faults in others, but do not worry about our own flaws or vices, which may indeed be worse.

Many speak about the conscience. They say that its voice resounds continuously in our ears. If this is true, we have to recognize in humanity a defect or an incurable ailment.

A great pity that a race that has served as a model to make the Apollo Belvedere and the Venus de Medici, is deprived of the song of the nightingale and the sweet cooing of the turtledoves! Man has ears, but... does not listen! [124]

In the 19th century, those infallible men and of marvelous specifics; the century of charlatanism and those of the greatest discoveries, one that has managed to link the sublime with the ridiculous; epoch of the antithesis, decade of anomalies in which two titanic gladiators called fanaticism and advancement, light and shadow, blind faith and analytical science fight desperately in the circus of progress. In this energetic century, the remedy has been found for the tenacious deafness that humanity suffers; the homeopathy of the soul, that has been rejected and ridiculed like homeopathy that heals the body, because the foolishness of man reaches to such extreme that he denies all that his clumsy intelligence cannot understand.

Dr. Lopez de la Vega has said, and has said it very well, that homeopathy is the physical regeneration of humanity, and I say, that Spiritism is also regeneration of the morality and intellect of man. [125]

Yes, it is; because Spiritism makes us see and hear, in spite of ourselves, with strength; and since there is no worse deaf person than the one who does not want to hear, a rough battle is maintained between the evidence of the facts and the malicious denials of obscurantism. [126]

Spiritism makes us accept justice within our home, in our body, in our way of being, within our special conditions, in short, in everything.

---

[124] Famous and beautiful sculpted statues.

[125] Medical doctors could not help Ms. Soler's eyesight, but she says her eyesight improved with homeopathic doctors, yet she had trouble with her eyes all her life. Homeopathy (using natural herbs, etc.) was popular in the 19th century, especially since official medical practices included blood-letting, etc. Spiritism brings knowledge that we are all spirits, there is no true death as we live on in the spirit world, and through evolution of the soul with increased goodness and wisdom humanity will transform.

[126] Obscurantism – opposition to the spread of knowledge. She is speaking of knowledge of spiritual matters.

It is the law of equality put into action. The monarch can be a beggar and this one an emperor. Everyone can reach the Promised Land: the wise and the fool, the believer and the atheist. Descartes [127] solely finds space and time in Nature; the latter is the treasure of humanity. Time is the inexhaustible mine whose lodes never end. It is the volcano whose crater always finds heat.

An Arab poet said that a dream was the wealth of a mortal, and I say that Time is the Holy Ark where man always finds refuge.

The materialists are the disinherited of the Earth; for them life has a limit, then ... they are solely left with nothing.

How sad will be their last hours!... If unfortunately, they have had one of those slow and terrible diseases in which their physical body has been disintegrating through forces of horrible pain, they have to say, as Zorrilla said, before the tomb of Larra [Mariano José de Larra]:[128]

Sadness presented for certain
Leaves one a bitter life,
to abandon a desert;
and to say goodbye
to the ugly garment of a dead one.

Certainly, it is hurtful to look at a cadaver. Remember that before I became a Spiritist I improvised the following verses, contemplating a young military man in his funeral coffin:

Seeing a dead man saddens;
the matter alone, is frightening,
without the sacrosanct vitality
with which God fortifies it;
when the soul disappears,
from our poor organism,

---

[127] French philosopher, mathematician and scientist René Descartes famously stated, "I think, therefore I am."

[128] Jose Zorrilla y Moral was a famous 19th century Romantic poet and playwright from Spain; a popular poem of his was *Del Joven Literato D. Mariano Jose de Larra* [*To the Unfortunate Memory of the Young Writer*]

we contemplate the abyss
in this transitory life,
which is a dream without memory
that conducts one to atheism.

Yes, atheism; the most profound desperation. What is life without a tomorrow; the sketch of a painting, the prologue of a story, a voice without echo, a flower without aroma? On the other hand, when hope encourages us, what unlimited horizons present themselves before our eyes! The death of the one who waits, is the death of the just, as the Catholics say, sweet and tranquil.

The true Spiritist that has suffered with resignation the hardships of life, dies with the satisfaction of having paid a debt; and he who pays rests (says the adage), and it is a great truth.

Ms. Soler relays a story:

In the last days of the year 1874, I saw a proof of this in the death of a woman whose last year of life on Earth was a prolonged agony.

It seems that I still see her. She was a woman of medium height, about 55 years of age, of humble and pleasant appearance, of an expressive look and of affable relations. A Spiritist from the heart, she attended with religious silence the mediumship sessions that were conducted in her house.

One night I noticed her absence. I asked about her and her family told me that she was sick with a tumor, that made her suffer a lot. I proposed that the session be suspended so that the murmur of our voices would not bother her.

"Oh, no madam!" they told me. The first thing she had asked is that we continue without interruption in our tasks, because while these last, they were the only moments when she finds herself better.

We continued to meet; the sick woman getting worse, suffering with amazing valor the painful cures; an ulcerated fistula devoured her organism and neither a complaint nor a sigh came from her lips. The months passed, and the poor martyr (who belonged to a family of the middle class, but were going through one of those supreme crises in which there is not even air to breathe) asked to be taken to a hospital. They had to accede to her wishes, and in a benevolent institution she continued to die slowly.

The day she left the Earth, she tranquilly said goodbye to one sister, saying, "Go, I'm going to sleep a very beautiful dream! ..." Very beautiful it was, without a doubt, because her organism had finished breaking down.

Her family, that had watched with silent amazement and profound pain, the prolonged martyrdom of a woman whose life had been a model of meekness and virtue, wondered. What could she have done yesterday, to suffer so much today, remaining a skeleton with sunken eyes, protruding cheekbones, blackened skin, cadaverous hands and a hoarse voice? Wanting to be without doubts, they evoked her protector spirits and their sister, to see if she had come out of her confusion soon, and with deep emotion they received the following communication through a beautiful young woman [a medium], who in a trance state said:

Spirit communication:

"I am very happy that you have gathered, my siblings, for me to communicate with you and to tell you, though limited, the causes that motivated my hard tests during my last existence on that planet.

"Listen to me, mainly my sister, as you were so distressed by my illness and have so much felt my death at the same time.

"In my previous incarnation I was a man. I was a doctor and I was in charge of a hospital in M ...

"Among the sick people who were in such a sad place there was one who complained bitterly because I did not take care of her like the others. Indeed, that unhappy creature, without knowing why, inspired within me a deep aversion that I could not explain, but that really existed.

"I came to neglect her so much that, she defended herself to one of the nurses, who then informed the director of the hospital of my wrongdoing. Then he, making sure himself of the seriousness of the case, dismissed me from my job; I defeated by the sick woman who, due to my carelessness, would soon cease to exist. I prayed, begged and promised to make amends, and use all my [knowledge] of science to remedy the damage I had caused. At last, the director took me in again. However, far from fulfilling what he had offered and believing that this woman was the cause of my ruin, I saw my aversion grow in an awful way; until it became a bleeding hatred, that when she died, left me very happy because she had ceased to exist.

"They fired me again, and the memory of that unhappy one, tormented me and caused me remorse, because my conscience constantly screamed, 'Assassin…, a new Cain… What have you done to your brother?'

"When I reincarnated, I had asked to suffer the same that I had made that poor being suffer. I had the same ailment and died like her in a hospital. But this test I have undergone with resignation, which, when parting from my last sleep, I experienced such joy, to see me free of my poor and rickety body. I cannot express it with words.

"Goodbye, my family, I will continue communicating with you."

Ms. Soler's final comments:

After listening to the previous story, if it is possible that pain [of grief] calms down in the first moments, it is calmed down effectively in those beings who remembered with sorrow the long torment of a being so dear to them.

Melancholy extended its mantle, and in its shadow, they see the days go by wishing that they could communicate again with the one that so loved them on the Earth. Can there be anything more comforting than Spiritism?

Does any positive religion respond to the moans of the soul with such precision and with so much justice?

None until now; none. Those with their implacable God, the others with hereditary sin, those with their redemption and their grace, those with minutes of repentance; all with a false base, with murky arguments, with undecipherable mysteries; with one who knows what, of darkness and confusion, that reason rejects and that only awakens doubt that end with a freezing of the heart.

Voltaire said, if there were no God it would be necessary to create one in order to live. [129]

---

[129] During the 18th century of the Enlightenment, Voltaire was a French writer, historian and philosopher famous for his wit, and was especially critical of the Catholic Church.

As for me, I say that if the revelation from beyond the grave was not a fact, we would have to magnetize our thoughts and ask fantasy to make us wait and believe.

Is there anything much grander, and that so elevates mankind than the intimate conviction that we are all equal?

The day that humanity is convinced of this undeniable truth there will be no races or privileges, then everyone will work; but not to accumulate treasures of metal.

That dawn of peace is still faraway; only some men, whom are called crazy, live quietly in their modest home, suffering resigned the condemnation they deserve, and pity the many who, like Cain, are fratricidal.

Unfortunate for those who only see the Earth! Fortunate are those, who say, "There is no fault, without a penalty...!"

Blessed be Spiritism, supreme illumination, eternal light, a secular cedar to whose aged trunk is linked justice, truth and reason! [130]

Translator's Final Note:

Ms. Soler is expressing that there is no suffering without some *just cause* because the Creator is All Love; she says, "there is no penalty without a fault." As imperfect as we all are, even any type of imperfection or deficit (whether moral, intellectual, emotional, etc.) requires effort towards improvement, towards perfecting. And, this process generally involves some kind of discomfort or various types of pain; whether repaying a debt, a selfless sacrifice of any kind (minor or major), tests of being a leader, our efforts helping others, and improving ourselves in any way (whether done grudgingly or with love), all this involves EFFORT and WORK, even if done out of love.

According to the spirits, pain in all its forms suffered upon the earth washes away our impurities, elevates our soul; providing for our soul's evolution. That is the purpose of material life. It is mostly during struggle and suffering when sentiments that were not there, are awakened within us, so we can have a greater appreciation and further comprehension of compassion, forgiveness, sympathy, empathy, benevolence, and finally unconditional charity and fraternal love.

---

[130] As a symbol, the cedar tree has had great spiritual significance for a thousand years, generally representing strength, and is mentioned in many passages of the Bible as such.

WHY SHOULD WE STUDY
SPIRIT COMMUNICATIONS?

What one person considers proof of something, another may not. Throughout these many centuries, at least since the mid-1800s, there have undoubtedly been many prestigious scientists who have determined, after their own careful study, that different types of so-called psychic phenomena exist and that there are certain persons who have the ability to initiate and/or provide these phenomena, as well as receive what are allegedly communications from entities (spirits) not of this material world.[131] This being the case, while the scientific establishment continues to study these phenomena because they are as yet not universally accepted as fact by them, does that preclude us from studying whatever "spirit messages" we can receive from these individuals we call mediums? The answer should be, no.

The reason we should continue to concurrently study the messages from these mediums, as well as continue studying spirit phenomena, is because these messages may have something important to say. If we ignore them and these "spirit messages" are indeed real and come from a legitimate and true source, then we would have ignored something of possibly vast proportions and considerable impact on humanity. We know this to be true because the three major religions were founded on what individuals believed were messages from outside the material plane. All the prophets, and even Jesus, would have to be considered delusional according

---

[131] I highly recommend Michael Tymn's books *The Articulate Dead* (2008) and *Resurrecting Leonora Piper – How Science Discovered the Afterlife* (2013) for information on these notable scientists.

to general scientific standards had they appeared and relayed their messages after the Scientific Age.

However, in studying these "spirit messages" we must use good reason, common sense and determine if there is a pattern or a certain harmony in regard to them. We need to ask ourselves is there a consistent message that is being brought forth. If a myriad of spirit communications coming from numerous mediums from all over the world are continuously saying the same things, does this not provide a phenomenon worth studying?

The purpose of science is to understand the universe around us no matter where it will lead. Anything that is determined to be false will fall by the wayside eventually, and that which stands the test of time after confirmation upon confirmation should be accepted until something else comes along that may alter or change our assumptions of the facts. Such a thing occurred when our ideas were changed regarding Newtonian physics and Einstein came along.

If something is encountered that seems to destroy the latest paradigm of thinking in the scientific establishment, so be it. Scientists who deride or do not want to accept as a legitimate study of what may provide to be a radical new idea that may move humanity forward in its advancement in knowledge of itself and the universe and its workings, I believe, are not being true to their supreme purpose. Nevertheless, we can still each study them for ourselves.

Yvonne Crespo Limoges

YOU ARE NEVER ALONE!

Spirit communication received by Yvonne Crespo Limoges

The effects of war, violence, natural disasters, sickness of mind, body and soul…afflict all the inhabitants of your world, one way or another.

Yet, in the midst of all your heartbreak, sorrow, fear, pain and anguish – you are never alone.

Your *spirit protector* is ever by your side instilling, within you and about you, their beneficial spiritual vibrations of calmness, goodness, inspiration and courage; and, emitting the special Love that comes from the Divine Source to help uphold your through all of your many struggles, pains, tribulations, traumas and the daily drudgery widespread on your material world.

Also, from the spirit world are the *spirits of your families and dear friends*, from present and past lives, doing their part to help ease your distress, anxieties, doubts and loneliness; trying hard to comfort and console you; their empathy allows them to know your pain, and they see your tears!

In addition, when your physical body sleeps, these spirits directly interact with yours, when it returns to the spirit world each night. They reach out to provide guidance, counseling and healing, as well as to remind you of the just cause (the why) of what you are going through, the kind of life you chose; the one you pledged to undergo with strong determination in your present existence.

Knowing all this, please try to open up your hearts to all these loving spirits who care so very much for you personally and for your spiritual progress!

They reach out to help you, although you may not see them – they are there! At moments of pure desperation – you may feel their loving sweet impressions! So, try your best to be emotionally and mentally be receptive to their loving, valuable and productive influences.

Be reminded that pain in all its forms suffered upon the earth washes away the impurities of your soul; all the trials, tests and atonements elevate your spirit. In this way, sentiments can be awakened in order for you to have more of an inner appreciation and further comprehension of compassion, forgiveness, sympathy, empathy, benevolence, charity and fraternal love.

Dear ones, as you advance, your suffering will be less and you will eventually reach true happiness. The Divine evolutionary process provides for your spirit's enlightenment, enhancing your intellectual and moral elevation. So be strong!

The Creator is All Love and you are always provided with spiritual assistance to fulfill your soul's journey!

(From September 2019 newsletter of the *Spiritist Society of Florida* - online at www. spiritistsocietyfl.com)

SUGGESTED READINGS
(BOOKS IN ENGLISH)

ALLAN KARDEC (Spiritism) spirit phenomena, mediumship and spirit teachings
> *The Spirits' Book*
> *The Mediums' Book*
> *The Gospel according to Spiritism*
> *Heaven and Hell, or Divine Justice according to Spiritism*
> *Spiritist Prayers* (handy pocket book)

AMALIA DOMINGO SOLER (translated by Edgar Crespo)
> *Memoirs of Father Germain* (Full of moral lessons, Amalia's spirit guide relays story of his earthly life via mediumship; stories full of intrigue, adventure, true love, human emotion and morality)

MIGUEL VIVES (translated by Edgar Crespo)
> *A Practical Guide for the Spiritist* (how any person should be before the Creator, oneself, family, Humanity, how to deal with the trials and tribulations of life, etc. – only 61 pages)

LEON DENIS (books translated by Jussara Korngold and/or U.S. Spiritist Federation)
> *After Death* (nature of human beings, purpose of material life, reincarnation)
> *The Problem of Life and Destiny* (life, destiny, power of the soul)
> *Into the Unseen* (Mediumship and Spiritism)

JON AIZPURUA (clinical psychologist)

Fundamentals of Spiritism (modern textbook on all aspects of psychic phenomena, mediumship, reincarnation, spirit communication, spirit influence & obsession, spiritual healing, and more)

JAMES VAN PRAAGH (a spiritual medium)

Reaching to Heaven: A Spiritual Journey Through Life and Death
Looking Beyond: A Teen's Guide to the Spiritual World
(True personal stories, mediumship, spirits, our psychic abilities, reincarnation, purpose of material life, etc.)

MICHAEL E. TYMN (an authority on the history of scientific study of mediums)

The Articulate Dead – They Brought the Spirit World Alive (The best scientists study mediums)
Resurrecting Leonora Piper – How Science Discovered the Afterlife

DIVALDO FRANCO (medium)

Happy Life (pocket book of short spirit communications to help guide and support us in our daily lives)

AUTHORS – for informative books on Reincarnation:
Joseph Head and S.L. Cranston; Brian L. Weiss, M.D.; Robert Schwartz; Ian Stevenson, M.D.; Jim B. Tucker, M.D.; James G. Matlock, Ph.D.; Erlendur Haraldsson, Ph.D.

Printed in the United States
by Baker & Taylor Publisher Services